WESTERN MAN AND ENVIRONMENTAL ETHICS
Attitudes Toward Nature and Technology

Edited by IAN G. BARBOUR
Carleton College

WESTERN MAN AND ENVIRONMENTAL ETHICS
Attitudes Toward Nature and Technology

ADDISON-WESLEY PUBLISHING COMPANY
Reading, Massachusetts · Menlo Park, California
London · Amsterdam · Don Mills, Ontario · Sydney

This book is in the
ADDISON-WESLEY SERIES IN HISTORY

Consulting Editor
Robin W. Winks

ISBN 0-201-00387-2
  FGHIJKLM-DO-7987

To Deane

CONTENTS

PART THREE: TECHNOLOGY AND ECOLOGY

INTRODUCTION
IAN G. BARBOUR

It is widely known that western industrial nations are polluting their rivers, contaminating the soil, exterminating wildlife, and using up the world's natural resources. Acrid air and foul water testify to our failure to recognize man's interdependence with nature. They testify also to the failures of a social order in which technological policy has been determined more by private profit than by human welfare. The purpose of this book is to examine how attitudes toward nature and technology have led to the environmental crisis, and how new attitudes might contribute to survival and the quality of life on earth.[1]

This book does not repeat the familiar lists of statistics and horror stories concerning ecological destruction. Instead, it examines the basic presuppositions about nature, man, and society which influence the way man treats the earth. It focuses attention on the social priorities, value judgments, and ethical issues involved in policy decisions about the environment. It seeks what Paul Goodman calls "a transformation of conscience," a new environmental ethic, a new recognition of the limits of growth in population and consumption.

Four very diverse historical roots of the environmental crisis can be distinguished, and corresponding to each there is a distinctive kind of response today:

1. *Attitudes toward nature* have in the past been influenced by western religious and cultural assumptions. If such assumptions

Ian G. Barbour is Professor of Religion and Professor of Physics at Carleton College, Northfield, Minnesota. He was a recent Guggenheim Fellow. His books include *Science and Secularity: The Ethics of Technology, Issues in Science and Religion,* and, as editor, *Earth Might Be Fair.*

have indeed contributed to man's devastation of the earth, we must try to encourage a less exploitative outlook today.

2. *Economic institutions* prevailing since the Industrial Revolution have engendered ecologically destructive practices. If this is the case, we must propose legislative and political changes which will make industrial policy more responsive to the welfare of man and nature.

3. *Technologies* have developed which use raw materials and create waste products in vast quantities. Accordingly, we must today seek technological improvements to conserve natural resources, reduce pollution, and recycle wastes.

4. *Growth in population and living standards* has produced an ever-increasing environmental demand. Exponential growth in consumption of natural resources will probably be the crucial factor in the years ahead. Far-reaching changes in values and social institutions are required if stability rather than growth is to become our goal.

Technological solutions to a succession of particular environmental problems are important, but their results will be short-lived unless the forces which have led men to ravage the earth are altered. Action requires adequate motivation. One powerful motive for action is self-interest and the threat of destruction. Perhaps only a series of major catastrophes will awaken people to the seriousness of their plight. But it is possible that significant changes in attitudes and values can occur without such catastrophes.

There are many kinds of source for environmental ethics. This collection is deliberately interdisciplinary. Chapters on fiction and poetry are included, for example, underscoring the importance of experience, feeling and emotion in contrast to abstract ideas about nature. Novels and poems can express new forms of self-awareness and new ways of experiencing the world. Who would deny the power of imagination in forming the sensibilities which affect behavior? Again, religious beliefs have influenced fundamental assumptions about man and nature, and have modified the goals and motives of human action. The humanities as well as the natural and social sciences have a significant place here.

Five themes of the volume may be summarized at the outset:

1. *Interdependence.* Evidence of the interconnectedness of the

community of life comes particularly from the biological sciences, but the theme is mentioned in almost every chapter. Ecology—the study of organisms in environments—has made us aware of the interactions within natural systems: the complex cycles of chemical elements, the food chains linking diverse species, the delicate balances among organisms. Human intervention has far-reaching repercussions, of which many are cumulative and a few irreversible. These findings have engendered a new respect for the integrity of biotic systems, and a realization that one cannot deal with any part in isolation from the larger whole. There is a new recognition of man's dependence on his environment, and acknowledgment of the limited capacity of the earth to absorb the by-products of civilization.

2. *Man's unity with nature.* Selections from a variety of disciplines present variations on this theme. From American history come diverse examples: Thoreau's religion of nature, the early conservation movement, the current attempts of youth to recover harmony with nature in individual experience and communal life. A literary critic traces in several American novels a pattern wherein the hero turns from an urban to a pastoral setting to find a sense of order and purpose. A theologian affirms the goodness of the created order to which man belongs, and celebrates its beauty and mystery. In nature poetry, man is united with the earth, responding in wonder and appreciation. A city planner tries to take into account man's need for natural as well as artificial environments. From each discipline comes the same message: man is inseparable from nature.

3. *Finite resources.* There are fixed limits to all natural resources— tillable land, oil reserves, mineral ores, air, water, and so forth. These limits will eventually be exceeded by any demand which grows exponentially (i.e. at a constant percentage rate, which means that in successive intervals it will have increased by factors of 2, 4, 8, 16, 32, etc.). The "doubling time" for electric power consumption in the U.S. is 9 years; the population of India is doubling every 28 years, and that of Costa Rica, every 18 years. In the concluding chapter, two members of the M.I.T. systems dynamics group, affiliated with the Club of Rome, give computer simulation curves showing how the critical limits might be exceeded in the future, under a variety of assumptions, unless drastic changes occur in the growth rates of population, consumption, and pollution. Several

other essays challenge the prevalent view that growth means progress, and criticize the idea of an ever-expanding gross national product.

4. *The control of technology.* Running throughout the book is the idea that uncontrolled technology has been one of the main threats to the earth. Environmental ethics entails communal responsibility as well as individual conscience. Several authors insist that the social costs of any product must be paid for by its users, and point to new accounting methods and tax proposals to make this possible. They call for strict national standards on air and water effluents and solid wastes, and new technologies for recycling materials. New decision-making mechanisms are discussed, such as technology assessment boards to evaluate the consequences of new innovations before they are developed into vested interests.

5. *Social justice.* Poverty and pollution are linked as products of our economic institutions. Exploitation of man and of nature are two sides of the same coin; they reflect a common set of cultural values and a common set of social structures. Moreover, the dispossessed receive proportionately less of the benefits of technology and more of its harmful effects. The guiding principles proposed here for the redirection of technology are ecological wisdom and social justice in meeting basic human needs. We have invested far more in aerospace and military technology than in public transportation, urban housing, and environmental protection. Changes in political power seem to be necessary before technology can become an equitable instrument for human welfare.

Lest it appear that these authors agree about everything, I will mention a few of their points of disagreement, about which the reader will have to come to his own conclusions:

• Has the biblical doctrine of man's dominion over nature been a major source of western man's exploitative attitudes towards the world? Or was the rise of industrial capitalism more significant among the historical roots of environmental destruction?

• In accounting for historical change in the past, or in trying to bring about change in the future, should attention be directed to beliefs and attitudes? Or are changes in social and economic institutions primary?

● Is the ecology movement a cop-out from more urgent problems of poverty, race and the ghetto; is it a middle-class evasion of the glaring inequities of our society? Or can we seek the goals of ecological wisdom and social justice at the same time?

● Are the new life-styles and forms of awareness among the youth of the counter-culture grounds for optimism that the next generation will be less destructive of the environment? Or is the anti-technological outlook of many young people a luxury which only an affluent elite can afford, an irresponsible neglect of the needs of most of mankind?

● Can social justice in the redirection of technology be achieved within established political structures? Or does genuine equality require a radical redistribution of power which only more revolutionary methods can effect? Or should we perhaps start from changes in personal and communal life-styles, and the abolition of domination and hierarchy in interpersonal relationships (women's liberation, free schools, cooperative industries, etc.)? What are the political implications of ecology? All these questions are discussed in the course of the volume.

I. HISTORICAL ROOTS

The opening selection by historian Lynn White has been widely quoted. White sees "the orthodox Christian arrogance toward nature" as the main source of western man's alienation from the natural world. Consequently, "Christianity bears a huge burden of guilt for environmental deterioration." In particular, White asserts that the idea of man's dominion over nature led to the anthropocentric (man-centered) outlook and domineering attitude typical of the West. The key passage is Genesis 1:28, in which man is told to "fill the earth and subdue it, and have dominion over the fish of the sea and over the birds of the air and over every living thing."

The same charge against biblical religion recurs in two essays later in the volume. Ian McHarg holds that Western anthropocentrism and disregard for the environment can be traced back to the biblical notion of man's dominion and the assumption that the world of nature is "a mere backdrop for the human play." And Wendell Berry, in discussing contemporary poetry, maintains that the Christian tradition articulated a dualism of man against nature, as well as a body-soul dualism within man, which encouraged other-worldliness and contempt for the world. Whereas White looks to St. Francis for a corrective to the main tradition of the West, McHarg looks to ecological science and a holistic philosophy to overcome man's alienation from the earth; Berry, in turn, finds in nature poetry a "secular pilgrimage," a "religious quest" apart from institutional religion, which can help to reunite man and the natural world.

Three types of reply to White's thesis are presented by other writers in this collection. First, non-Christian cultures seem to have harmed natural environments as much as Christian ones. Sociologist Lewis Moncrief maintains that man has been altering his environment in all cultures since antiquity. Biologist René Dubos indicates that in ancient Chinese, Greek and Western civilizations there was disastrous deforestation, soil erosion and over-grazing. Christian cultures, past and present, have had no monopoly on ecological damage.

Second, there are diverse strands in the Bible. Dubos points to the second chapter of Genesis, in which man is instructed to "dress and keep the garden." As patron saint for the ecology movement he nominates not St. Francis, who responded to the created order with reverence, but St. Benedict, who was willing to use nature respectfully. The Benedictine monks worked hard, drained swamps, managed the land soundly, and changed the face of Europe. This was "creative intervention," says Dubos, not simply the protection of untouched nature. He concludes: "We certainly must reject the attitude which asserts that man is the only value of importance and that the rest of nature can be sacrificed to his welfare and whims. But we cannot escape, I believe, an anthropocentric attitude which puts man at the summit of creation while still a part of it."

The biblical theme of responsible stewardship is also set forth in the later contribution by theologian Gabriel Fackre. He argues that the Genesis account does not endorse unlimited dominion. Man is viewed as a trustee, manager, or caretaker, accountable for his treatment of the earth. Moreover, says Fackre, Genesis strongly proclaims the goodness of creation, and in other portions of the Bible the affirmation and appreciation of nature is prominent. He shows that the early church rejected gnostic dualism, which looked on the world as evil. There were undoubtedly strong notes of other-worldliness and world-denial in medieval thought, but these had their origin more in Hellenistic ideas than in biblical ones. In the

Bible itself, man is called to be the responsible steward of a good creation.

Third, the rise of capitalism and industry must be assigned major roles in the origins of the environmental crisis. Moncrief discusses private ownership of resources, the motive of commercial profit, and the development of technology and urbanization. He claims that these factors were only indirectly related to the Judeo-Christian tradition, and are found in other cultures today. In a similar vein, several later essays (Fackre, Faramelli, Ecology Action East) see the rape of the earth today as the product not of deficient views of nature but of inadequate social institutions; they blame a technocratic society and an economic system in which man and nature are exploited for profit. These critics tend to stress institutions more than beliefs, in looking at both the past and the future.

Lynn White has written for this volume a reply to some of these criticisms, which carries a step further the debate touched off by his earlier article. He reaffirms the importance of a society's underlying assumptions and value structures in the dynamics of social change. Men's beliefs and priorities shape political patterns; Marx's moral indignation at injustice and oppression, for instance, has been as influential as his theory of social institutions. Concerning the specific idea of "man's dominion over nature," White distinguishes the historian's task of studying the way a scriptural passage was interpreted and emphasized in earlier generations, from the contemporary task of recovering biblical themes which may have been overlooked. Thus he cites further evidence of the distinctive moral approval of technological innovation in medieval Christianity. But he also acknowledges occasional expressions of reverence for life, and even for non-living forms, both before and after St. Francis. He concludes that an ecological ethic must today rest, not simply on man's enlightened self-interest (we endanger ourselves when we endanger the biotic system), but on recognition of obligation toward all creatures.

II. MAN AND NATURE

The second group of selections deals with attitudes toward nature, and their relation to attitudes toward society and technology, from the perspective of several academic disciplines. In *American history*, as Paul Santmire's article shows, one can trace two contrasting strands. On the one hand, there has been a persistent theme of retreat to nature, of which Thoreau's *Walden*, John Muir's writings, and today's communes in the wilderness are very diverse expressions; these movements have usually been associated with a rejection of the city and its problems. On the other hand, utilitarian capitalism and the technological mentality have treated all of nature as a commodity, an object to be manipulated; the nation thought its Manifest Destiny was to subdue a continent in the name of progress. Santmire suggests that these two attitudes—retreat to nature and compulsive manipulation—appear contradictory, yet both represent evasions of the demands of social justice. Both reflect a conservative social ideology and a failure to change the status quo. Santmire holds that we should be concerned about nature and about civilization, but he finds few models for such a double concern in American history.

A similar ambiguity about nature and civilization is evident in *American literature.* Leo Marx identifies in a number of novels (*Moby Dick, Huckleberry Finn*, Ernest Hemingway's stories, for instance) a recurrent pattern which starts as a withdrawal from the city and a reaction against technology, symbolized by the machine. There is an idyllic interlude of peace, the romantic pastoralism of a life closer to nature, a psychic and moral renewal, a quasi-religious search for order and meaning. The pattern ends with the hero returning to society as man's true home, in acknowledgment that the pastoral retreat can never be permanent. Professor Marx sees here expressions of man's need for both nature and civilization, and the limitations of pursuing either one alone.

The resources in *Western religious thought* for motivating environmental action are explored by Gabriel Fackre. We have already noted his affirmation of nature and his defense of responsible stewardship. He also discusses the biblical recognition of the self-interest of groups, a view which would encourage realism about the power of vested interests today. For Fackre, the villain of the piece is "the technocratic juggernaut that has rolled over the helpless in man and nature." But he urges "taming technology, not disdaining it, and harnessing it to the purposes of personal, social, and environmental healing." He endorses new life-styles manifesting cooperation and restraint in place of competition and growth.

Perhaps *modern poetry* can also contribute distinctively to the renewal of man's sensitivity to nature. Wendell Berry shows how the tradition of earlier nature poets (Blake, Wordsworth, Whitman,

Robert Frost, D. H. Lawrence) is taken up today by Denise Levertov, A. R. Ammons, Gary Snyder, and others. Their poems express a sense of humility, awe and appreciation, imagination and openness of spirit. They portray a profound bond between man and the earth, "an impulse of reverence moving toward the world." Moreover, the respect for nature which these immediate personal responses communicate need not exclude concern for the wider social context in which much of our interaction with nature occurs.

The *biological sciences* are obviously a crucial source for environmental ethics. William Murdoch and Joseph Connell present some general conclusions from ecology—for instance, that diverse ecosystems containing many species are less vulnerable than simple systems containing few species. They summarize the ecological wisdom which is relevant to the future of man: the environment and its resources are finite, and its capacity to absorb the by-products of technology is very limited. No "technical solutions" which allow the general growth of technology to proceed unhindered will work for long. The goal, as they see it, is a non-growth economy and a stable population.

Ian McHarg brings to the problems of *city planning* a similar ecological awareness of man's dependence on his environment. The distribution of water (rivers, marshes, flood plains, ground water) is a key factor in the intelligent planning of land use (location of agriculture, recreation, residences, industry). Again, parks and gardens fulfill man's need, not simply for recreation, but also for beauty, openness and interaction with diverse surroundings. "When we find the place of nature in the city of man," says McHarg, "we may return to that enduring inquiry—the place of man in nature." There are, then, a variety of disciplines which can encourage respect for the environment without a romantic retreat from the problems of society.

III. TECHNOLOGY AND ECOLOGY
The last section of the book deals with the relation of technology to the environmental crisis. There are two extreme positions which are *not* represented among these selections:

"*Better technology is the solution.*" The technological optimists are impressed by the human genius for improvisation. They are sure that if we can reach the moon we can easily clean up our rivers. If we run out of one energy source, we'll find another. They hold that when we know what environmental mistakes to avoid, we can design improved technologies. But the technological optimists overlook the fact that the solution to one problem often creates new problems. For instance, oil spills at sea were dispersed with detergents, which in turn proved to be destructive to marine life. New technologies use further resources, create further wastes, and always use up energy and release heat. Moreover new inventions are likely to be utilized for the purposes of particular industrial interests. Confidence in purely technical solutions seems unfounded.

"Technology itself is the culprit." At the opposite extreme, the pessimists say that technology is inherently destructive of both environmental and human values. Jacques Ellul, among others, has argued that it is inevitably dehumanizing. In his eyes, technology drives toward the single value of efficiency; it is an autonomous and uncontrollable process in which man and nature are enslaved by the machine. Another kind of anti-technological stand is taken by a portion of the youth counter-culture. But the pessimists forget that the renunciation of science and technology would condemn most of the globe to a life of poverty and hunger. Furthermore, the evils attributed to technology itself seem to be mainly the products of the way it has been used and the social order within which it has developed.

My own viewpoint lies between these two extremes: technology should be neither uncritically embraced nor totally rejected, but redirected. If I were proposing a set of principles to guide this redirection, I would start from a number of general *values*, including survival (a prerequisite of all other values), human fulfillment, freedom and justice, in addition to the welfare of nonhuman species. *Human fulfillment* would require elaboration in terms of physical needs (food, housing, etc.), psychological needs (security, recognition, love), and beyond these in terms of personal creativity and interpersonal community. Fulfillment or self-realization is the development of what one takes to be the distinctive characteristics of human existence. It would be a dreary world indeed if we achieved pure air and water but lost the capacity for play and celebration, for example.

Freedom can be defined as the opportunity for individual choice and self-determination. But in a technological society, the freedom of one man or group can jeopardize the fulfillment of many men, and can produce inequalities which make a mockery of justice. The freedom of a corporation to pursue profits can leave hills devastated by strip mines or denuded of forests. In place of an individualistic concept of freedom as independent action and the absence of restraints, I believe we need to stress freedom as participation in the decisions which affect us. Only through political processes can technology be redirected toward human fulfillment and justice. Together we choose whether we breathe or suffocate.

Starting from these general values, I would propose two principles for environmental ethics today. Because man's physical needs, and perhaps survival itself, as well as human fulfillment, will be threatened if the world continues on its present course, the first principle is *ecological wisdom*, which includes the ideas of inter-dependence and finite resources mentioned earlier. And because there are such huge inequities within the U.S. and between nations, the second guiding principle is *social justice*, especially with respect to equality in economic and political power.

But *ecology* and *equality* often seem to lead in opposite directions. The essay by Norman Faramelli contrasts two revolutions now in progress. The pre-affluent revolution of the poor and the blacks is concerned about self-determination, economic opportunity and the distribution of political power. The post-affluent revolution of the young and the environmentalists is concerned about over-consumption and new life-styles. The poor and the blacks distrust the ecology movement. They want exactly what many of the affluent young are rejecting, and they have no interest in a pollution-free repressive society. Doing something about rat-infested apartments comes before bird sanctuaries in their priorities. Ecologists, on the other hand, have often ignored the particular problems of the ghetto. I suggest, however, that both ecology and equality are important and that they are not mutually exclusive. Consider the following issues in which both these principles can receive concrete application:

1. *National priorities in technology.* Research and development should be reoriented toward fundamental human needs. We have invested huge sums in military and space technology, but meager support has been given to the technologies of low-cost housing, health care, and environmental protection. Public transportation systems are called for by both ecological wisdom and distributive justice. The ghetto gets more than its share of dirt, smog, and

noise; the integrity of the biosphere is essential to the well-being of every man. Priorities for technology must be based on human and environmental considerations rather than on national pride or commercial profit.

2. *Allocation of the costs of pollution.* Justice prompts us to ask who reaps the benefits and who pays the indirect costs of a technology (for example, a freeway used mainly by suburban commuters may pollute an inner-city neighborhood and isolate one block from another). Ecological wisdom prompts us to look at the hidden, long-range social costs. Air and water can no longer be treated as free commodities for industry. Private ownership of natural resources can no longer include the right to do with them as one pleases. There are new methods of social accounting and taxation which allow the cost of disposing of all wastes from a product to be assessed against its manufacturer. We must stop rewarding unecological behavior. A tax on both the extraction of raw materials and the disposal of the end-products would provide a double incentive to recycle materials.

3. *Restraint in consumption of resources.* In the American dream, bigger is better, and growth is progress. We expect an endless expansion of production. With $23 billion spent on advertising each year, appetites for greater consumption are constantly increased. Ecological responsibility recognizes the finite limits of resources and the wastefulness of current practices. We should therefore encourage a simpler standard of living among the affluent and more careful use of energy and materials. Economic growth should occur mainly in selective areas, such as the social services, which do not make heavy demands on the environment. In the past, growth seemed to offer a way of bringing the dispossessed up without bringing the rich down; in a growing economy, everyone was supposed to get richer. But a more stabilized economy will tend to freeze the level of low-income families; therefore, in the name of social justice, we must also seek a redistribution of national income, perhaps through some form of guaranteed annual income.

4. *A global perspective.* While this volume concentrates on Western man and not on the distinctive problems of the Third World, any notion of justice must take into account the scandal of global inequalities. The U.S., with six percent of the world's population, uses from 30 to 45 percent of various natural resources used in the

whole world each year. We have plundered the non-renewable raw materials of other countries. An American uses enough resources to sustain between 50 and 100 persons living in India. At present, the growth of technology is increasing the gap between rich and poor nations. Clearly justice requires that economic and technological development should occur mainly in the newly emerging nations and be directed to basic human needs.

5. *Political mechanisms for controlling technology.* New methods of policy-making are needed if technological decisions are to be instruments of social justice. The basic question is: Who decides? There are often value judgments implicit in what seem to be technical decisions made by industrial management or government agencies of limited public visibility. The chapter by political scientist James Carroll defends "technology assessment" boards which would study the social and environmental impact of a proposed innovation in advance—before financial interests in it are strongly established. On such a board would sit spokesmen for various groups affected, since different segments of the public may evaluate these wider implications quite differently. The goal is a broader participation in all decisions by those who will be most affected by them—as workers, as consumers, and as citizens. Decisions will involve tradeoffs among benefits and costs; in a pluralistic society, wide representation is essential. We cannot entrust our future to a technical elite.

6. *Action by citizens.* There are many channels for environmental action by individuals. A person can work for the enactment of legislative measures—such as enforceable national standards for air and water effluents, pesticides, detergents, radiation, thermal pollution, etc. Another approach is action through the courts; citizen lawsuits can now be introduced as "class actions" on behalf of a public interest, even when no private economic damages are claimed. Citizen groups have forced scrutiny of many environmental problems. One can, moreover, try to bring one's own personal life-style and habits of consumption into closer conformity with ecological wisdom.

Two of the selections in this volume propose more radical measures. Paul Goodman attacks the whole "establishment": the military-industrial complex, big corporations, big government, big universities. He feels that the West is over-technologized, and recommends that we innovate sparingly, allowing only modest interventions into nature. He calls for a decentralization of technology which would use local materials and allow community participation. Goodman concludes that to save man and nature there must be not only a fundamental change in values and priorities, but also a restructuring of society, a rejection of "the entrenched world-wide system of corrupt power."

The article by "Ecology Action East" argues that the exploitation of nature is a by-product of the exploitation of man. It maintains that the starting point of change must be the rejection of all modes of domination and all hierarchical relations—between owner and worker, man and woman, parent and child, teacher and student. Liberation of nature will follow from human liberation and the abolition of institutions of domination—private property, competitive education, paternalistic families. The first step is a revolution in life-styles, in which individuals and groups take control of their own lives and create communities which express ecological attitudes toward both man and nature. Whereas other authors see some hope of working "within the system" to reform it, this selection urges the formation of independent communities based on radically different assumptions.

The topic of this book is environmental ethics; the population explosion deserves a separate volume. Nevertheless the two problems are inseparable, since each additional person must be carried by the environment. The interactions of population, pollution, and resource depletion are vividly illustrated in the final chapter by Jørgen Randers and Donella Meadows, who are members of the M.I.T. systems dynamics group studying computer models of global systems as part of a project for the Club of Rome. They give computer simulations of growth curves under a variety of alternative assumptions. In many of these projections, population continues to rise, but then falls drastically because of crises in resources, pollution or food production in the early decades of the next century. But some kinds of change now could lead to a stable equilibrium— value changes which would decrease birth rates and economic growth, and technological changes which would decrease natural resource depletion and pollution generation.

The Club of Rome computer project has been criticized for

being "oversimplified" and "based on many assumptions." The computer model does indeed leave out a large number of variables. But it is less oversimplified than the alternatives, namely the mental models by which most people think of the future. The great advantage of the computer is that it can keep track of the interaction between variables usually studied in isolation. It is indeed based on assumptions. But the assumptions are explicitly stated and can therefore be debated and improved. What most of the critics have failed to note is that the general trends and the shape of the curves are determined more by the basic interaction patterns and feedback loops than by the particular parameters assumed. As long as population and consumption per capita grow exponentially, technological improvements only postpone the crisis. As long as there are built-in delays, the population will tend to overshoot and collapse; thus after the birth rate is stabilized at the replacement rate (two children per couple), the population may continue to grow for up to 70 years because of the age distribution, and thereby exceed the carrying capacity. Yet these computer projections are not, as some critics have said, "predictions of doom." They are not predictions, but analyses of alternative modes of behavior; and the message is not doom, but hope for intelligent action.

Randers and Meadows conclude that the actions needed to avert these crises require a reorientation of our ethical judgments to give greater weight to the future. The welfare of generations yet unborn as well as the welfare of the living must be our concern if the world is to make the transition to a steady state without major catastrophes. If this is the case, the application of the principles which I have proposed for environmental ethics—ecological wisdom and social justice—must be not only global in scope, but long-range in temporal span. This would require an extension of the time horizon of our moral responsibility to include several generations in the future.

Do we start, then, by trying to change attitudes, or behavior, or institutions? People will never act to reform social institutions until they are motivated to do so by new attitudes. Yet prevailing institutions powerfully mold men's attitudes and influence their behavior. Surely we must work on all these fronts. There are no easy solutions. But the particular concern of this volume is the possibility of new attitudes toward nature and technology which might lead to new behavior and new institutions.

Advocated here is a recognition of the interdependence of all creatures and a respect for life in all its forms. Man can learn to live in harmony with nature and as part of the community of life. Technology can be redirected in accordance with ecological wisdom and social justice. A shift in values is called for: from individualism and competition to communality and cooperation. A change is needed from a frontier mentality of using up and moving on, to a spaceship mentality of living together on a fixed set of resources. But unlike a man-made spaceship built for man alone, our spaceship earth supports the life of a rich variety of creatures.

The United Nations Conference on the Human Environment, held in Stockholm in 1972, dramatized the gap between rich and poor countries and the need for a more equitable distribution in resource usage. It made clear the need for new kinds of technological development—following neither the self-perpetuating patterns of poverty of most nations in the past, nor the environmentally destructive and socially exploitative path of Western industrial nations. For countries of the Third World, health, food and economic development have higher priority than environmental preservation, yet even among them there is a new concern for the quality of life as well as for improved economic standards. There is no greater challenge to mankind than the task of combining ecological wisdom and social justice on a world-wide scale.

The image of the earth as a spaceship symbolizes both our finite resources and our global interdependence. On this frail planet we travel together to a common destiny. The pictures of our spinning globe from 100,000 miles out in space show the incredible richness and beauty of our earth, a blue and white gem among the barren planets. All the disciplines of the human mind can contribute to the task of preserving its life.

NOTES

1. I am grateful to a number of persons who have made suggestions concerning the selection of articles for this collection: Frederick Ferré (Dickinson College), Edward Long (Oberlin College), Jon Seger (Smithsonian Institution), Don Shriver (North Carolina State University), and Myron Teske (Purdue). I am particularly indebted to Richard Baer (Earlham College), and to students in my classes at Carleton College.

Part One

HISTORICAL ROOTS

2

THE HISTORICAL ROOTS OF OUR ECOLOGIC CRISIS
LYNN WHITE, JR.

A conversation with Aldous Huxley not infrequently put one at the receiving end of an unforgettable monologue. About a year before his lamented death he was discoursing on a favorite topic: Man's unnatural treatment of nature and its sad results. To illustrate his point he told how, during the previous summer, he had returned to a little valley in England where he had spent many happy months as a child. Once it had been composed of delightful grassy glades; now it was becoming overgrown with unsightly brush because the rabbits that formerly kept such growth under control had largely succumbed to a disease, myxomatosis, that was deliberately introduced by the local farmers to reduce the rabbits' destruction of crops. Being something of a Philistine, I could be silent no longer, even in the interests of great rhetoric. I interrupted to point out that the rabbit itself had been brought as a domestic animal to England in 1176, presumably to improve the protein diet of the peasantry.

All forms of life modify their contexts. The most spectacular and benign instance is doubtless the coral polyp. By serving its own ends, it has created a vast undersea world favorable to thousands of other kinds of animals and plants. Ever since man became a numerous species he has affected his environment notably. The hypothesis that his fire-drive method of hunting created the world's great grasslands and helped to exterminate the monster mammals of the Pleistocene from much of the globe is plausible, if not proved. For 6 millennia at least, the banks of the lower Nile have been a human

Lynn White is Professor of History at the University of California, Los Angeles. This article, which has become something of a classic already, appeared originally in *Science*, Vol. 155, p. 1203–1207 (10 March, 1967). Copyright 1967 by the American Association for the Advancement of Science.

artifact rather than the swampy African jungle which nature, apart from man, would have made it.   The Aswan Dam, flooding 5000 square miles, is only the latest stage in a long process.   In many regions terracing or irrigation, overgrazing, the cutting of forests by Romans to build ships to fight Carthaginians or by Crusaders to solve the logistics problems of their expeditions, have profoundly changed some ecologies.   Observation that the French landscape falls into two basic types, the open fields of the north and the *bocage* of the south and west, inspired Marc Bloch to undertake his classic study of medieval agricultural methods.   Quite unintentionally, changes in human ways often affect nonhuman nature.   It has been noted, for example, that the advent of the automobile eliminated huge flocks of sparrows that once fed on the horse manure littering every street.

The history of ecologic change is still so rudimentary that we know little about what really happened, or what the results were.   The extinction of the European aurochs as late as 1627 would seem to have been a simple case of overenthusiastic hunting.   On more intricate matters it often is impossible to find solid information.   For a thousand years or more the Frisians and Hollanders have been pushing back the North Sea, and the process is culminating in our own time in the reclamation of the Zuider Zee.   What, if any, species of animals, birds, fish, shore life, or plants have died out in the process?   In their epic combat with Neptune, have the Netherlanders overlooked ecological values in such a way that the quality of human life in the Netherlands has suffered?   I cannot discover that the questions have ever been asked, much less answered.

People, then, have often been a dynamic element in their own environment, but in the present state of historical scholarship we usually do not know exactly when, where, or with what effects man-induced changes came.   As we enter the last third of the 20th century, however, concern for the problem of ecologic backlash is mounting feverishly.   Natural science, conceived as the effort to understand the nature of things, had flourished in several eras and among several peoples.   Similarly there had been an age-old accumulation of technological skills, sometimes growing rapidly, sometimes slowly.   But it was not until about four generations ago that Western Europe and North America arranged a marriage between science and technology, a union of the theoretical and the empirical approaches to our natural environment. The emergence in widespread practice of the Baconian creed that scientific knowledge means technological power over nature can scarcely be dated before about 1850, save in the chemical industries, where it is anticipated in the 18th century. Its acceptance as a normal pattern of action may mark the greatest event in human history since the invention of agriculture, and perhaps in nonhuman terrestrial history as well.

Almost at once the new situation forced the crystallization of the novel concept of ecology; indeed, the word *ecology* first appeared in the English language in 1873. Today, less than a century later, the impact of our race upon the environment has so increased in force that it has changed in essence. When the first cannons were fired, in the early 14th century, they affected ecology by sending workers scrambling to the forests and mountains for more potash, sulfur, iron ore, and charcoal, with some resulting erosion and deforestation. Hydrogen bombs are of a different order: a war fought with them might alter the genetics of all life on this planet. By 1285 London had a smog problem arising from the burning of soft coal, but our present combustion of fossil fuels threatens to change the chemistry of the globe's atmosphere as a whole, with consequences which we are only beginning to guess. With the population explosion, the car-cinoma of planless urbanism, the now geological deposits of sewage and garbage, surely no creature other than man has ever managed to foul its nest in such short order.

There are many calls to action, but specific proposals, however worthy as individual items, seem too partial, palliative, negative: ban the bomb, tear down the billboards, give the Hindus contra-ceptives and tell them to eat their sacred cows. The simplest solution to any suspect change is, of course, to stop it, or, better yet, to revert to a romanticized past: make those ugly gasoline stations look like Anne Hathaway's cottage or (in the Far West) like ghost-town saloons. The "wilderness area" mentality invariably advocates deep-freezing an ecology, whether San Gimignano or the High Sierra, as it was before the first Kleenex was dropped. But neither atavism nor prettification will cope with the ecologic crisis of our time.

What shall we do? No one yet knows. Unless we think about fundamentals, our specific measures may produce new backlashes more serious than those they are designed to remedy.

As a beginning we should try to clarify our thinking by looking, in some historical depth, at the presuppositions that underlie modern technology and science. Science was traditionally aristocratic, speculative, intellectual in intent; technology was lower-class, empirical, action-oriented. The quite sudden fusion of these two, towards the middle of the 19th century, is surely related to the slightly prior and contemporary democratic revolutions which, by reducing social barriers, tended to assert a functional unity of brain and hand. Our ecologic crisis is the product of an emerging, entirely novel, democratic culture. The issue is whether a democratized world can survive its own implications. Presumably we cannot, unless we rethink our axioms.

THE WESTERN TRADITIONS OF TECHNOLOGY AND SCIENCE
One thing is so certain that it seems stupid to verbalize it: both modern technology and modern science are distinctively *Occidental*. Our technology has absorbed elements from all over the world, notably from China; yet everywhere today, whether in Japan or in Nigeria, successful technology is Western. Our science is the heir to all the sciences of the past, especially perhaps to the work of the great Islamic scientists of the Middle Ages, who so often outdid the ancient Greeks in skill and perspicacity: al-Rāzī in medicine, for example; or ibn-al-Haytham in optics; or Omar Khayyám in mathematics. Indeed, not a few works of such geniuses seem to have vanished in the original Arabic and to survive only in medieval Latin translations that helped to lay the foundations for later Western developments. Today, around the globe, all significant science is Western in style and method, whatever the pigmentation or language of the scientists.

A second pair of facts is less well recognized because they result from quite recent historical scholarship. The leadership of the West, both in technology and in science, is far older than the so-called Scientific Revolution of the 17th century or the so-called Industrial Revolution of the 18th century. These terms are in fact outmoded and obscure the true nature of what they try to describe —significant stages in two long and separate developments. By A.D. 1000 at the latest—and perhaps, feebly, as much as 200 years earlier—the West began to apply water power to industrial processes other than milling grain. This was followed in the late 12th century by the harnessing of wind power. From simple beginnings, but with remarkable consistency of style, the West rapidly expanded its skills in the development of power machinery, labor-saving devices, and automation. Those who doubt should contemplate that most monumental achievement in the history of automation: the weight-driven mechanical clock, which appeared in two forms in the early 14th century. Not in craftsmanship but in basic technological capacity, the Latin West of the later Middle Ages far outstripped its elaborate, sophisticated, and esthetically magnificent sister cultures, Byzantium and Islam. In 1444 a great Greek ecclesiastic, Bessarion, who had gone to Italy, wrote a letter to a prince in Greece. He is amazed by the superiority of Western ships, arms, textiles, glass. But above all he is astonished by the spectacle of waterwheels sawing timbers and pumping the bellows of blast furnaces. Clearly, he had seen nothing of the sort in the Near East.

By the end of the 15th century the technological superiority of Europe was such that its small, mutually hostile nations could spill out over all the rest of the world, conquering, looting, and colonizing. The symbol of this technological superiority is the fact that Portugal, one of the weakest states of the Occident, was able to become, and to remain for a century, mistress of the East Indies. And we must remember that the technology of Vasco da Gama and Albuquerque was built by pure empiricism, drawing remarkably little support or inspiration from science.

In the present-day vernacular understanding, modern science is supposed to have begun in 1543, when both Copernicus and Vesalius published their great works. It is no derogation of their accomplishments, however, to point out that such structures as the *Fabrica* and the *De revolutionibus* do not appear overnight. The distinctive Western tradition of science, in fact, began in the late 11th century with a massive movement of translation of Arabic and Greek scientific works into Latin. A few notable books—Theophrastus, for example—escaped the West's avid new appetite for science, but within less than 200 years, effectively the entire corpus of Greek and Muslim science was available in Latin, and was being eagerly read and criticized in the new European universities. Out of criticism arose new observation, speculation, and increasing distrust of ancient authorities. By the late 13th century Europe had seized global scientific leadership from the faltering hands of Islam.

It would be as absurd to deny the profound originality of Newton, Galileo, or Copernicus as to deny that of the 14th century scholastic scientists like Buridan or Oresme on whose work they built. Before the 11th century, science scarcely existed in the Latin West, even in Roman times. From the 11th century onward, the scientific sector of Occidental culture has increased in a steady crescendo.

Since both our technological and our scientific movements got their start, acquired their character, and achieved world dominance in the Middle Ages, it would seem that we cannot understand their nature or their present impact upon ecology without examining fundamental medieval assumptions and developments.

MEDIEVAL VIEW OF MAN AND NATURE

Until recently, agriculture has been the chief occupation even in "advanced" societies; hence, any change in methods of tillage has much importance. Early plows, drawn by two oxen, did not normally turn the sod but merely scratched it. Thus, cross-plowing was needed and fields tended to be squarish. In the fairly light soils and semi-arid climates of the Near East and Mediterranean, this worked well. But such a plow was inappropriate to the wet climate and often sticky soils of northern Europe. By the latter part of the 7th century after Christ, however, following obscure beginnings, certain northern peasants were using an entirely new kind of plow, equipped with a vertical knife to cut the line of the furrow, a horizontal share to slice under the sod, and a moldboard to turn it over. The friction of this plow with the soil was so great that it normally required not two but eight oxen. It attacked the land with such violence that cross-plowing was not needed, and fields tended to be shaped in long strips.

In the days of the scratch-plow, fields were distributed generally in units capable of supporting a single family. Subsistence farming was the presupposition. But no peasant owned eight oxen: to use the new and more efficient plow, peasants pooled their oxen to form large plow-teams, originally receiving (it would appear) plowed strips in proportion to their contribution. Thus, distribution of land was based no longer on the needs of a family but, rather, on the capacity of a power machine to till the earth. Man's relation to the soil was profoundly changed. Formerly man had been part of nature; now he was the exploiter of nature. Nowhere else in the world did farmers develop any analogous agricultural implement.

Is it coincidence that modern technology, with its ruthlessness toward nature, has so largely been produced by descendants of these peasants of northern Europe?

This same exploitive attitude appears slightly before A.D. 830 in Western illustrated calendars. In older calendars the months were shown as passive personifications. The new Frankish calendars, which set the style for the Middle Ages, are very different: they show men coercing the world around them—plowing, harvesting, chopping trees, butchering pigs. Man and nature are two things, and man is master.

These novelties seem to be in harmony with larger intellectual patterns. What people do about their ecology depends on what they think about themselves in relation to things around them. Human ecology is deeply conditioned by beliefs about our nature and destiny—that is, by religion. To Western eyes this is very evident in, say, India or Ceylon. It is equally true of ourselves and of our medieval ancestors.

The victory of Christianity over paganism was the greatest psychic revolution in the history of our culture. It has become fashionable today to say that, for better or worse, we live in "the post-Christian age." Certainly the forms of our thinking and language have largely ceased to be Christian, but to my eye the substance often remains amazingly akin to that of the past. Our daily habits of action, for example, are dominated by an implicit faith in perpetual progress which was unknown either to Greco-Roman antiquity or to the Orient. It is rooted in, and is indefensible apart from, Judeo-Christian teleology. The fact that Communists share it merely helps to show what can be demonstrated on many other grounds: that Marxism, like Islam, is a Judeo-Christian heresy. We continue today to live, as we have lived for about 1700 years, very largely in a context of Christian axioms.

What did Christianity tell people about their relations with the environment?

While many of the world's mythologies provide stories of creation, Greco-Roman mythology was singularly incoherent in this respect. Like Aristotle, the intellectuals of the ancient West denied that the visible world had had a beginning. Indeed, the idea of a beginning was impossible in the framework of their cyclical notion of time. In sharp contrast, Christianity inherited from

Judaism not only a concept of time as nonrepetitive and linear but also a striking story of creation. By gradual stages a loving and all-powerful God had created light and darkness, the heavenly bodies, the earth and all its plants, animals, birds, and fishes. Finally, God had created Adam and, as an afterthought, Eve to keep man from being lonely. Man named all the animals, thus establishing his dominance over them. God planned all of this explicitly for man's benefit and rule: no item in the physical creation had any purpose save to serve man's purposes. And, although man's body is made of clay, he is not simply part of nature: he is made in God's image.

Especially in its Western form, Christianity is the most anthropocentric religion the world has seen. As early as the 2nd century both Tertullian and St. Irenaeus of Lyons were insisting that when God shaped Adam he was foreshadowing the image of the incarnate Christ, the Second Adam. Man shares, in great measure, God's transcendence of nature. Christianity, in absolute contrast to ancient paganism and Asia's religions (except, perhaps, Zoroastrianism), not only established a dualism of man and nature but also insisted that it is God's will that man exploit nature for his proper ends.

At the level of the common people this worked out in an interesting way. In Antiquity every tree, every spring, every stream, every hill had its own *genius loci*, its guardian spirit. These spirits were accessible to men, but were very unlike men; centaurs, fauns, and mermaids show their ambivalence. Before one cut a tree, mined a mountain, or dammed a brook, it was important to placate the spirit in charge of that particular situation, and to keep it placated. By destroying pagan animism, Christianity made it possible to exploit nature in a mood of indifference to the feelings of natural objects.

It is often said that for animism the Church substituted the cult of saints. True; but the cult of saints is functionally quite different from animism. The saint is not *in* natural objects; he may have special shrines, but his citizenship is in heaven. Moreover, a saint is entirely a man; he can be approached in human terms. In addition to saints, Christianity of course also had angels and demons inherited from Judaism and perhaps, at one remove, from Zoroastrianism. But these were all as mobile as the saints themselves. The spirits *in* natural objects, which formerly had protected nature from man, evaporated. Man's effective monopoly on spirit in this world was confirmed, and the old inhibitions to the exploitation of nature crumbled.

When one speaks in such sweeping terms, a note of caution is in order. Christianity is a complex faith, and its consequences differ in differing contexts. What I have said may well apply to the medieval West, where in fact technology made spectacular advances. But the Greek East, a highly civilized realm of equal Christian devotion, seems to have produced no marked technological innovation after the late 7th century, when Greek fire was invented. The key to the contrast may perhaps be found in a difference in the tonality of piety and thought which students of comparative theology find between the Greek and the Latin Churches. The Greeks believed that sin was intellectual blindness, and that salvation was found in illumination, orthodoxy—that is, clear thinking. The Latins, on the other hand, felt that sin was moral evil, and that salvation was to be found in right conduct. Eastern theology has been intellectualist. Western theology has been voluntarist. The Greek saint contemplates; the Western saint acts. The implications of Christianity for the conquest of nature would emerge more easily in the Western atmosphere.

The Christian dogma of creation, which is found in the first clause of all the Creeds, has another meaning for our comprehension of today's ecologic crisis. By revelation, God had given man the Bible, the Book of Scripture. But since God had made nature, nature also must reveal the divine mentality. The religious study of nature for the better understanding of God was known as natural theology. In the early Church, and always in the Greek East, nature was conceived primarily as a symbolic system through which God speaks to men: the ant is a sermon to sluggards; rising flames are the symbol of the soul's aspiration. This view of nature was essentially artistic rather than scientific. While Byzantium preserved and copied great numbers of ancient Greek scientific texts, science as we conceive it could scarcely flourish in such an ambience.

However, in the Latin West by the early 13th century natural theology was following a very different bent. It was ceasing to be the decoding of the physical symbols of God's communication with man and was becoming the effort to understand God's mind by discovering how his creation operates. The rainbow was no longer simply a symbol of hope first sent to Noah after the Deluge: Robert

Grosseteste, Friar Roger Bacon, and Theodoric of Freiberg produced startlingly sophisticated work on the optics of the rainbow, but they did it as a venture in religious understanding.   From the 13th century onward, up to and including Leibnitz and Newton, every major scientist, in effect, explained his motivations in religious terms. Indeed, if Galileo had not been so expert an amateur theologian he would have got into far less trouble: the professionals resented his intrusion.   And Newton seems to have regarded himself more as a theologian than as a scientist.   It was not until the late 18th century that the hypothesis of God became unnecessary to many scientists.

It is often hard for the historian to judge, when men explain why they are doing what they want to do, whether they are offering real reasons or merely culturally acceptable reasons.   The con sistency with which scientists during the long formative centuries of Western science said that the task and the reward of the scientist was "to think God's thoughts after him" leads one to believe that this was their real motivation.   If so, then modern Western science was cast in a matrix of Christian theology.   The dynamism of religious devotion, shaped by the Judeo-Christian dogma of creation, gave it impetus.

AN ALTERNATIVE CHRISTIAN VIEW

We would seem to be headed toward conclusions unpalatable to many Christians.   Since both *science* and *technology* are blessed words in our contemporary vocabulary, some may be happy at the notions, first, that, viewed historically, modern science is an extrapolation of natural theology and, second, that modern technology is at least partly to be explained as an Occidental, voluntarist realization of the Christian dogma of man's transcendence of, and rightful mastery over, nature.   But, as we now recognize, somewhat over a century ago science and technology—hitherto quite separate activities—joined to give mankind powers which, to judge by many of the ecologic effects, are out of control.   If so, Christianity bears a huge burden of guilt.

I personally doubt that disastrous ecologic backlash can be avoided simply by applying to our problems more science and more technology.   Our science and technology have grown out of Christian attitudes toward man's relation to nature which are almost universally held not only by Christians and neo-Christians but also by those who fondly regard themselves as post-Christians. Despite Copernicus, all the cosmos rotates around our little globe. Despite Darwin, we are *not*, in our hearts, part of the natural process. We are superior to nature, contemptuous of it, willing to use it for our slightest whim. The newly elected Governor of California, like myself a churchman but less troubled than I, spoke for the Christian tradition when he said (as is alleged), "when you've seen one redwood tree, you've seen them all." To a Christian a tree can be no more than a physical fact. The whole concept of the sacred grove is alien to Christianity and to the ethos of the West. For nearly 2 millennia Christian missionaries have been chopping down sacred groves, which are idolatrous because they assume spirit in nature.

What we do about ecology depends on our ideas of the man-nature relationship. More science and more technology are not going to get us out of the present ecologic crisis until we find a new religion, or rethink our old one. The beatniks, who are the basic revolutionaries of our time, show a sound instinct in their affinity for Zen Buddhism, which conceives of the man-nature relationship as very nearly the mirror image of the Christian view. Zen, however, is as deeply conditioned by Asian history as Christianity is by the experience of the West, and I am dubious of its viability among us.

Possibly we should ponder the greatest radical in Christian history since Christ: St. Francis of Assisi. The prime miracle of St. Francis is the fact that he did not end at the stake, as many of his left-wing followers did. He was so clearly heretical that a General of the Franciscan Order, St. Bonaventura, a great and perceptive Christian, tried to suppress the early accounts of Franciscanism. The key to an understanding of Francis is his belief in the virtue of humility—not merely for the individual but for man as a species. Francis tried to depose man from his monarchy over creation and set up a democracy of all God's creatures. With him the ant is no longer simply a homily for the lazy, flames a sign of the thrust of the soul toward union with God; now they are Brother Ant and Sister Fire, praising the Creator in their own ways as Brother Man does in his.

Later commentators have said that Francis preached to the birds as a rebuke to men who would not listen. The records do not read so: he urged the little birds to praise God, and in spiritual ecstasy they flapped their wings and chirped rejoicing. Legends of

saints, especially the Irish saints, had long told of their dealings with
animals but always, I believe, to show their human dominance over
creatures. With Francis it is different. The land around Gubbio
in the Apennines was being ravaged by a fierce wolf. St. Francis,
says the legend, talked to the wolf and persuaded him of the error
of his ways. The wolf repented, died in the odor of sanctity, and
was buried in consecrated ground.

What Sir Steven Runciman calls "the Franciscan doctrine of the
animal soul" was quickly stamped out. Quite possibly it was in part
inspired, consciously or unconsciously, by the belief in reincarnation
held by the Cathar heretics who at that time teemed in Italy and
southern France, and who presumably had got it originally from
India. It is significant that at just the same moment, about 1200,
traces of metempsychosis are found also in western Judaism, in the
Provençal *Cabbala*. But Francis held neither to transmigration of
souls nor to pantheism. His view of nature and of man rested on a
unique sort of pan-psychism of all things animate and inanimate,
designed for the glorification of their transcendent Creator, who, in
the ultimate gesture of cosmic humility, assumed flesh, lay helpless
in a manger, and hung dying on a scaffold.

I am not suggesting that many contemporary Americans who
are concerned about our ecologic crisis will be either able or willing
to counsel with wolves or exhort birds. However, the present increasing disruption of the global environment is the product of a
dynamic technology and science which were originating in the
Western medieval world against which St. Francis was rebelling in
so original a way. Their growth cannot be understood historically
apart from distinctive attitudes toward nature which are deeply
grounded in Christian dogma. The fact that most people do not
think of these attitudes as Christian is irrelevant. No new set of basic
values has been accepted in our society to displace those of Christianity. Hence we shall continue to have a worsening ecologic crisis
until we reject the Christian axiom that nature has no reason for
existence save to serve man.

The greatest spiritual revolutionary in Western history, St.
Francis, proposed what he thought was an alternative Christian
view of nature and man's relation to it: he tried to substitute the idea
of the equality of all creatures, including man, for the idea of man's
limitless rule of creation. He failed. Both our present science and

our present technology are so tinctured with orthodox Christian arrogance toward nature that no solution for our ecologic crisis can be expected from them alone. Since the roots of our trouble are so largely religious, the remedy must also be essentially religious, whether we call it that or not. We must rethink and refeel our nature and destiny. The profoundly religious, but heretical, sense of the primitive Franciscans for the spiritual autonomy of all parts of nature may point a direction. I propose Francis as a patron saint for ecologists.

3

THE CULTURAL BASIS OF
OUR ENVIRONMENTAL CRISIS

LEWIS W. MONCRIEF

One hundred years ago at almost any location in the United States, potable water was no farther away than the closest brook or stream. Today there are hardly any streams in the United States, except in a few high mountainous reaches, that can safely satisfy human thirst without chemical treatment. An oft-mentioned satisfaction in the lives of urbanites in an earlier era was a leisurely stroll in late afternoon to get a breath of fresh air in a neighborhood park or along a quiet street. Today in many of our major metropolitan areas it is difficult to find a quiet, peaceful place to take a leisurely stroll and sometimes impossible to get a breath of fresh air. These contrasts point up the dramatic changes that have occurred in the quality of our environment.

It is not my intent in this article, however, to document the existence of an environmental crisis but rather to discuss the cultural basis for such a crisis. Particular attention will be given to the institutional structures as expressions of our culture.

SOCIAL ORGANIZATION

In her book entitled *Social Institutions*,[1] J. O. Hertzler classified all social institutions into nine functional categories: (i) economic and industrial, (ii) matrimonial and domestic, (iii) political, (iv) religious, (v) ethical, (vi) educational, (vii) communications, (viii) esthetic, and (ix) health. Institutions exist to carry on each of these functions in all

Lewis W. Moncrief teaches in the Department of Park and Recreation Resources at Michigan State University. This reply to Lynn White's article was published in *Science,* Vol. 170, p. 508–512 (30 October, 1970). Copyright by the American Association for the Advancement of Science.

cultures, regardless of their location or relative complexity. Thus, it is not surprising that one of the analytical criteria used by anthropologists in the study of various cultures is the comparison and contrast of the various social institutions as to form and relative importance.[2]

A number of attempts have been made to explain attitudes and behavior that are commonly associated with one institutional function as the result of influence from a presumably independent institutional factor. The classic example of such an analysis is *The Protestant Ethic and the Spirit of Capitalism* by Max Weber.[3] In this significant work Weber attributes much of the economic and industrial growth in Western Europe and North America to capitalism, which, he argued, was an economic form that developed as a result of the religious teachings of Calvin, particularly spiritual determinism.

Social scientists have been particularly active in attempting to assess the influence of religious teaching and practice and of economic motivation on other institutional forms and behavior and on each other. In this connection, L. White[4] suggested that the exploitative attitude that has prompted much of the environmental crisis in Western Europe and North America is a result of the teachings of the Judeo-Christian tradition, which conceives of man as superior to all other creation and of everything else as created for his use and enjoyment. He goes on to contend that the only way to reduce the ecologic crisis which we are now facing is to "reject the Christian axiom that nature has no reason for existence save to serve man." As with other ideas that appear to be new and novel, Professor White's observations have begun to be widely circulated and accepted in scholarly circles, as witness the article by religious writer E. B. Fiske in the *New York Times* earlier this year.[5] In this article, note is taken of the fact that several prominent theologians and theological groups have accepted this basic premise that Judeo-Christian doctrine regarding man's relation to the rest of creation is at the root of the West's environmental crisis. I would suggest that the wide acceptance of such a simplistic explanation is at this point based more on fad than on fact.

Certainly, no fault can be found with White's statement that "Human ecology is deeply conditioned by beliefs about our nature and destiny—that is, by religion." However, to argue that it is the primary conditioner of human behavior toward the environment is much more than the data that he cites to support this proposition will bear. For example, White himself notes very early in his article that there is evidence for the idea that man has been dramatically altering his environment since antiquity. If this be true, and there is evidence that it is, then this mediates against the idea that the Judeo-Christian religion uniquely predisposes cultures within which it thrives to exploit their natural resources with indiscretion. White's own examples weaken his argument considerably. He points out that human intervention in the periodic flooding of the Nile River basin and the fire-drive method of hunting by prehistoric man have both probably wrought significant "unnatural" changes in man's environment. The absence of Judeo-Christian influence in these cases is obvious.

It seems tenable to affirm that the role played by religion in man-to-man and man-to-environment relationships is one of establishing a very broad system of allowable beliefs and behavior and of articulating and invoking a system of social and spiritual rewards for those who conform and of negative sanctions for individuals or groups who approach or cross the pale of the religiously unacceptable. In other words, it defines the ball park in which the game is played, and, by the very nature of the park, some types of games cannot be played. However, the kind of game that ultimately evolves is not itself defined by the ball park. For example, where animism is practiced, it is not likely that the believers will indiscriminately destroy objects of nature because such activity would incur the danger of spiritual and social sanctions. However, the fact that another culture does not associate spiritual beings with natural objects does not mean that such a culture will invariably ruthlessly exploit its resources. It simply means that there are fewer social and psychological constraints against such action.

In the remainder of this article, I present an alternative set of hypotheses based on cultural variables which, it seems to me, are more plausible and more defensible as an explanation of the environmental crisis that is now confronting us.

No culture has been able to completely screen out the egocentric tendencies of human beings. There also exists in all cultures a status hierarchy of positions and values, with certain groups partially or totally excluded from access to these normatively desirable goals.

Historically, the differences in most cultures between the "rich" and the "poor" have been great. The many very poor have often produced the wealth of the few who controlled the means of production. There may have been no alternative where scarcity of supply and unsatiated demand were economic reality. Still, the desire for a "better life" is universal; that is, the desire for higher status positions and the achievement of culturally defined desirable goals is common to all societies.

THE EXPERIENCE IN THE WESTERN WORLD

In the West two significant revolutions that occurred in the 18th and 19th centuries completely redirected its political, social, and economic destiny.[6]   These two types of revolutions were unique to the West until very recently.   The French revolution marked the beginnings of widespread democratization.   In specific terms, this revolution involved a redistribution of the means of production and a reallocation of the natural and human resources that are an integral part of the production process.   In effect new channels of social mobility were created, which theoretically made more wealth accessible to more people.   Even though the revolution was partially perpetrated in the guise of overthrowing the control of presumably Christian institutions and of destroying the influence of God over the minds of men, still it would be superficial to argue that Christianity did not influence this revolution.   After all, biblical teaching is one of the strongest of all pronouncements concerning human dignity and individual worth.

At about the same time but over a more extended period, another kind of revolution was taking place, primarily in England.   As White points out very well, this phenomenon, which began with a number of technological innovations, eventually consummated a marriage with natural science and began to take on the character that it has retained until today.[7]   With this revolution the productive capacity of each worker was amplified by several times his potential prior to the revolution.   It also became feasible to produce goods that were not previously producible on a commercial scale.

Later, with the integration of the democratic and the technological ideals, the increased wealth began to be distributed more equitably among the population.   In addition, as the capital to land ratio increased in the production process and the demand grew for labor to work in the factories, large populations from the agrarian hinter-lands began to concentrate in the emerging industrial cities. The stage was set for the development of the conditions that now exist in the Western world.

With growing affluence for an increasingly large segment of the population, there generally develops an increased demand for goods and services. The usual by-product of this affluence is waste from both the production and consumption processes. The disposal of that waste is further complicated by the high concentration of heavy waste producers in urban areas. Under these conditions the maxim that "Dilution is the solution to pollution" does not withstand the test of time, because the volume of such wastes is greater than the system can absorb and purify through natural means. With increasing population, increasing production, increasing urban concentrations, and increasing real median incomes for well over a hundred years, it is not surprising that our environment has taken a terrible beating in absorbing our filth and refuse.

THE AMERICAN SITUATION

The North American colonies of England and France were quick to pick up the technical and social innovations that were taking place in their motherlands. Thus, it is not surprising that the inclination to develop an industrial and manufacturing base is observable rather early in the colonies. A strong trend toward democratization also evidenced itself very early in the struggle for nationhood. In fact, Thistlewaite notes the significance of the concept of democracy as embodied in French thought to the framers of constitutional government in the colonies.[8]

From the time of the dissolution of the Roman Empire, resource ownership in the Western world was vested primarily with the monarchy or the Roman Catholic Church, which in turn bestowed control of the land resources on vassals who pledged fealty to the sovereign. Very slowly the concept of private ownership developed during the Middle Ages in Europe, until it finally developed into the fee simple concept.

In America, however, national policy from the outset was designed to convey ownership of the land and other natural resources into the hands of the citizenry. Thomas Jefferson was perhaps more influential in crystallizing this philosophy in the new nation than anyone else. It was his conviction that an agrarian society made up of small landowners would furnish the most stable foundation for building the nation. This concept has received support up to the present and, against growing economic pressures in recent years, through government programs that have encouraged the conventional family farm. This point is clearly relevant to the subject of this article because it explains how the natural resources of the nation came to be controlled not by a few aristocrats but by many citizens. It explains how decisions that ultimately degrade the environment are made not only by corporation boards and city engineers but by millions of owners of our natural resources. This is democracy exemplified!

CHALLENGE OF THE FRONTIER

Perhaps the most significant interpretation of American history has been Frederick Jackson Turner's much criticized thesis that the western frontier was the prime force in shaping our society.[9]   In his own words,

If one would understand why we are today one nation, rather than a collection of isolated states, he must study this economic and social consolidation of the country. . . . The effect of the Indian frontier as a consolidating agent in our history is important.

He further postulated that the nation experienced a series of frontier challenges that moved across the continent in waves. These included the explorers' and traders' frontier, the Indian frontier, the cattle frontier, and three distinct agrarian frontiers. His thesis can be extended to interpret the expansionist period of our history in Panama, in Cuba, and in the Philippines as a need for a continued frontier challenge.

Turner's insights furnish a starting point for suggesting a second variable in analyzing the cultural basis of the United States' environmental crisis. As the nation began to expand westward, the settlers faced many obstacles, including a primitive transportation system, hostile Indians, and the absence of physical and social security. To many frontiersmen, particularly small farmers, many of the natural resources that are now highly valued were originally perceived more as obstacles than as assets. Forests needed to be cleared to permit farming. Marshes needed to be drained. Rivers needed to be controlled. Wildlife often represented a competitive threat in addition to being a source of food. Sod was considered a nuisance—to be burned, plowed, or otherwise destroyed to permit "desirable" use of the land.

Undoubtedly, part of this attitude was the product of perceiving these resources as inexhaustible. After all, if a section of timber was put to the torch to clear it for farming, it made little difference because there was still plenty to be had very easily. It is no coincidence that the "First Conservation Movement" began to develop about 1890. At that point settlement of the frontier was almost complete. With the passing of the frontier era of American history, it began to dawn on people that our resources were indeed exhaustible. This realization ushered in a new philosophy of our national government toward natural resources management under the guidance of Theodore Roosevelt and Gifford Pinchot. Samuel Hays[10] has characterized this movement as the appearance of a new "Gospel of Efficiency" in the management and utilization of our natural resources.

THE PRESENT AMERICAN SCENE

America is the archetype of what happens when democracy, technology, urbanization, capitalistic mission, and antagonism (or apathy) toward natural environment are blended together. The present situation is characterized by three dominant features that mediate against quick solution to this impending crisis: (i) an absence of personal moral direction concerning our treatment of our natural resources, (ii) an inability on the part of our social institutions to make adjustments to this stress, and (iii) an abiding faith in technology.

The first characteristic is the absence of personal moral direction. There is moral disparity when a corporation executive can receive a prison sentence for embezzlement but be congratulated for increasing profits by ignoring pollution abatement laws. That the absolute cost to society of the second act may be infinitely greater than the first is often not even considered.

The moral principle that we are to treat others as we would want to be treated seems as appropriate a guide as it ever has been. The rarity of such teaching and the even more uncommon instance of its being practiced help to explain how one municipality can, without scruple, dump its effluent into a stream even though it may do irreparable damage to the resource and add tremendously to the cost incurred by downstream municipalities that use the same water. Such attitudes are not restricted to any one culture. There appears to be an almost universal tendency to maximize self-interests and a widespread willingness to shift production costs to society to promote individual ends.

Undoubtedly, much of this behavior is the result of ignorance. If our accounting systems were more efficient in computing the cost of such irresponsibility both to the present generation and to those who will inherit the environment we are creating, steps would undoubtedly be taken to enforce compliance with measures designed to conserve resources and protect the environment. And perhaps if the total costs were known, we might optimistically speculate that more voluntary compliance would result.

A second characteristic of our current situation involves institutional inadequacies. It has been said that "what belongs to everyone belongs to no one." This maxim seems particularly appropriate to the problem we are discussing. So much of our environment is so apparently abundant that it is considered a free commodity. Air and water are particularly good examples. Great liberties have been permitted in the use and abuse of these resources for at least two reasons. First, these resources have typically been considered of less economic value than other natural resources except when conditions of extreme scarcity impose limiting factors. Second, the right of use is more difficult to establish for resources that are not associated with a fixed location.

Government, as the institution representing the corporate interests of all its citizens, has responded to date with dozens of legislative acts and numerous court decisions which give it authority to regulate the use of natural resources. However, the decisiveness to act has thus far been generally lacking. This indecisiveness cannot be understood without noting that the simplistic models that depict the conflict as that of a few powerful special interests versus "The People" are altogether inadequate. A very large proportion of the total citizenry is implicated in environmental degradation; the responsibility ranges from that of the board and executives of a utility company who might wish to thermally pollute a river with impunity to that of the average citizen who votes against a bond issue to improve the efficiency of a municipal sanitation system in order to keep his taxes from being raised. The magnitude of irresponsibility among individuals and institutions might be characterized as falling along a continuum from highly irresponsible to indirectly responsible. With such a broad base of interests being threatened with every change in resource policy direction, it is not surprising, although regrettable, that government has been so indecisive.

A third characteristic of the present American scene is an abiding faith in technology. It is very evident that the idea that technology can overcome almost any problem is widespread in Western society. This optimism exists in the face of strong evidence that much of man's technology, when misused, has produced harmful results, particularly in the long run. The reasoning goes something like this: "After all, we have gone to the moon. All we need to do is allocate enough money and brainpower and we can solve any problem."

It is both interesting and alarming that many people view technology almost as something beyond human control. Rickover put it this way:[11]

It troubles me that we are so easily pressured by purveyors of technology into permitting so-called "progress" to alter our lives without attempting to control it—as if technology were an irrepressible force of nature to which we must meekly submit.

He goes on to add:

It is important to maintain a humanistic attitude toward technology; to recognize clearly that since it is the product of human effort, technology can have no legitimate purpose but to serve man—man in general, not merely some men: future generations, not merely those who currently wish to gain advantage for themselves: man in the totality of his humanity, encompassing all his manifold interests and needs, not merely some one particular concern of his. When viewed humanistically, technology is seen not as an end in itself but a means to an end, the end being determined by man himself in accordance with the laws prevailing in his society.

In short, it is one thing to appreciate the value of technology; it is something else entirely to view it as our environmental savior—which will save us in spite of ourselves.

CONCLUSION

The forces of democracy, technology, urbanization, increasing individual wealth, and an aggressive attitude toward nature seem to be directly related to the environmental crisis now being confronted in the Western world. The Judeo-Christian tradition has probably influenced the character of each of these forces. However, to isolate religious tradition as a cultural component and to contend that it is the "historical root of our ecological crisis" is a bold affirmation for which there is little historical or scientific support.

To assert that the primary cultural condition that has created our environmental crisis is Judeo-Christian teaching avoids several hard questions. For example: Is there less tendency for those who control the resources in non-Christian cultures to live in extravagant affluence with attendant high levels of waste and inefficient consumption? If non-Judeo-Christian cultures had the same levels of economic productivity, urbanization, and high average household incomes, is there evidence to indicate that these cultures would not exploit or disregard nature as our culture does?

If our environmental crisis is a "religious problem," why are other parts of the world experiencing in various degrees the same environmental problems that we are so well acquainted with in the Western world? It is readily observable that the science and technology that developed on a large scale first in the West have been adopted elsewhere. Judeo-Christian tradition has not been adopted as a predecessor to science and technology on a comparable scale. Thus, all White can defensibly argue is that the West developed modern science and technology *first*. This says nothing about the origin or existence of a particular ethic toward our environment.

In essence, White has proposed this simple model:

I	→	II	→	III
Judeo-Christian tradition		Science and technology		Environmental degradation

I have suggested here that, at best, Judeo-Christian teaching has had only an indirect effect on the treatment of our environment. The model could be characterized as follows:

I	→	II	→	III	→	IV
Judeo-Christian tradition		1) Capitalism (with the attendant development of science and technology) 2) Democratization		1) Urbanization 2) Increased wealth 3) Increased population 4) Individual resource ownership		Environmental degradation

Even here, the link between Judeo-Christian tradition and the proposed dependent variables certainly have the least empirical support. One need only look at the veritable mountain of criticism of Weber's conclusions in *The Protestant Ethic and the Spirit of Capitalism* to sense the tenuous nature of this link. The second and third phases of this model are common to many parts of the world. Phase I is not.

Jean Mayer,[12] the eminent food scientist, gave an appropriate conclusion about the cultural basis for our environmental crisis:

It might be bad in China with 700 million poor people but 700 million rich Chinese would wreck China in no time. . . . It's the rich who wreck the environment . . . occupy much more space, consume more of each natural resource, disturb ecology more, litter the landscape . . . and create more pollution.

NOTES

1. J. O. Hertzler, *Social Institutions* (McGraw-Hill, New York, 1929), pp. 47–64.
2. L. A. White, *The Science of Culture* (Farrar, Straus and Young, New York, 1949), pp. 121–145.
3. M. Weber, *The Protestant Ethic and the Spirit of Capitalism,* translated by T. Parsons (Scribner's, New York, 1958).
4. L. White, Jr., *Science* **155**, 1203 (1967).
5. E. B. Fiske, "The link between faith and ecology," *New York Times* (4 January, 1970), section 4, p. 5.
6. R. A. Nisbet, *The Sociological Tradition* (Basic Books, New York, 1966), pp. 21–44. Nisbet gives here a perceptive discourse on the social and political implications of the democratic and industrial revolutions to the Western world.
7. It should be noted that a slower and less dramatic process of democratization was evident in English history at a much earlier date than the French revolution. Thus, the concept of democracy was probably a much more pervasive influence in English than in French life. However, a rich body of philosophic literature regarding the rationale for democracy resulted from the French revolution. Its counterpart in English literature is much less conspicuous. It is an interesting aside to suggest that perhaps the industrial revolution would not have been possible except for the more broad-based ownership of the means of production that resulted from the long-standing process of democratization in England.

8. F. Thistlewaite, *The Great Experiment* (Cambridge University Press, London, 1955), p. 34, 60.
9. F. J. Turner, *The Frontier in American History* (Henry Holt, New York, 1920 and 1947).
10. S. P. Hays, *Conservation and the Gospel of Efficiency* (Harvard University Press, Cambridge, Massachusetts, 1959).
11. H. G. Rickover, *American Forests* **75**, 13 (August, 1969).
12. J. Mayer and T. G. Harris, *Psychology Today* **3**, 46 and 48 (January, 1970).

4

A THEOLOGY OF THE EARTH
RENÉ DUBOS

Shortly after the return to earth of Apollo 8 the science editor of the Columbia Broadcasting System, Earl Ubell, interviewed the crew over the CBS network. Through skillful and persistent questioning he tried to extract from the astronauts what had been their most profound impression during their trip through space. What turned out was that their deepest emotion had been to see the earth from space. The astronauts had been overwhelmed by the beauty of the earth as compared with the bleakness of space and the grayness of the moon.

On the whole, I have been rather skeptical concerning the scientific value of the man-in-space program. But, while listening to the Apollo 8 crew, I became interested in that effort because I felt that it would pay unexpected dividends—namely, make us objectively aware, through our senses as it were, of the uniqueness of the earth among other bodies in the sky.

The incredible beauty of the earth as seen from space results largely from the fact that our planet is covered with living things. What gives vibrant colors and exciting variety to the surface of the earth is the fact that it is literally a living organism. The earth is living by the very fact that the microbes, the plants, the animals, and man have generated on its surface conditions that occur nowhere else, as far as we know, in that part of the universe that we can hope to reach. The phrase "theology of the earth" thus came to me from the Apollo 8 astronauts' accounts of what they had seen from their

René Dubos, professor at the Rockefeller University, is a microbiologist and experimental pathologist. This lecture, which includes his response to Lynn White's article, was given on 2 October, 1969, at the Smithsonian Institution in Washington, D.C.

space capsule, making me realize that the earth is a living organism.

My presentation will be a mixture of the emotional response of my total being to the beauty of the earth, and of my mental processes as a scientist trying to give a rational account of the earth's association with living things. The phrase "theology of the earth" thus denotes for me the scientific understanding of the sacred relationships that link mankind to all the physical and living attributes of the earth.

I shall have to touch on many different topics because I want to convey my belief that we have collectively begun to engage in a kind of discovery of ourselves—who we are, where we belong, and where we are going. A few lines from T. S. Eliot in his poem "Four Quartets" seems to me the ultimate expression of what I shall try to express emotionally and to analyze scientifically:

> *We shall not cease from exploration*
> *And the end of all our exploring will be*
> *To arrive where we started*
> *And know the place for the first time*[1]

All archaic peoples, all ancient classical cultures, have practiced some form of nature religion. Even in our times a large number of isolated, primitive tribes in Australia, in Africa, and in South America still experience a feeling of holiness for the land in which they live. In contrast, respect for the earth and for nature has almost completely disappeared from industrialized people in most of the countries that have accepted the ways of western civilization.

Primitive religion, with its sense of holiness of the environment, was always linked with magic. It is easy to understand how there can be links between primitive religious beliefs and the attempts to control nature through the mysterious influences of the world. Even though they always have coexisted among primitive people, religion and magic represent two very different kinds of attitudes.

In the words of the anthropologist Malinowsky: "Religion refers to the fundamental issues of human existence while magic turns round specific, concrete and practical problems."

Most of my remarks this evening will be based on the conviction that the ecological crisis in the modern world has its root in our failure to differentiate between the use of scientific technology as a kind of modern magic and what I shall call modern religion, namely, knowledge as it relates to man's place in the universe and, especially, his relation to the earth.

All ancient peoples personified a locality or a region with a particular god or goddess that symbolized the qualities and the potentialities of that place. Phrases such as "the genius of the place" or "the spirit of the place" were commonly used in the past. All followers of ancient cultures were convinced that man could not retain his physical and mental health and fulfill his destiny unless he lived in accordance with the traditions of his place and respected the spirit of that place. I believe it was this attitude that helped ancient peoples to achieve rich and creative adjustment to their surroundings. Now you may say: "Spirit of place; genius of place? This is no longer for us. We are far too learned and sophisticated."

Yet, rationalistic and blasé as we may be, we still feel, deep in our hearts, that life is governed by forces that have their roots in the soil, in the water, and in the sky around us. The last part of Lawrence Durrell's book *Spirit of Place* deals with this very topic. There is not one among us who does not sense a deep meaning in phrases such as "the genius of New England" or "the spirit of the Far West." We still sense that there is some kind of uniqueness to each place, each location, which gives it a very special meaning in our minds. But while we pine for the sense of holiness in nature, we do not know how to introduce this sense in our social structure. I am convinced that this has much to do with the ecological crisis.

I am not the first to express the feeling that we shall not be able to solve the ecological crisis until we recapture some kind of spiritual relationship between man and his environment. Some two years ago, for example, the learned American scholar Lynn White, Jr., a professor at the University of California in Los Angeles, delivered before The American Association for the Advancement of Science a special lecture titled "The Historical Roots of Our Ecologic Crisis." This lecture must strike a very sensitive chord in the minds of Americans because it has been reproduced again and again in several journals—ranging from *The Oracle*, the organ of the Hippie movement in San Francisco, to the plush magazine *Horizon*. Among the many interesting and important things White says, I single out a particular item with which I disagree in part. He stated that, in his opinion, the lack of reverence for nature on the part of modern industrial man, especially in the United States, and the desecration of nature by technology are consequences of biblical teachings. He traced them to the first chapter of Genesis in which it is said that man and woman were given the right and the duty to replenish the earth, subdue it, and have dominion over all living things. According to White, this biblical teaching has had such a profound and lasting influence on western civilization that it has made modern man lose any feeling for nature and to be concerned only with the conquest of nature for his own benefit. Also, White sees no hope of retracing our steps through science and technology because both exemplify the authority expressed in that statement in the first chapter of Genesis. The only solution to the ecological crisis, therefore, is to try to recapture the worshipful attitude that the monks of the Franciscan Order had toward nature in the thirteenth century. The last sentence of White's lecture is, if my memory serves me right, "I propose Francis as a patron saint for ecologists."

All of us have some kind of sentimental, romantic sympathy with Lynn White's thesis. All of us are happy that there have been practical expressions of this attitude in the development of the national parks and in the attempts to preserve as much wildlife as possible. By preserving the state of certain wilderness areas, with their animals and plants, their rocks and marshes, mankind symbolizes that it has retained some form of respect for the natural world. In passing, it is not without interest that the United States—the country which has certainly been the most successful and has done the most toward achieving dominion over the earth through technology—is also the one country which is doing the most to save some fragments of wilderness. I wonder at times whether Glacier Park and Monument Valley do not represent a kind of atonement for God's own junkyard.

Despite my immense admiration for Lynn White's scholarship, I find it difficult to believe that the Judeo-Christian tradition has been as influential as he thinks in bringing about the desecration of the earth. One does not need to know much history to realize that the ancient Chinese, Greek, and Moslem civilizations contributed their share to deforestation, to erosion, and to the destruction of nature in many other ways. The goats of primitive peoples were as efficient as modern bulldozers in destroying the land. In any case, the Judeo-Christian attitude concerning the relation of man to nature is not expressed only in the first chapter of Genesis. The second chapter of Genesis states that man, after he had been placed in the Garden of Eden, was instructed by God to dress it and to keep it—a statement which has ecological implications. To dress and keep the land means that man must be concerned with what happens to it.

Man is rarely, if ever, just a worshiper of nature, a passive witness of its activities. He achieved his humanness by the very act of introducing his will into natural events. He became what he is while giving form to nature. For this reason I believe that ecologists should select St. Benedict as a much truer symbol of the human condition than Francis of Assisi. Most of you probably know little about St. Benedict, perhaps even less about the history of the Benedictine Order. So allow me to elaborate on them because they represent a topic that is crucial to my personal attitude toward conservation.

St. Benedict created the first great monastery in the western world on Monte Cassino, in Italy, in the sixth century. He must have been a wise man, because when he formulated the rules of conduct for Monte Cassino—rules which became a model for monastic life all over the world—he decided that the monks should not only pray to God but also should work. Moreover, he urged that the monastery be self-sufficient. The rule of work and the need for self-sufficiency led the Benedictine monks to master a multiplicity of practical arts, especially those relating to building and to architecture. The monks learned to manage the land in such a manner that it supplied them with food and clothing, and in such a manner that it retained its productivity despite intensive cultivation. Moreover, they developed an architecture which was lasting, well-suited to the country in which they lived as well as to their activities, and which for these reasons had great functional beauty. Those of you who have traveled over the world know that the Benedictine monasteries are marvels of medieval architecture.

It seems to me that the Benedictine rule implies ecological concepts which are much more in tune with the needs of the modern world than is the worshipful attitude of St. Francis. Perhaps most influential among the monks who followed the Benedictine rule were those of the Cistercian Order. For reasons that I shall not discuss, the Cistercians established their monasteries in the lowlands and swamps: consequently, they had to learn to drain the land, and therefore they learned to use water power. And, through these technological practices, they converted areas of swamps and forests (that were not suitable for human habitation because of the prevalence of malaria) into wonderful fertile land which now makes up much of Europe's countryside.

If I have talked so long about St. Francis and St. Benedict it is not to give you a course in the history of medieval religion. Rather it is to illustrate two contrasting—but, I believe equally important—attitudes toward nature: on the one hand, passive worship; on the other, creative intervention.

I have no doubt that the kind of worship symbolized by St. Francis helps man to retain his sanity by identifying himself with the totality of creation from which he emerged. Preserving the wilderness and all forms of wildlife is essential not only for esthetic and moral reasons but also for biological reasons.

Unfortunately, it will become increasingly difficult in the modern world to protect the wilderness from human use. In fact, no longer can there be any true wilderness. No fence is tight enough to shut out radiation clouds, air and water pollution, or noise from aircraft. Some ten or twenty years ago we could still escape from the insults of technological civilization by moving to the Rocky Mountains, to the Greek islands, or to the islands of the Pacific Ocean, but now the national parks and the isolated islands are almost as crowded and as desecrated as Coney Island. The only solution left to us is to improve Coney Island. In his short novel *Candide*, Voltaire pointed out that Candide discovered at the end of his adventures that the surest formula for happiness was to cultivate one's own garden. I believe that our Garden of Eden will have to be created in our own backyards and in the hearts of our cities. Just as the Benedictine monasteries had to apply, although empirically, ecological principles so as to remain self-supporting and viable, so must we learn to manage the earth in such a manner that every part of it becomes pleasant.

The achievements of the Cistercian monks serve to illustrate another aspect of modern ecologic philosophy. As I mentioned before, the swamps in which they established their monasteries were unfit for human life because of insects and malaria. But monastic labor, skill, and intelligence converted these dismal swamps into productive agricultural areas, many of which have become centers for civilization. They demonstrate that transforming of the land, when intelligently carried out, is not destructive but, instead, can be a creative art.

My speaking of medieval times in Europe was not meant to convey the impression that only then have there been great achievements in the management of the land. One need only look at the Pennsylvania Dutch country to see a striking demonstration of land that has been created out of the forest, that became highly productive, and that has been well preserved. One could cite many similar feats all over the world. But the tendency at present is to determine the use of lands and waters, mountains and valleys, only on the basis of short-range economic benefits. And yet one can safely assert that sacrificing ecological principles on the altar of financial advantage is the road to social disaster, let alone esthetic degradation of the countryside. I shall now present a few remarks about how we can create land. By this I mean taking nature as it is presented to us and trying to do with it something which is both suitable for human life and for the health of nature.

To do this it is essential that we identify the best "vocation" for each part of our spaceship. In Latin the word for "vocation" refers to the divine call for a certain kind of function. I wish we could apply this word, and indeed I shall apply it, to the different parts of the earth because each part of the earth has, so to speak, its vocation. It is our role as scientists, humanists, and citizens, and as persons who have a feeling for the earth, to discover the vocation of each part of it.

Certain parts of the earth, like certain persons, may have only one vocation. For example, there may be only one kind of thing that can be done with the Arctic country; there may be only a limited range of things that can be done with certain tropical lands. But in practice most places, like most persons, have several vocations, several options, and this indeterminism adds greatly to the richness of life. To illustrate with a few concrete examples what I have in mind, I ask that you consider what has happened to the primeval forest in the temperate parts of the world. I am not going to speak about the tropics, I am only going to speak of western Europe and the United States—the two parts of the world that I know best.

Much of the primeval forest in temperate countries has been transformed into farmland, but what is interesting is that each part of this primeval forest transformed into farmland has acquired its own agricultural specialization, social structure, and esthetic quality. On the other hand the temperate forest need not become agricultural land. In Scotland and England such lands progressively were transformed into moors—the famous moor country of the Scottish Highlands and eastern England. This happened largely through lumbering activities and also through the sheep grazing of the Benedictine monks. The moors are not very productive from the agricultural point of view, but their charm has enriched the life of Great Britain and played a large part in literature. In North America, much of the primeval forest was transformed into prairie country as a result of the fires set by the preagricultural Indians. The prairies have now been converted in large part into agricultural land, but they have left a lasting imprint on American civilization.

I have quoted a few transformations of the land from one ecological state to another which have been successful, but I hasten to acknowledge that many other such transformations have not been as successful. Much of the country around the Mediterranean has been almost destroyed by erosion, and very little is left of the famous cedars of Lebanon. The transformation from one ecological state to another has given desirable results, especially where it has occurred slowly enough to be compatible with adaptive processes either of a purely biological nature or when it involved the adaptation of man to the new conditions. This is the case for the moors in Great Britain. In this case the creation of romantic moors out of forest land took a thousand years, so there was a chance for all the adjustments that always occur in nature, when there is enough time, to come about. Contrast this with what happened in many parts of the United States where massive and hasty lumbering has been responsible for ghost towns and for eroded land.

From now on most of the transformations of the earth's surface will occur so rapidly that we may often create those terrible situations resulting in erosion and destruction of the land. It therefore is urgent that we develop a new kind of ecological knowledge to enable us to predict the likely consequences of massive technological intervention, and to provide rational guides as substitutes for the spontaneous and empirical adjustments that centuries used to make possible.

I have spoken so far chiefly of the transformations of the forest into new ecological structures that have economic value. But utilitarian considerations are only one aspect of man's relation to the earth. The widespread interest in the preservation of wildlife and primeval scenery is sufficient evidence that man does not live by bread alone and wants to retain some contact with his distant origins. In practice, however, the only chance that most people have to experience and enjoy nature is by coming into contact with its humanized aspects—cultivated fields, parks, gardens, and human settlements. It is, of course, essential that we save the redwoods, and Everglades, and as much wilderness as possible, but it is equally important that we protect the esthetic quality of our farmland, and to use this image again, that we improve Coney Island.

I wish there were time to discuss at length the factors that make for a beautiful landscape. Clearly, there is a kind of magic splendor and magnitude which gives a unique quality to certain landscapes. The Grand Canyon, the Painted Desert, and Niagara Falls are examples of scenery to which man's presence never adds anything, and may detract a great deal. In most cases, however, the quality of the landscape consists, in a sense, of fitness between man and his surroundings. This fitness accounts for most of the charm of ancient settlements, not only in the Old World but in the New World as well. The river villages of the Ivory Coast in Africa, the Mediterranean hill towns, the pueblos of the Rio Grande, the village greens of New England, and all the old cities so well organized around peaceful rivers represent many different types of landscapes that derive their quality not so much from topographical or climatic peculiarities as from an intimate association between man and nature.

Among the many factors that play a role in the sense of identification between man and nature, let me just mention in passing how history and climate condition the architecture and the materials of dwellings and churches. Also, how the climate determines the shape and the botany of gardens and parks.

The formal gardens of Italy and France didn't just happen through accidents or through the fancy of some prince or wealthy merchant. These wonderful parks and gardens were successful because they fitted very well into the physical, biological, and social atmosphere of Italy and France at the time of their creation. Such formal parks and gardens also flourished in England, especially during the seventeenth century, but the English school achieved its unique distinction by creating an entirely different kind of park. The great and marvelous English parks of the late seventeenth and eighteenth centuries were characterized, as we all know, by magnificent trees grouped in meadows and vast expanses of lawn. This style was suited to the climate of the British Isles, to the abundance of rain, and to the fact that insolation is sufficiently limited to permit certain types of growth. In France many attempts were made in the eighteenth century to create gardens and parks in the English style. Except in a few cases, however, English-type parks and gardens were not very successful in France.

On this topic, there is an interesting letter of Horace Walpole, who was one of the prophets of the English landscape school. He traveled in France and after his return he expressed a critical opinion of the attempts to duplicate the English park on the Continent. "The French will never have lawns as good as ours until they have as rotten a climate," he wrote in a letter. This witticism expresses the biological truth that landscape styles can be lastingly successful only if they are compatible with the ecological imperatives of the countries in which they develop. This is what Alexander Pope summarized in his famous line, "In everything respect the genius of the place." The word "genius" here express the total characteristics and potentialities of a particular area.

We should have Horace Walpole's phrase in mind when we look at what is being done in our large cities toward creating parks and gardens. Just as the climate in France cannot produce the green magnificence of the English parks, so in general the atmosphere in most of our large cities is unable to support most plant species. This does not mean that plant life is out of place in our cities, only that much more effort should be made to identify and propagate for each particular city the kinds of trees, flowers, and ground cover that can best thrive under its own particular set of climatic and other constraints. When I look on New York City parks and notice how their ordinary grass can appear so pathetic, and when I see how monotonous row after row of plain trees can be, I feel that botanists and foresters should be encouraged to develop other plant species congenial to urban environment. This is a wonderful field for plant ecologists because, in the very near future, pioneers of plant ecology are likely to be much more needed in the city than in the wilderness.

To summarize my remarks, let me restate that the "genius" or the "spirit of the place" is made up of all the physical, biological, social, and historical forces which, taken together, give uniqueness to each locality. This applies not only to the wilderness but also to human settlements—Rome, Paris, London, Hamburg, New York, Chicago, San Francisco—and I have selected these cities as representatives of very different types. Each of these cities has a genius that transcends its geographical location, commercial importance, and population size. The great cities of the world contribute to the richness of the earth by giving it the wonderful diversity that man adds to the diversity of nature. The "genius of the place" will be found in every part of the world if we look for it.

In the final analysis the theology of the earth can be expressed scientifically in the form of an enlarged ecological concept. Since this theology will be formulated by human minds it inevitably will involve man's interplay with nature. We certainly must reject the attitude which asserts that man is the only value of importance and that the rest of nature can be sacrificed to his welfare and whims. But we cannot escape, I believe, an anthropocentric attitude which puts man at the summit of creation while still a part of it. Fortunately, one of the most important consequences of enlightened anthropocentricism is that man cannot effectively manipulate nature without loving nature for her own sake. And here I shall have to summarize a set of complex biological concepts in the form of general and dogmatic statements which, I hope, will convey some feeling of what I would have liked to state more scientifically.

It is not just a sentimental platitude to say that the earth is our mother. It is biologically true that the earth bore us and that we endanger ourselves when we desecrate her. The human species has been shaped biologically and mentally by the adaptive responses it has made to the conditions prevailing on the earth when the planet was still undisturbed by human intervention. Man was shaped biologically and mentally while responding to wild nature in the course of his evolution. The earth is our mother not only because she nurtures us now but especially because our biological and mental being has emerged from her, from our responses to her stimuli.

Furthermore, the earth is our mother in more than an evolutionary sense. In the course of our individual development from conception to death, our whole being is constantly influenced by the stimuli that reach us from the environment. In other words, we constantly are being modified by the stimuli that reach us from nature and also from what we have done to the earth. To a great extent, we therefore come to reflect what we create. As Winston Churchill said:

"We shape our buildings and afterward our buildings shape us."

This means that everything we create, good and bad, affects our development and, more importantly, affects the development of children. In his notes of a *Native Son* James Baldwin expressed even more vividly the influence of our environment on our biological and mental characteristics. Here are three phrases:

"We cannot escape our origins however hard we try, those origins which contain the key, could we but find it, to all that we later become."

"It means something to live where one sees space and sky, or to live where one sees nothing but rubble or nothing but high buildings."

"We take our shape within and against that cage of reality bequeathed us at our birth."

In the light of the remarks that I have presented to you, I have come to a sort of general philosophy about the meaning of the word "conservation"; and it is with a brief statement of this philosophy that I end. Conservation programs, whether for wilderness or for man-made environments, usually are formulated and conducted as if their only concern were to the human species and its welfare. Yet they can be effective only if they incorporate another dimension, namely, the earth and her welfare. This is not sentimentality but hard biological science. Man and the earth are two complementary components of an indivisible system. Each shapes the other in a wonderfully creative symbiotic and cybernetic complex. The theology of the earth has a scientific basis in the simple fact that man emerged from the earth and then acquired the ability to modify it and shape it, thus determining the evolution of his own future social life through a continuous act of creation.

NOTES

1. From T. S. Eliot, *Four Quartets.* Used by permission of the publisher, Harcourt Brace Jovanovich, Inc.

5

CONTINUING THE CONVERSATION
LYNN WHITE, JR.

The roots of my personal theology of ecology go back to a time before I had heard the word *ecology*. It was 1926, and I was in Ceylon. British colonial officials were making new roads in the jungles so that the crop of the great tea plantations could go to market more efficiently. In the red cuts slashed through the dark green vegetation I saw cones of earth left standing and asked what they were for. "Those are snakes' nests," I was told. They were spared not because the workmen were afraid of snakes—everybody in Ceylon learns to live with snakes—but because of a feeling by the workers that the snake had a right to its house so long as it wanted to stay there. Ceylon's is a Hinayana Buddhist culture believing in metempsychosis, and any given snake may well be one's late great uncle. With all the noise and activity of road building, the snake would soon decide to move to a more desireable neighborhood. After that the cone of earth would be removed. There was no particular hurry, and the officials let the diggers handle the digging in their own way.

Many of the officials seemed to be Scots, and it occurred to me that if the men with the shovels in their hands likewise had been Presbyterians the snakes would have fared less well. Only later, after I had read Max Weber, did I begin to wonder whether autonomous Buddhist Singhalese would ever have laid out those tea plantations and consequently built those roads. It was not that they lacked energy or imagination: their temples and ceremonial dancing surpassed Edinburgh's kilted dancers. Different cultures expend

---

Lynn White, Professor of History at the University of California, Los Angeles, has written especially for this volume a reply to the critics of his earlier article, "The Historical Roots of our Ecologic Crisis."

their capital, energy and imagination in very different proportions upon different sorts of creativity.

Scholars who rummage into the reasons for these remarkable variations talk about contrasting "value structures" that presumably guide the priorities of groups of people. The study of value structures, however, is slippery business because a society's own verbal formulations of its values may be unconsciously deceptive for two reasons. First, assumptions universally held may be so axiomatic that everybody forgets to mention them. Second, every complex society—including our own—reveres a more or less amorphous body of writings and certain modes of expression inherited from the past, with the result that efforts to verbalize contemporary values are normally obscured by a prestige-carrying veneer of obsolete ideas and words. The understanding of a society's value structure must be based less on what that society says about itself than on what it actually does, and on what it expresses in pictures and other symbols less involved in formal education than words are.

New exigencies, however, may occasionally compel people to formulate novel ideals that are crushed by the baggage of old values. America today is deep in ecologic crisis. I have not discovered anyone who publicly advocates pollution. Everybody says that he is against it. Yet the crisis deepens because all specific measures to remedy it are either undercut by "legitimate" interest groups, or demand kinds of regional cooperation for which our political system does not provide. We deserve our increasing pollution because, according to our structure of values, so many other things have priority over achieving a viable ecology.

The gap between our words and our deeds is not hypocrisy. It is something more dangerous: self-deception. We shall not cope with our ecologic crisis until scores of millions of us learn to understand more clearly what our real values are, and determine to change our priorities so that we not only wish but also are able to cope effectively with all aspects of pollution.

This means far more than simply rethinking and revising our economic and political systems. Organizations for making and implementing decisions, whether about producing and distributing goods or about governing, are human artifacts in the same sense that a skyscraper, a symphony orchestra, or a mathematical equation is an artifact. Human societies produce artifacts in quite different styles for many reasons. Their geographic and climatic contexts range widely; but groups in similar environments often adapt to them in strangely different ways. They inherit different materials from predecessor groups; but what living societies decide to do with their legacies from the past is incredibly variable. The artifacts of a society, including its political, social and economic patterns, are shaped primarily by what the mass of individuals in that society believe, at the sub-verbal level, about who they are, about their relation to other people and to the natural environment, and about their destiny. Every culture, whether it is overtly religious or not, is shaped primarily by its religion.

There has long been a tendency—of which Marxist theory is only one of the manifestations—to assume that the economic-social-political component of human relationships is basic to all the rest of what a society does and produces: its art, religion, literature, science, technology and so on. This does not explain why changes in economic-social-political relationships take place. World Communism was produced not by Karl Marx's social analysis but by his immense moral indignation at injustice and oppression. He changed the values of millions of people. Marx stood in the prophetic tradition, and Marxism believes that an irresistable destiny, a cosmic rightness, is leading our world toward the socialist millennium. This faith has produced vast numbers of martyrs who have died in its mission. The history of Marxism demonstrates that what can only be called religious values are fundamental in the dynamics of cultural and social change.

Professional historians, delving into the complexity of the human past, seldom use the word *cause*. The search for causes is like peeling the proverbial onion: there is always a deeper cause. What is more, it seems that for any change of great magnitude there is usually more than one cause. It is this sense of pluralism, and the various strata of historical "causation," that lead me to prefer the metaphor of *roots*. As I have peeled onions and grubbed for roots, I have more and more converged upon religion, including crypto-religion, as a source for historical explanations.

No sensible person could maintain that all ecologic damage is, or has been, rooted in religious attitudes. It is doubtful whether the dinosaurs had even a crypto-religion; nevertheless a disastrous crumbling of their ecology reduced them to token survival. A cloud of grasshoppers denuding a field is not theologically minded. Silver from Laurion helped to build the Parthenon; smelting that silver and timbering the mine shafts helped to produce the deforestation of Attica that Plato lamented. Religion in Greece affected ecology, yet that deforestation can scarcely be blamed in any direct way on the cult of Athene. And so one might comment indefinitely. But in the end one returns to value structures.

Today's ecologic situation is the by-product of a forward surging technology that first emerged during the Middle Ages in the area of the Latin church and has continued to the present. Since both the Hellenistic-Roman world and China also witnessed vigorous technological advances, Christianity obviously is not the necessary base for a dynamic technology. All that can be said—but it is not a negligible thing to say—is that Christianity *in its Latin form* (which includes Protestantism, as any Eastern Orthodox theologian can easily demonstrate) provided a set of presuppositions remarkably favorable to technological thrust. Since America's religion, and also its crypto-religion, are still Latin Christianity rather than its Greek version, let me mention a few of the items illustrating the distinctively Western medieval value structure that fostered technology.[1]

In the ninth century a picture drawn near Reims shows mankind divided into two contending camps: the righteous and the unrighteous. In each camp a sword is being conspicuously sharpened. The ungodly are content to use a large whetstone, whereas the godly possess the first rotary grindstone (or sharpener) known anywhere, and it is being turned by the first crank outside China. Since the replacement of reciprocating motion by continous rotary motion is at the heart of modern machine design, this illumination is a major monument in the history of technology. But even more instructive is the clear statement by the Benedictine monk who drew the picture that technological advance is morally good.

Similarly, in the middle of the fifteenth century the artists of northern France and Burgundy invented a novel iconography for the seven Virtues. For intricate reasons, by that time Temperance (or Moderation) had displaced Charity as the supreme Virtue. In the new iconography Temperance—and she alone—is associated with the new technology. On her head she wears a mechanical clock (invented in the 1330s), the most significant and elaborate recent bit of automation; in her right hand she holds eyeglasses (invented in the 1280s), the greatest boon to the mature intellectual; on her heels she wears rowel spurs (of about 1290); and she stands on a tower windmill (of about 1390), the most spectacular new power machine of the age. The message could scarcely be more emphatic: technological advance is superlatively virtuous.

No such statements were produced from the area of Eastern Christianity. Quite the contrary. Before the mechanical clock, the pipe organ was the most complex machine. Continuing Hellenistic-Roman traditions, organs were used in Byzantium for secular festivities. The Greek church, however, rigorously excluded all instruments from its worship: only the unaccompanied human voice could rival the cherubim in God's praise. Since the maintenance of organs demands a continuity of craftsmanship impossible in chaos, organs vanished from the West during the very early Middle Ages. In the ninth century they were reintroduced to the West for secular music, but with amazing speed they penetrated into Latin churches. The first giant organ was built by the Benedictines of Winchester in the late tenth century: its 400 pipes were blown by 26 bellows pumped by 70 men. At first organs accompanied processions, sequences and the like, but by the thirteenth century their music was used with the canon of the Mass itself.

Justinian had put sundials and clepsydras on and in a separate building adjacent to Hagia Sophia, but the Eastern church has strongly resisted putting any time-measuring device on or in its shrines themselves: to place them there would contaminate eternity with time. Mechanical clocks were invented in the West primarily to serve the needs of medical astrologers, with the result that many of them were not only timekeepers but also immensely intricate planetaria. The Latin church, far from being repelled, immediately seized upon the clock for its homiletic value; within a few decades astronomical clocks were found in and on churches all over Europe, placed there partly to tell the time but more particularly to illustrate the orderliness of God's Creation. The metaphor of the clockmaker God was invented by a great French bishop who died in 1382.

Clearly, Latin Christianity came to feel that an advancing technology was an aspect of high spirituality. The medieval Greeks did not. Men commit their lives to what they consider good. Because Western Christianity developed strong moral approval of technological innovation, more men of talent in the West put more resources, energy and imagination into the advancement of technology than was the case among Greek Christians or indeed in any other society, including the Chinese. The result was an unprecedented technological dynamism of which our present technological movement (with its attendant consequences) is the unbroken extension. There may have been other factors contributing to this advance, but the novel Western medieval value structure is central and essential to our understanding of it.

The iconography of Genesis 1:28, in which God gives dominion over nature to man, underscores my point. The Greek pictures are in marked contrast to the Latin. In Byzantine manuscripts Adam is shown at repose in his Garden; the animals are dispersed at random; sometimes God's hand appears from a cloud blessing the situation. The mood is relaxed, idyllic. The Western manuscripts show a very different scene. With his left hand God has seized Adam's wrist, and he is shaking his right index finger at Adam with great earnestness, giving detailed instructions as to his ruling of the fief that has been given him. There is a mood of imminent action, urgency. At one side the animals are huddled, looking a bit frightened. Considering the outcome, they have every right to be.

Not only modern technology but also the unhesitatingly exploitative approach to nature that has characterized our culture are largely reflections of value structures emerging from the matrix of Latin Christianity. When I published this hypothesis in 1967,[2] a bishop wrote to me: "I agree with you completely, and I am deeply troubled by it." Others were less acquiescent. I was denounced, not only in print but also on scraps of brown paper thrust anonymously into envelopes, as a junior Anti-Christ, probably in the Kremlin's pay, bent on destroying the true faith. The most common charge was that I had ignorantly misunderstood the nature of "man's dominion" and that it is not an arbitrary rule but rather a stewardship of our fellow creatures for which mankind is responsible to God.

In its doctrine of the Holy Spirit, Christianity fortunately makes provision for continuing revelation. Or, to phrase the matter in a more orthodox way, it recognizes the progressive unfolding of truths inherent in an original deposit of revelation. The Christian wants to know what Scripture says to him about a puzzling problem. The historian wants to know what Christians in various times and places have thought Scripture was saying to them. The history of Biblical exegesis is sometimes troubling. It would be hard to find a Christian of any species at present defending slavery on Scriptural grounds; yet until about two hundred years ago the overwhelming body of Christians accepted slavery as a part of God's economy. So, if one points to the fact that historically Latin Christians have generally been arrogant toward nature, this does not mean that Scripture read with twentieth-century eyes will breed the same attitude. Perhaps the Holy Ghost is whispering something to us.

In every complex religious tradition there are recessive genes which in new circumstances may become dominant genes. In my 1967 discussion I referred to St. Francis's abortive challenge to the anthropocentric concept of God's world. Scattered through the Bible, but especially the Old Testament, there are passages that can be read as sustaining the notion of a spiritual democracy of all creatures. The point is that historically they seem seldom or never to have been so interpreted. This should not inhibit anyone from taking a fresh look at them.

The most remarkable by far is the *Benedicite, omnia opera domini, domino* (O All ye Works of the Lord, bless ye the Lord) found in the Vulgate because it appears in the Septuagint version of Daniel 3:57–90. Lamentably it was eliminated from Protestant Bibles because it is not part of the Hebrew text of Daniel. It survived, however, in the Anglican prayerbook because from early times it had been used liturgically. Yet it contradicts the historically dominant Judeo-Christian anthropocentrism. It is a jubilant exhortation to all created things to glorify their Maker. It makes no distinctions between categories of creatures: the angels, the heavenly bodies, winds and rain, ice and snow, fire and heat, night and day, seas and rivers, mountains and hills, whales and birds and beasts, men and the souls of the dead, and finally the singers themselves, are urged to praise him and magnify him forever.

After my 1967 article appeared, a distinguished professor of forestry wrote to me: "We save redwood groves because people enjoy them. If St. Francis thought we should save them for squirrels, then he was preaching a religion for squirrels, not for men." I could only reply that St. Francis worshipped a God who was the God both of squirrels and of men. The author of the *Benedicite* seems to have had the same faith. There being, it seems, no present consensus among Biblical scholars about who wrote it, we may speculate that it was composed in the second century before Christ by a Hellenized Alexandrian Jew—of the community that produced the Septuagint —who felt that there were spiritual values in Greek animism that should be reconciled with the rigid monotheism of his ancestral tradition. The result smelt a bit of heresy, so both the rabbis and the more rigorous Reformers rejected it. Catholicism, both Greek and Latin, has been more patient of paradoxes so that the recessive genes of the *Benedicite* survived even though they have not thus far moderated Christian ruthlessness toward our environment. The *Benedicite* may have more of a future than a past.

Yet a man-nature dualism is deep-rooted in us, as the letter from the professor of forestry shows. Until it is eradicated not only from our minds but also from our emotions, we shall doubtless be unable to make fundamental changes in our attitudes and actions affecting ecology. The religious problem is to find a viable equivalent to animism.

During the past few generations, kindness to animals (as distinct from pets) has become a virtuous sentiment in Western culture. It is now widely regarded as Christian, although there is little or no basis for it in the Christian tradition. The Save the Redwoods League and similar groups have been extending kindness from animals to vegetables. Albert Schweitzer's concept of "reverence for life" continues to spread. But is it only to living creatures that we should be kind?

My late friend Wendell Stanley was properly honored with a Nobel Prize for crystalizing the tobacco mosaic virus: in doing so he smashed the artificial conceptual frontier between organic and inorganic matter. Stanely had religious concerns deeper than he often cared to show. Fearing that his work might start a battle as futile as that over Darwinism had been, he consulted several reputable theologians. They told him not to worry: until the time of Pasteur most people had thought that toads were generated spontaneously from mud: all he had done was to erase a recent and faulty distinction between the living and the non-living parts of God's creation.

Unfortunately most people are not very good theologians. And perhaps not all the theologians have thought their way into the ethical implications of such ideas. Do people have moral obligations towards sea otters, even though these latter eat some abalones, or to the integrity of the ecologic system of a tundra threatened by a pipeline? (Incidentally, it is amusing that the romantic brand of ecologic buff often sets up a mirror-image of the old man-nature dualism by insisting that men have no "rights" at all against those of caribou.) More and more of us are inclined to think that we should have a decent respect for our living fellow creatures, although the arguments are usually prudential: if we damage the biotic system, won't it produce a backlash that will hurt *us*? We should ask whether a prudential ethic can rightly be called an ethic. Isn't it simply a rule of enlightened self-interest to be junked if feared results cannot be shown to occur?

The problem grows if we ask "Do people have ethical obligations toward rocks?" To an ancient Greek, to an American Indian, or perhaps to certain kinds of Buddhists, the question would have meaning. For quite different reasons they would probably reply "Yes," and the replies would reflect not prudential ethics but their ideas about the nature of reality. But today to almost all Americans, still saturated with ideas historically dominant in Christianity (although perhaps not necessarily so), the question makes no sense at all. If the time comes when to any considerable group of us such a question is no longer ridiculous, we may be on the verge of a change of value structures that will make possible measures to cope with the growing ecologic crisis. One hopes that there is enough time left.

The auguries are not encouraging. Nothing touched the American spirit more deeply than our astronauts' reaction to this planet seen from outer space: it was "Spaceship Earth." The metaphor is, in fact, ecologically terrifying. A spaceship is completely a human artifact, designed to sustain human life and for no other purpose. It is no accident that some of our space men read from Genesis while on their voyage to the moon: the traditional Judeo-Christian view of the creation is precisely that it was planned in every detail for man's use and edification, and for no other purpose. This indifference to the possibility of autonomy in other creatures has much facilitated our style of technology and thus has been a major force in polluting our globe.

The spaceship mentality is the final sophistication of this disastrous man-centered view of the nature of things and the things of nature, and it has the present allurement of seeming to offer ecologic solutions without sacrifice of the old presuppositions. We are in worse danger than we seem.

NOTES

1. For details of the following, see my "The Iconography of *Temperantia* and the Virtuousness of Technology" in *Action and Conviction in the Early Modern Europe: Essays in Memory of E. H. Harbison,* ed. T. K. Rabb and J. E. Seigel (Princeton: Princeton University Press, 1969), pp. 197–219, and "Cultural Climates and Technological Advance in the Middle Ages," *Viator* 2 (1971). I have not yet published the materials on the iconography of Man's Dominion. See also my *Machina ex Deo: Essays in the Dynamism of Western Culture* (Cambridge, Massachusetts: M.I.T. Press, 1968).

2. The first detailed statement of such a view was made, so far as I know, by Ernst Benz, the great medieval historian at the University of Marburg, in his "Fondamenti cristiani della tecnica occidentale" in *Tecnica e casistica,* ed. E. Castelli (Rome, 1964), pp. 241–263. As may be seen in my *Viator* article (see above), I do not agree in all respects with Benz.

Part Two

MAN AND NATURE

6

HISTORICAL DIMENSIONS
OF THE AMERICAN CRISIS
H. PAUL SANTMIRE

Our ecological crisis has historical dimensions which we cannot afford to neglect if we are to understand *and* influence contemporary attitudes and patterns of behavior toward nature. Above all, we must be able to identify and to deal with *the ecological schizophrenia of the American mind.* On the one hand, we Americans venerate nature passionately, camping, hiking, sailing, surfing, and fighting for conservation whenever we can find the time. On the other hand, no less passionately, we venerate the Gross National Product as a criterion of national health and virtue, when increasing production regularly means the exhaustion and pollution of nature. It seems clear that we will not be able to solve our ecological crisis unless we have first resolved our ecological schizophrenia. How can we so intensely adore and yet so violently abuse the land of our destiny? I want to try to respond to that question.

I. NATURE VERSUS CIVILIZATION
When we contemplate and manipulate nature today in America, we are heirs of the nineteenth century much more than we usually realize. In the nineteenth century the American mind was captivated by two apparently contradictory religious or quasi-religious approaches to nature, each one with deep roots in Western history: Nature versus Civilization, and Civilization versus Nature. Perry Miller has aptly referred to the coexistence of these two themes as the "obsessive American drama."[1]

H. Paul Santmire is Chaplain and Lecturer in Religion at Wellesley College. This article from the Summer, 1970 issue of *Dialog* was adapted from his book, *Brother Earth* (Thomas Nelson, Inc.). Copyright, 1970 by H. Paul Santmire.

Thoreau's philosophy—increasingly popular today—is the prototype of the first theme, Nature versus Civilization.[2] Positively, this theme means the individual seeks Deity, virtue, and vitality in nature, especially wild nature, and that he strives for personal purity and vitality of soul through communion with the world of nature. So intense is the relationship to nature which this theme occasions that there is usually little psychic energy left for sustained intellectual and moral involvement in the practical political arena, whether that be with a view to upholding, transforming, or overthrowing the inherited order. That is the negative side of the nineteenth century religion of nature in America, a withdrawal from the organized city of man. That city is generally viewed as the godless, virtueless, artificial arena of the mechanized, mindless, heartless mass-man.

Thoreau believed that the wilderness was the town's source of life, a source which it could not afford to forsake. In nature, not in the "pomp and parade" of the town, he says in *Walden*, the individual may "walk with the Builder of the Universe." "Our village life," he continues, "would stagnate if it were not for the unexplored forests and meadows which surround it. . . . We need the tonic of wilderness. . . . We can never have enough of nature. We must be refreshed by the sight of inexhaustible vigor, vast and titanic features. . . ."

Thoreau also saw nature as a teacher of humility and a sense of finitude: "We need to witness our own limits transgressed and some pasturing freely where we never wander." Similarly, he viewed nature as a teacher of simplicity and virtue. Of his stay at Walden Pond, for example, he comments: "I am convinced, that if all men were to live as simply as I did, thieving and robbery would be unknown." Nature, then, was the existential substance of his life, and he was convinced that it should be of the same import for all America. In his own experience, however, he continually felt hemmed in by "the dirty institutions" of men and by their pressures on him "to belong to their desperate odd fellow society."[3] This led him ever more passionately to look beyond civilization to the wilderness. As he wistfully concludes his account of his journey to Cape Cod, depicting the Cape's easternmost shore, at the sea, at the very edge of "Naked Nature": "A man may stand there and put all America behind him."[4]

As I have suggested, the nineteenth century religion of nature was permeated with a conservative social ideology, at least by implication, since adoration means being totally captivated by the object, at the expense of other objects. The other side of the adoration of nature was an ethic of withdrawal from the town, sometimes even contempt for the town. And the result of that, as a matter of course, was that lovers of nature consistently refused to participate regularly in movements for social, political, and economic betterment in the town, which finally resulted in a tacit but firm acceptance of the urban status quo.

This is most vividly and at the same time most paradoxically expressed in the writings of Thoreau. He was a man of deep moral feeling and was particularly hostile toward the institution of slavery. This moral sensitivity is not in question here; his ethic is. We can only be thankful that Thoreau felt as strongly as he did about slavery and related issues. But how does that intense moral feeling flow from his articulated ethic? In fact, the feeling seems to have only the most tenuous of relationships to the ethic. Thoreau states, "The only obligation which I have right to assume is to do at any time what I think right."[5] And what he thought right in practice as well as in principle was *dis*engagement. His ethic is predicated on the idea of a *renunciation of sustained political involvement*—that kind of involvement which was the prior condition for the abolition of slavery and the resolution of other social ills.

Thoreau's articulated social ethic is an ethic of withdrawal from institutions and of striving for individual moral purity. By going to Walden Pond, he states, he chose "not to live in this restless, nervous, bustling, trivial Nineteenth Century, but to stand or sit thoughtfully while it goes by." Still more explicitly, he remarks in his essay on civil disobedience, "It is not a man's duty, as a matter of course, to devote himself to the eradication of any, even the most enormous, wrong . . . but it is his duty, at least, to wash his hands of it, and, if he gives it no thought longer, not to give it practically his support." One's life thus becomes "a counter-friction to stop the machine," he suggests, by turning away from it. So, quite consistently, this man who has such a deep repugnance toward slavery advises the abolitionists to "withdraw their support, both in person and in property, from the government of Massachusetts," and not to worry about winning votes.[6]

It is the pure child of nature who speaks here, the one who has found the Deity in the light and darkness of vital natural forces, not in the historical call to a community of men for moral obedience by a God who works his just purposes in history.   For Thoreau, if society is corrupt, leave it be; forsake it for the sake of your own moral purity, which can then be undergirded by the original virginity and fecundity of nature.   That is the indifferent political face behind the attractive mask of nature worship in this American drama.   That is the irresponsible political ethic of withdrawal espoused by the child of nature, who, it so happens, also has such admirably intense adult convictions about such issues as slavery.

The message came through, sometimes clearly, sometimes more by implication, in the writings and speeches by many of America's growing force of conservationists, particularly toward the end of the nineteenth century.   Perhaps the most forceful and most influential member of this group was the naturalist John Muir.   Roderick Nash rightly calls Muir the publicizer of the wilderness in America.[7] Although Muir, in many respects, restated the gospel of Thoreau, Muir's works have the added significance that they achieved a popularity Thoreau's had never known.   His books were minor best sellers, as Nash points out, and the foremost periodicals of the day bid for his articles.

Muir adored the wilderness—where he spent most of his life alone—and he scorned the city.   He was at home only in "the hospitable Godful wilderness."[8]   The wilderness, he believed, is Divine balm for a wounded, decadent society.   "If you are traveling for health," he advised, "play truant to doctors and friends, fill your pockets with biscuits, and hide in the hills of the Hollow, lave in its waters, tan in its golds, bask in its flower-shine, and your baptisms will make you a new creature indeed.   Or, choked in the sediments of society, so tired of the world, here will your hard doubts disappear, your carnal incrustations melt off, and your soul breathe deep and free in God's shoreless atmosphere of beauty and love."[9]   True, Muir fought tenaciously for national parks, and to that extent he was a participant in national political life.   But the goal of his politics was to draw the hearts of his fellow citizens away from the city to the wilderness.   As he wrote concerning the national parks, "The tendency nowadays to wander in wildernesses is delightful to see. Thousands of tired, nerve-shaken, over-civilized people are beginning to find out that going to the mountains is going home; that wilderness is a necessity; and that mountain parks and reservations are useful not only as fountains of timber and irrigating rivers, but as fountains of life."[10] His own heart, clearly, was where he wanted the nation's to be, not with the "clocks, almanacs, orders, duties, etc.," of urban routine, not with the "lowland care and dust and din, where Nature is covered and her voice smothered," but with "the freedom and glory of God's wilderness."[11] In the wilderness, which he so adored, he saw "life at work everywhere, obliterating all memory of the confusion of man."[12] And that was the ethic he lived and the gospel he proclaimed across the nation.

II. CIVILIZATION VERSUS NATURE

The city of man was burgeoning. During the nineteenth century the combination of invention, immigration, and vast stores of natural resources set loose momentous economic forces which eventually were to bulldoze the virgin American land into amazingly new contours. The symbol of the new age was the steam locomotive. As Leo Marx has observed, the locomotive became "a kind of national obsession."[13]

The nation sang about it, made political speeches about it, and wrote countless articles about it. America confessed a new faith—in words like these, from a magazine article on the Pacific Railroad cited by Marx: "And the Iron Horse, the earth-shaker, the fire-breather, which tramples down the hills, which outruns the laggard winds, which leaps over the rivers, which grinds the rocks to powder and breaks down the gates of the mountains, he too shall build an empire and an epic. Shall not solitudes and waste places cry for gladness at his coming?"[14] This was the second act of the obsessive American drama we have been considering, an act that went on simultaneously with the first, but which reversed its terms. This is the theme Civilization versus Nature.

The way for this theme was paved by a number of cultural and economic forces, which we should note here in view of their continuing influence. Intellectually, the mechanical view of nature, championed by Descartes and Newton, and widely accepted by educated men in the nineteenth century, was a powerful, if indirect, influence. According to this view, nature is analogous to a machine; or in the more popular version nature *is* a machine. Nature is composed of hard, irreducible particles which have neither color nor smell nor taste. Such qualities are "secondary." Simply expressed, beauty and value in nature are in the eye of the beholder.

In itself nature is valueless. *God,* moreover, is the supreme initiator of the world-machine. But God is little more than that. For the most part, nature the machine runs by itself, by its own intrinsic forces. God, often likened to a watchmaker, remains "back there" at the temporal beginning of the world, or "up there" in a wholly transcendent heaven; he does not really need to "meddle" with nature now. Man, likewise, is set apart from nature, at least in his spiritual aspects. For him, nature is "out there." Nature is the dead *res extensa*, perceived by his mind, which observes nature from a position of objective detachment. Nature in itself is basically a self-sufficient, self-enclosed complex of merely physical forces acting on colorless, tasteless, and odorless particles of hard, dead matter. That is the mechanical view of nature as it was popularly accepted in the circles of the educated in the nineteenth century.

The way for the theme Civilization versus Nature was also prepared by the Puritan doctrine of the dominion of man over nature. The Puritans strongly emphasized that text from Genesis which depicts God commanding man to subdue the earth and to have dominion over all creatures. The Puritans also believed that they were called upon to show the fruits of their election by their works, and so to glorify God. This, in broad outline, is what Max Weber referred to as the Protestant Ethic. Generations of Americans were instructed by their Churches that nature is properly man's sphere of lordship, given to him by God, and now at his disposal to use, by the sweat of his brow, in order to bring honor to the name of God.

From its earliest days, this Puritan doctrine tended to coalesce with what Weber further called the Spirit of Capitalism. The many spokesmen for capitalism argued, after the fashion of Adam Smith, that the ideal social system is the one which allows individual entrepreneurs freedom to develop and expand their supply of natural resources, guided chiefly by their own self-interest. While the Puritan used nature to glorify God by the fruitful exercise of his Divinely bestowed dominion, the capitalist used nature to enhance his own enterprise and so to fulfill what he considered to be his own Divinely ordained destiny. For both, then, the chief criterion for man's dealing with nature was *utility*. Hence we can conveniently refer to this coalescing of the Puritan doctrine with the apology for capitalism as the utilitarian view of nature. When all has been said, it is not surprising to note, this view depicts nature as a reality defined—this is the mind-set—by its openness to manipulation and exploitation.

It is evident how harmoniously the Puritan and capitalistic approaches to nature (the utilitarian view), on the one hand, and the mechanical view of nature, on the other hand, fit together. The common motif is that nature is valueless in itself and essentially open to human manipulation, and that nature is defined by its quantitative aspects: its existence as that colorless, tasteless, odorless *res extensa*. As Lewis Mumford has observed, "the power that was science [i.e., mechanistic Newtonian science] and the power that was money were, in the final analysis, the same kind of power; the power of abstraction, measurement, quantification."[15] And, we may add, the power that was science and money together was also the power that was religious motivation, the power of the Puritan's ingrained drive to manipulate the world he encountered, whether that be by objective study or by economic development. Thus the mechanical view of nature, which had its fount in the universities, the Puritan approach to nature, borne along by the Churches, and the capitalistic attitude toward nature, sustained by the ever-expanding class of entrepreneurs, all came together to pave the way for a religion of "civilization."

Positively, this religion means that society seeks to overcome the ancient enemies of mankind: natural disaster, disease, and, above all, hunger. It also means that men strive to build a society with a level of economic productivity and a breadth of popular distribution of goods which will provide the underpinning for political institutions which, in turn, will prohibit the enslavement of the individual. Poverty is the door to serfdom; remove the first and the second will disappear as well. This was the popular logic.

Positively, then, the theme Civilization versus Nature was egalitarian, whereas the theme Nature versus Civilization was conservative. Similarly, in a religious context, the faith in civilization was progressive, founded on a vision of a commonwealth that is yet to come, whereas the faith in nature generally was regressive, structured on a vision of a peaceable kingdom that has been lost or that is in the process of being lost through the incursions of civilization. Deity in particular is near at hand in the affairs of men, according to the religion of civilization; nearer anyway to man, the rational creature, than to nature, the brute, self-enclosed mechanism. "The kingdom of God is within you" might be chosen as the key biblical text for this theme.

Men were encouraged to work and to build, to show by their deeds that God is with them and so to glorify God. Men were *not* urged to go out to the hills, and to survey the glorious firmament in order to find the presence of God. On the contrary, they were instructed that God is with *them*—or that the moral force of history is with them—in their work and in their struggle with the elements. Correspondingly, according to the religion of civilization, virtue and vitality were not located in the wilderness as such, so much as they were thought to be produced by the challenge posed by the machine.

When the religion of civilization was articulated in the nineteenth century those positive, progressive elements came to the fore as a matter of course. And they did so usually in the form of the venerable Enlightenment notions, reason, progress, and moral Deity, which had so permeated the American consciousness in the eighteenth century.

But this religion of civilization, laudable in many respects, also had its pervasively negative aspects, as we who daily live with polluted air and water know so well. This was already apparent to some by the middle of the nineteenth century. We can see the sense of foreboding, for example, in the novels of Cooper. "In his mingling of anxieties and exultations," Perry Miller comments, "Cooper is indeed the central interpreter of his period; even while glorifying the forest-born virtue of America, he had also portrayed the brutal Skinners in *The Spy* and the settlers in *The Pioneers* who wantonly slaughter Nature's pigeons."[16] This irony of American history was stated well by Irving Babbit in 1930, looking back at the preceding century. "No age ever grew so ecstatic over natural beauty as the nineteenth century," Babbit wrote, "at the same time no age ever did so much to deface nature."[17]

Ironically, toward the end of the nineteenth century the capitalistic devastation of men, women, and children in the cities and of resources in the wilderness came to be justified by appeals to—nature. This time, however, it was not the genteel nature extolled by an Emerson, it was a newly discovered world: nature evolving by the principle of the survival of the fittest. This "Social

Darwinism" became the new ideology of many entrepreneurs. Raw nature, with its forces of darkness as well as light, which Thoreau so idolized as he turned his back on the city, had now penetrated into the city, in the form of a pernicious, pseudo-scientific, social dogma.

This, then, is the historical shape of the American schizophrenia: in the nineteenth century the traditional Western theme, Nature versus Civilization, becomes obsessive. It develops into a religion of nature, a passionate fixation on wild nature and, to a lesser extent, cultivated nature, and a religion turning away from the incursions of the machine and the politics of the city. During the same century the traditional Western theme, Civilization versus Nature, also becomes obsessive. It develops into a religion of civilization, a thoroughgoing commitment to dominate nature for the sake of "progress," accompanied by what was usually an unreflective—though sometimes deliberate—devastation of the resources of nature.

III. THE CULT OF THE SIMPLE RUSTIC LIFE
By the second half of our century, it would seem, that obsessive American drama between nature and civilization has begun to play itself out. American society seems to have resolved to deal with the problems of the city and the intimately related problems arising from modern technology. Even the most passionate nature-lover today cannot readily ignore the city, as it explodes in rebellions and spreads its polluted air across the land. In this respect the antiurban force of the religion of nature seems to have been blunted. At the same time, few Americans today are unaware of the problems of the depletion of natural resources. Even the most insensitive of the entrepreneurs seem to be beginning to realize that the "myth of abundance" of resources in America is just that, a myth. It appears that more than a few contemporary leaders of industry have begun to think about preserving our natural wealth for the sake of their enterprises and even conserving it for the sake of their employees' ever-increasing leisure time.

Nevertheless, and contrary to these recent developments, the obsessive American drama, sad to say, is *not* over. And that is why we so desperately need historical understanding as we respond to our ecological crisis today. The American drama has left an indelible mark on the American unconscious. When Morton and Lucia White conclude in *The Intellectual Versus the City* that "romantic antiurbanism cannot be regarded as a permanent fixture of the American mind," they may well be right—but only insofar as they are referring to certain representatives of the post-Civil War intelligensia.[18] The mass culture of the affluent majority today, in any case, is something else.

The religion of nature not only survives, but it thrives, in the form of a romanticizing popular ideology, conveyed and reenforced by the mass media. We can call this the *cult of the simple rustic life*. Likewise the religion of civilization is sustained by a mostly unreflective pattern of behavior, but on a vast scale. We can call this the *cult of compulsive manipulation*.

The cult of the simple rustic life is evident in the exclusive attention given to the natural life in the hundreds of smaller national magazines on camping, boating, fishing, and hunting; in the journals of the scores of conservation groups; and in the widely circulated publications of the National Geographic Society. It appears in our commercial advertising suffusively. Our advertising regularly tries to push cigarettes, shaving cream, automobiles, and virtually any other product, by highlighting the rugged individualist in the rugged country, the mountain climber, the deep sea diver, or the cowhand. Men are offered masculinity in nature as tough "Marlboro Men," and couples are offered bliss in the country with Salem cigarettes.

In a not dissimilar way the cult of the simple rustic life appears memorably in the immensely popular creations of Walt Disney and his firm. Concerning Disney's view of the world, one sensitive critic, Peter Michelson, has written: "He prefers animals before men. His good guys are either animals or men living in the jaws of nature, more kindly brutes than men—e.g., the seven dwarfs." Disney's world "is shot through with nostalgia for the happy time prior to man's corruption, to which we can return if we will be instructed by the natural laws of the land God gave us."[19] We can also see the outline of the same cult in the activities of the popular rustic organizations for young people in this country, the Cub Scouts, the Boy Scouts, Explorer Scouts, Girl Scouts, and Camp Fire Girls.

Perhaps the most striking aspect of this cult *is* that it is largely unarticulated. It is much more a presupposition of contemporary

American life, at least in its dominant affluent sectors, than a professed ideology. The Coopers and Parkmans and Thoreaus are no longer prominent, but vast numbers remain unconscious adherents to a watered-down version of their religion: the flight to wild nature, the rejection of urban life. This is not to suggest that the cult of the simple rustic life has no exponents. Indeed it has more than a few, but they generally are not writers of the stature of their nineteenth century forebears, and they are frequently in close rapport with the popular cult, hardly ever assuming the radical stance of a Thoreau over against the whole of society and its "dirty institutions."

The cult of the simple rustic life, interestingly, is not immediately so noticeable in the lives of the children of the affluent masses. Although they have been nurtured by the message of Walt Disney and other like-minded molders of the public imagination, and although they have been tutored by the style of life dramatized by romanticizing Old West television programs such as "Bonanza," they nevertheless seem to be able to attune themselves to the pulse of urban life much more closely than their parents do. This is evident in their rock music, their light shows, and their experimental films, not to speak of their radical political activities. Whether they are thereby embracing or protesting against urban life is another question, but at least they have some kind of personal stake in it. This would seem to represent something of a shift in the values of the affluent classes; that is, if these young people do not return to the traditional cult as they grow older.[20]

On the other hand, the lives of many American young people reflect their parents' cult of the simple rustic life, occasionally in remarkable ways. In some cases the cult has been internalized, so that the youthful individual tries to escape from the distressing problems of urban life not by motoring to the country or the seashore, but by "taking a trip" to an equally idealized inner world, with the help of consciousness-expanding drugs. His goal, as this is sometimes articulated, is to "turn on, tune in, and drop out." More often than not, he longs for a place with the hippies, where "flower power" is supreme, where the simple virtues are a reality. He also seeks his Walden. This quest may be undertaken with only a few friends, passing a "joint" around ritualistically—as they passed the Indian "peace pipe" when they were kids—and in this way realizing a simple natural community which the atomization and bureaucratization of technocratic society apparently prohibits. Or the quest occasionally can be a massive community trip, such as the celebrated events of Woodstock in 1969, where thousands sat around in the mud, turned on, and generally lived out the simple elementary life in nature.

Closely related to this, though usually much more private, others take their "trip" to the simple rustic world through a highly intense, highly idealized sex life. The appeal of the "naturalness" of the Living Theatre, the attractiveness of nakedness as a form of honesty not possible in our machine-society, is but one manifestation of this. Perhaps the most popular exponent of this kind of life *au naturale* is D. H. Lawrence, who is still widely read by the affluent younger generation today.

The beards and the blue-jeans worn by students at such urbane institutions as Harvard and Yale tell much the same story, as does the almost universal appeal of the Peace Corps—that life which is rugged, simple, and self-reliant, away, far away from Boston and New York. Many of these students can properly be termed "alienated." Yet they continue to manifest a longing for a life-style which is much like their parents' cult of the simple rustic life. Burdened by the weight of the "system" or the "machine" (the latter term is still used on occasion), they often seek refuge in a lonely life "on the road."

According to Kenneth Keniston, close study of them shows that "as a group, the alienated are wanderers, walkers, and hitchhikers: when confronted with a major or even a minor problem they are likely to 'take off,' sometimes for a long midnight walk, sometimes for a few years." "It is as if," Kenniston explains, "they were seeking some consoling contact with objects and things, contact more immediate and embracing than afforded by daily experience, and as if this contact could nourish and refresh them." They frequently have fantasies of mystical fusion with the universe—one thinks here of Emerson's likening himself in his mystical ecstasy to a transcendent eyeball. They manifest, as Keniston states, "the unconscious desire to lose all selfhood in some undifferentiated state with another or with nature, to be totally embraced and to be embraced totally."[21]

The latest manifestation of the cult of the simple rustic life is the much-celebrated commune movement. Recently, for example, *Parade* magazine ran a cover picture of a hippie family, husband, wife and infant, standing next to a tepee in the Western wilds of Taos, New Mexico. An estimated 2000 hippies have "renounced the comfortable life," according to the story, "and come out here to the Taos wilderness to live in comparative poverty." This is but one of hundreds of similar communes which have been established in the past few years across the country, especially in California. One can think here, too, of the growing number of much more sophisticated centers for sensitivity training and encounter groups. More often than not these centers, such as the now venerable Esalen or the newly established institute in Cumbres, New Hampshire, are set way off from civilization in the wilderness, where effete city people may revitalize themselves close to the bosom of mother nature.

As should be clear by now, the cult of the simple rustic life, like the nineteenth-century religion of nature, brings with it an implicit—sometimes explicit—social irresponsibility. It would be too much to say that the contemporary cult has been consciously developed in order to divert public attention from the pressing urban problems of the day. Indeed, in some cases a commitment to serve today's urban society is in evidence. Still, there can be little doubt that the cult of the simple rustic life does reenforce a prior commitment to the status quo, especially in the ranks of the small town, suburban, and affluent urban citizenry.

The vast sums expended on boating and camping, for example—think of those shiny "boat shows" and "camparinas" in the public auditoriums located in the midst of the decaying inner city—not to speak of the emotional investment, would surely be better spent, at least in part, in supporting low-income housing, in establishing efficient mass-transportation systems, and so on. As it is, however, the passion for boating is one of a number of similar drains on the nation's investment in its own "public sector." Or a somewhat different example: consider the popular devotion to leisure time in the forest and the mountains, particularly as that sometimes comes to a symbolic focus in conservation projects such as saving the California redwoods.

In January 1968, as President Johnson was delivering his State of the Union Message, he mentioned such urban concerns as civil rights, fair housing, and equal opportunity employment; and there was no noticeable reaction by the Congress. He then indicated his interest in saving the redwoods, and the whole Congress came alive witn loud applause. Surely, no sensitive citizen would want to see the magnificent redwood forests desecrated any more than they have been. But that silence for the city dwellers, and that applause for the trees, seemed to disclose some of the Congress' deeper feelings and, behind that, some of the deeper commitments of many whom the Congress represents.

And the story continued two years later. In his State of the Union Message, President Nixon—apparently very much in touch with the majority mood of the nation—proclaimed that the "great question of the seventies" is the environmental question: "Shall we . . . begin to make reparations for the damage we have done to our air, to our land and to our water?" In the same speech the President hardly so much as mentioned making reparations to our decaying and deprived cities and to the minority groups, particularly the blacks, who live there.

The conservatism implicit in this stance—the social ills of the city can wait, while we seek to heal the world of nature—is reflected, as we might expect, by the alienated children of the Silent Majority. This relatively small but representative group of middle class students shows a sustained contempt for political involvement in general and urban involvement in particular. For them, the thing to do is to *drop out* of society. As Keniston has written of these alienated students, "One basic, though usually hidden premise of much of their thinking is the principle of implicit conservatism. In alienated fantasies, we have seen repeatedly that revolution ends in disaster for all concerned. The ideological corollary of this fantasy is that one should seek to change the world as little as possible, for no matter how numerous its present evils, they will be succeeded by other evils just as devastating if not more so."[22]

On the other hand, as we have seen, this same group is as a general rule very much taken by the cult of the simple rustic life. This, then, is reminiscent of the nineteenth-century religion of nature, which also was essentially regressive, which depicted society as falling away from a pristine and virtuous life in nature.

There is a genuine pathos in all this, admittedly. Present-day urban, technological society is full of a thousand jagged edges. This has been amply documented by critics such as Lewis Mumford and Herbert Marcuse and by the writers of works like *1984* and *Brave New World*. In this sense, the cult of the simple rustic life might be interpreted as a protest. Yet if it is a protest, and that is by no means clear, in the last analysis it is an inarticulate, mostly unconscious, unconstructive, and therefore highly ineffective expression of discontent.

IV. THE CULT OF COMPULSIVE MANIPULATION

The other side of the cult of the simple rustic life, as the religion of civilization was the obverse side of the religion of nature, is the cult of compulsive manipulation. Americans today idolize, perhaps as never before, what Paul Tillich called technical reason. This is the cognitive faculty that calculates means for ends, which functions to "get the job done," as distinct from reflective reason which sets goals in the context of some larger structure of meaning. We Americans do not generally question why we should go to the moon; we leap to the decision and set thousands and thousands of technicians to work on the project. As Keniston has observed, "'Competence,' 'know-how,' 'efficiency,' and 'expertise' are prominent national virtues; and though we may consciously acknowledge that these are at best instrumental qualities, we often unconsciously pursue them as independent goals."[23] We are prone to manipulate our environment without question.

If we need a fast avenue from here to there, let it be. If that superhighway throws thousands of poor people out of their homes and destroys landscapes and forest preserves, so be it. If we need, or think we need, chemical weapons to fight the next war, we will have them and let the overflow fall where it may. Once Americans have the expertise to get a certain job done, all it usually takes is an impulsive decision to begin, and the project is well underway. Americans today are manipulators of the first order, compulsively.

Consider the immensely popular television series "Mission Impossible," which is the technological corollary to the simple, rustic "Bonanza." "Mission Impossible" reflects the *cool* technocratic generation: men and women without feelings (except for a cool efficient smile now and then), without sex, without playfulness, and also without noticeable moral convictions. They simply accept their instructions from the voice on the tape recorder and then, with great skill and technical imagination, get the job done, no matter what must be done. These robot people of "Mission Impossible" reveal both the sociological and the psychological pathos of the cult of manipulation.

It can be no surprise, then, that we who habitually manipulate our world and our inmost selves without much reflection, continue to deplete and deface the resources and the beauty of our natural environment much as our nineteenth-century forebears did. Behind this is the old Manifest Destiny attitude toward nature; now, however, it is clothed in cool technological garb. Our air, especially in places like New York City, Los Angeles, Detroit, and Gary, may well be cancer-inducing, as cigarette smoke is. Our milk and fish and hundreds of other foodstuffs are contaminated by DDT. Our water, almost everywhere in the nation, is both in short supply and more and more undrinkable.

The growing scientific consensus is that we in America are in danger of destroying our own natural foundations. "Mankind is living incredibly dangerously," a scientist told a Congressional committee two years ago. "We are living with and disturbing, disrupting, and attempting to manage the earth's surface," he continued, "without understanding the effects of our actions."[24] The American Association for the Advancement of Science issued similar warnings several years ago and repeated them at the end of 1969.

Like the cult of the simple rustic life, however, the cult of compulsive manipulation is largely without conscious articulation, and that makes it all the more difficult for the public to identify and to correct. It is much more a style of life than a philosophy of life. Few people today, surely, would be willing to defend the pollution of nature. On the other hand, few people are prepared to ask, to cite one example, whether the detergent they use is the indestructible variety that is foaming up in our streams and on our beaches. In the main, the cult of manipulation is an unconscious habit. Still, the habit is buttressed, as the nineteenth-century religion of civilization was buttressed, by three pervasive cultural forces: the mechanical view of nature, the Protestant doctrine of man's God-given dominion over nature, and the still venerated ideology of the entrepreneur. The last two need no comment at this point, since they function in the contemporary milieu much as they did in the nineteenth century, as ideological reenforcements for an already established pattern of life. The first of the three, the mechanical view of nature, also functions in the same way. But that is something of a surprise.

Contemporary physics has criticized, and passed beyond, the mechanical view of nature. One would think that that development would have influenced our approach to nature. But the impact of contemporary physics, which deals, of course, with unexperience-able subatomic particles, has not been felt in the context of the daily experience of most educated people. Even physicists will innocently say, upon occasion, that the classical mechanical view still is quite adequate for the items of everyday experience. It seems certain that if there is any one view of nature adhered to by educated people in America today, it is the mechanical view. If he does think reflectively about nature, the engineer or the research technician employed by the large company or by the government is much more likely to think of nature in mechanical terms than any other way. That is the mode of thought in which he has been trained and that is the mode of thought which is most congenial to "getting the job done." This is what his company or the government wants him to do. And it is the essence of the mechanical view, as we saw, to present nature itself as valueless, self-sufficient, and self-enclosed; also to present it as being separated from God and man for the most part.

So, for example, the engineer draws plans for or helps to build a supersonic transport, while he remains oblivious to the effects its sonic booms may have on society. The SST, after all, is and will remain (he thinks) part of his valueless, neutral "It-world" of mere mechanical things, and it will have its import there. That It-world is separate from the Thou-world of his personal circle, his family, friends, and acquaintances living in the green suburbs (he thinks). By extension of the same kind of logic, the It-world is also separate from society as a whole. In such ways, adherence to the mechanical view of nature continues to be a form of support for the cult of compulsive manipulation.

V. THE CHALLENGE OF SOCIAL JUSTICE

So we can see that nature, an historical dilemma for American society, remains a problem today. The American mind still suffers from a kind of schizophrenia: we continue both to worship nature and to exploit it, perhaps not so enthusiastically as our nineteenth-century predecessors, but just as relentlessly. Now, as then, to be sure, there are individual exceptions to the general rule. Not every-one, by any means, is a true believer in the cult of the simple rustic life. Not everyone, by any means, daily participates in the American liturgy of compulsive manipulation. But as far as our relationship to nature is concerned, both cults, like the religions of nature and civilization a century ago, continue to be the dominant colors in the fabric of American society.

Yet how can both exist in the same fabric in such dominant ways? Logically speaking, the cult of the simple rustic life and the cult of manipulation seem to be contradictory. And, as we recall the contours of the nineteenth-century religions of nature and civilization, we can quickly draw the same conclusion. The American approach to nature apparently has consistently been a contradiction in terms.

To explain how this apparent contradiction can be sustained, we might make some simple observations. In the nineteenth century, the two conflicting attitudes toward nature were characteristic of two relatively distinct groups: on the one hand, the nature philosophers and nature lovers who were fearful of the machine, and certain older aristocratic segments of society (like the boys who went to Harvard); on the other hand, the growing group of city-based entrepreneurs, an urban proletariat work force, and many real frontiersmen who were inclined to view the actual frontier not as a friend, but as an enemy, not as a landscape, but as a life-and-death challenge. The religions of nature and civilization were thus sustained, generally speaking, by two different social groups.

The explanation for the contradiction today might be somewhat different, since the adherents of the cult of the simple rustic life are mainly suburbanites and affluent urbanites, who are very much involved, where they work, in the mainstream economic and academic processes of our society. They are thereby priests of *both* the cult of the simple rustic life and the cult of compulsive manipulation. How can the same individual have two religions? To answer this question we could say that both cults are largely unarticulated, and that for this reason both lend themselves to easy compartmentalization. The suburbanite or the affluent urbanite works in the city; he dreams of the country. He works on a sonic-boom-producing SST, perhaps; he lives in a "ranch house." His life has two foci, and he does not feel compelled, nor is he, in fact, compelled, to relate the two reflectively

Here, then, it is not the case of two segments of society holding contradictory views; rather it is the case of a certain intraclass schizophrenia: one unreflective, compartmentalized suburban and affluent-urban mind-set. A revealing example of the success of that compartmentalization would be the state of our national parks, to which prosperous thousands flee for spiritual refreshment during the summer, and over which they litter tons of paper and soft-drink cans as they drive through.

Perhaps it is best to be content with this approach to the apparent contradiction in the American attitude toward nature, once we have identified it. But somehow to stop here is unsatisfying; something is missing. Simply to point to the schizophrenia does not really allow us to understand a man like Emerson who could both champion the locomotive and adore the world of nature. Also, and more important for the contemporary situation, it does not really account for the contemporary suburbanite and affluent urbanite, who can be so thoroughly taken by both cults. Does he not know that he is, and that he needs to be, the priest of two cults? Is he not aware, at some level of his personality, of his compartmentalized approach to his natural environment? Perhaps, then, there is a deeper explanation.

Here, however, we begin to touch on the province of existential psychology, metaphysics, and theology. Here we begin to deal with the fundamental intuitions and motives which prompt men to think and to act as they do. This province is a very subtle one, so we must proceed with caution. No observer can automatically identify why a certain individual's ultimate concern (Tillich), or why a certain group's ultimate concern, is focused precisely as it is. The best way to proceed at this point, therefore, is by suggestion. This does not mean that one is not required to give reasons for the suggestions he makes. It means that in such a delicate area as ultimate concern, which flows from the nonobjectifiable center of the self, it is more appropriate to proceed by imaginative suggestion— no easy task—than by empirical demonstration.

We might begin by introducing some Marxist categories in a somewhat oversimplified form. The religion of nature, we could say, whether it be the nineteenth-century version or the twentieth-century cult of the simple rustic life, was developed by the bourgeoisie as an opiate for the masses. The nineteenth-century evangelists of nature, it might be said, unconsciously or consciously wanted working people to live close to the land, and not in the cities, so that the workers would not come together as some "unruly mob" to press for radical changes in the status quo. Similarly today, this line of reasoning might continue, sending a worker to the woods for two weeks, or letting him buy his own boat or dream of himself as the cowboy in the Wild West, plasters over the boil of his resentment against the entrepreneurs. Likewise, the Marxist might say, the religion of nature functions to defuse social criticism and social protest in certain intellectual circles, directing them *away from* the concrete problems of social change in urban society, further solidifying the status quo by neutralizing the prophetic voice. Similarly, for Church leaders, insofar as they are also adherents of the religion of nature, the point of their message of conscience is also blunted. That, from this point of view, is how the religion of nature and the cult of the simple rustic life have functioned: as opiates.

At the same time, to continue this Marxist type of critique, the nineteenth-century religion of civilization and the contemporary cult of compulsive manipulation are direct expressions of the power and the ideology of the bourgeoisie. Plundering both things and people is not merely permitted by this theme of American life, the critique continues; plundering of things and people is even encouraged. The theme Civilization versus Nature prompts people to use each other as things and to use nature as a *mere* thing, as something which has no value apart from what it can do for the economic purposes of the upper classes. The philosophy of Social Darwinism, indeed, the Marxist could say, is actually the most honest expression of the underlying economic facts of American history.

So, this critique could conclude, we see the economic function of both themes in American history: the theme Nature versus Civilization serves to discourage social change and the theme Civilization versus Nature serves to justify the economic mores of the ruling classes. The apparent contradiction between the two themes is no contradiction at all, once one uncovers the economic substratum of intellectual and moral history. Clearly, such a Marxist critique could be quite illuminating, if it were to be documented in detail. But there is a more comprehensive theological explanation, which is also worth careful consideration.

It may well be that the American schizophrenia has its deepest roots in what may be called *the challenge of historical existence,* which is the challenge to man to be authentically the historical creature he has evolved to be. Through and through, man is an historical creature. But history brings with it anxieties and responsibilities which can weigh so heavily on man that he frequently tries to relinquish his historical destiny for something less, a sheerly natural destiny.

The challenge of historical existence emerged preeminently in the life of ancient Israel, a point illuminating for our present situation. As Tillich writes, "To the birth of man out of nature and against nature corresponds the birth of prophetism out of paganism and against paganism." As God of time, the biblical Yahweh is the God of history. "This means, first of all," Tillich explains, "that He is the God who acts in history toward a final goal. History has a direction, something new to be created in it and through it."[25] To express this differently: as God of history, Yahweh is the God of *change* and the oncoming *future*, as theologians Juergen Moltmann and Wolfhart Pannenberg have recently been arguing with great force.[26] In contrast, the gods of Israel's neighboring peoples were nature gods.[27] They were essentially intertwined with the recurring cycles of nature, particularly the seasons of the year. Hence they were gods of *stability*, both natural and civil. Similarly, with regard to social morality, Yahweh was a God of social justice and the gods of the nations, the Baalim, were gods of the status quo.

The biblical apperception of God and history, the affirmation of historical existence, produced a good deal of anxiety in the minds and hearts of those who adhered to it: a whole people was called to stake its life on a nondemonstrable Future, the coming Kingdom of God, which required moral obedience for the sake of social change leading to social justice. The anxiety this caused is reflected, for example, by the Deuteronomic historian in the introduction of his major work, when he notes how the people "would not go up," how they "murmured in [their] tents, and said, 'Because the Lord hated us he has brought us forth out of the land of Egypt, to give us into the hand of the Amorites to destroy us!'" (*Dt*.1:27) The people were not automatically willing to accept the challenge of historical existence, the challenge of leaving the secure status quo and of venturing out into an unknown and even threatening future.

The other side of the challenge of historical existence is the practically experienced failure of the historical people to be fully obedient to the claims of the coming future, the Kingdom of God. That Kingdom entails, in Jeremiah's words, executing justice one with another, not oppressing the alien, the fatherless, or the widow, not shedding innocent blood. (*Jer.* 7:5) But the people of Israel were, in fact, disobedient. As another prophet, Hosea, depicts the history of Israel, the fabric of pure Yahwism was torn, even shred, by economic self-seeking among the people of Yahweh: "It was I who knew you in the wilderness, in the land of drought; but when they had fed to the full, they were filled, and their heart was lifted up; therefore they forgot me." (*Hos.* 13:5-6) The fabric of pure Yahwism was also torn, as Hosea viewed it, by political self-seeking: "They made kings, but not through me." (*Hos.* 8:4) So, in Hosea's eyes, due to both economic and political aggrandizement, the underlying socio-religious foundations of Israelite society had begun to crumble.

In such a context, with anxiety before the future and disintegration of the essential moral response to Yahweh, the gods of the surrounding peoples in Canaan began to make inroads into Israelite life. Faced with uncertainty and fragmentation, many in the nation Israel began to be attracted to the predictableness and the stability offered by the gods of nature. Also, the very wealthy were undoubtedly concerned to hold on to their wealth—here the Marxist point emerges—so they had special reason to devote themselves to the Baalim and to encourage the masses to do so as well.

That was how the challenge of historical existence was experienced in ancient Israel. The prophets continually were calling the people to historical faithfulness to the God of history. The people were continually being pulled toward the predictableness and stability of the gods of nature. The gods of nature had their appeal both as an *escape* from the rigors of historical existence and as a *refuge*, for poor and wealthy alike (although for different reasons), in a time of socio-religious fragmentation.

The people of the New World, many centuries later, came to experience anew the challenge of historical existence in a thoroughgoing way. The American mind was shaped by an historical consciousness, first the "Exodus" from the Old World to the New, then the continuing "Errand Into the Wilderness," which Perry Miller has described so well. Along with this came the Enlightenment faith in progress—a secularization and to some extent a radical distortion of the biblical understanding of history—which underscored the historical consciousness of the nation. Progress presupposes history, clearly, since it looks forward to *the new* and to change for the better, in contrast to the recurring cycles of nature.

In this American context, then, as in the life of ancient Israel, there was both anxiety before an uncertain future and a sense that the nation had failed, or was failing, to live up to its promise. In addition, with the achievement of a certain level of prosperity, the wealthy understandably tended to desire a more stable order. Perhaps this anxiety and this sense of failure, together with the desire to protect a given economic order, were most dramatically evident in the Civil War and in the profound impact it had on the nation. During that period it was not clear whether the nation would survive, nor was it clear whether the nation would be a land of justice for all men, nor was it clear which given economic matrix would survive, the agrarian or the urban. Faced with the Civil War and with many similar occurrences during the nineteenth century, of which that war was more or less the culminating apex, the nation was understandably attracted to nature. Whereas the nation's history was being shaken to its foundations, the predictableness and the stability and— here we meet the peculiarly American motif—*the purity* of nature must have been profoundly attractive. It was indeed.

In our own time we can see a similar pattern operative, most clearly perhaps in the life-style of our "alienated students." For many of them the future is horrendously uncertain, symbolized by their fantasies of atomic holocaust. At the same time, they see our society as having failed radically to live up to its promise of justice for all men. And they hear a relentless cry for "law and order" from those who are threatened by continuing and accelerating social change. So they drop out, they take a trip, they wander across the nation, they join in communes in the wilderness, reliving the cult of the simple rustic life they learned from their affluent parents. For them the challenge of historical existence is felt most acutely, and the allure of the gods of nature is felt with corresponding power.

On the other side of the generational dividing line today, in the ranks of the older Silent Majority, we now hear both cries for "law and order" and pleas to pay "reparations to nature." This conjunction of slogans is only the most blatant verbal expression of a widespread refusal on the part of middle-class America to meet the challenge of historical existence. This is how the many-faceted, pervasive cult of the simple rustic life seems to function generally: closely allied with a thoroughgoing commitment to the political status quo. But the political status quo is disintegrating in our time, and this is a serious threat to those entrenched in power. So they focus their own attention even more on nature, particularly the stability of nature, and hope to seduce others with nature too. Whereas their children are dropping out of a society which the children detest, more or less, and in turn going to nature as an escape, the members of the Silent Majority cherish the received society, more or less, and therefore they are turning to nature, it seems, in the hope that somehow in this way society will disintegrate no further.

I am suggesting, then, that nature has functioned in nineteenth and twentieth century America, as in ancient Israel, both as an *escape* from anxiety before an uncertain and often threatening future, and as a *refuge* from a decaying "just" society (a refuge for those who are despairing over the society's failure to give justice to all; and a refuge for another large segment of society which has "made it" and which fears further social change). So the American schizophrenia is not completely new. On the contrary, its basic shape is as old as the history of Israel, when history and time first emerged potentially victorious over nature and space.

With the rise of modern industrial society, clearly, historical tendencies were forthcoming which were radically different from anything known in the Ancient Near East. At this point the parallel between the history of biblical Israel and modern America breaks down. The religion of exploitation and the cult of compulsive manipulation were simply not possible to any noticeable degree in Old Testament times. Still, in this instance we can also see nature functioning as an *escape* from the challenge of historical existence. Rather than face radically the openness of the future and the demand for social justice, we may say, men of power turned instead to a *war* against nature. Total commitment to exploitation of nature functioned for them much as total commitment to adoring nature functioned for others, as an existential alternative to openness to the future and commitment to social justice.

Instead of working for a just peace in the city of man, in other words, the bourgeoisie and their fellow travelers devoted most of their attention and expended most of their energy attacking the world of nature, in the last analysis in order to amass their own wealth and thereby to secure their own position. Their escape from history to nature took the form of aggression instead of adoration. Compulsive manipulation of nature, the twentieth-century American motif, is only a less dramatic manifestation of the same tendency:

men seeking "worldly security" (Bultmann) by excessive domination of nature, turning away from the insecurity of an open future and the demand for social justice.

This explains why middle-class Americans in the last two centuries have been able to shift so easily from the adoration to the exploitation of nature, from the cult of the simple rustic life to the cult of compulsive manipulation, and then back again, depending on the circumstances. Each approach to nature, Nature versus Civilization and Civilization versus Nature, represents a turning away from the challenge of historical existence. The American schizophrenia, in other words, is predicated on a rejection of authentic life in history.

I should add that there is clearly no schizophrenia, no twofold allegiance to nature and civilization, for the masses of the rural and urban poor today. They cannot afford the luxury of the cult of the simple rustic life. That would cost them resources which they do not have, and would not really have any existential function for them. They live too close to the subsistence level, or in some cases too close to starvation. If they have any identifiable relationship to nature it is clearly and surely utilitarian. They are understandably predisposed, as hungry men have been from the beginning of time, to "take what they can get." The religion of nature, whether it be the well-articulated faith of the nineteenth century or the mostly unarticulated contemporary cult of the simple rustic life, is a religion which actually appeals only to those who have entered the charmed circle of affluence.

If my suggestion is right, if in some sense the obsessive American drama with nature is a replaying of a story well known in the Old Testament, then I would like to suggest further that Americans today should reexamine how the prophets creatively resolved the dilemma with nature which they faced. Isaiah, for example, did not turn his back on the political arena and the Divine demand for social justice for all the poor. He challenged the Baalim. He affirmed the intrinsic rights of civilization. In this respect he stands with Marx, and against Thoreau. On the other hand, unlike Marx (who ironically was at this point very much in the camp of his bourgeois opponents), Isaiah did not approach nature as a mere thing, whose only *raison d'être* is to be dominated by man for the sake of economic justice. Isaiah looked for a Kingdom of peace and justice *in nature*, when the wolf shall dwell with the lamb, when nature's own bondage would be redeemed.

With Thoreau, and against Marx, Isaiah affirms the intrinsic rights of nature. It was one of Isaiah's closest disciples, indeed, who proclaimed the hope of "new heavens and a new earth," the ultimate vindication of the integrity and the worth of nature. *The prophetic tradition blends both social justice and cosmic redemption.* It affirms both civilization *and* nature, both the progressive forces implicit in human society *and* the rejuvenative powers implicit in the wilderness, without setting civilization or nature in opposition to the other. Hence, to speak to our situation: both the political radical and the conservationist can take their stand with Isaiah. Each one can glean from the prophetic tradition the essential concerns of his respective hero, Marx or Thoreau.

I do not want to hold up biblical prophecy as a cure for our ecological crisis. That would be preposterous. But insofar as biblical prophecy can nourish our most fundamental intellectual intuitions and our deepest existential commitments, and insofar as those intuitions and commitments shape our attitudes and our behavior, we might indeed discover that the ancient biblical tradition could help us grow out of our ecological schizophrenia.

NOTES

1. Perry Miller, *Errand Into the Wilderness* (Cambridge, Massachusetts: Belknap Press, 1956), p. 204.
2. Thoreau's thought is more subtle than I can indicate in this brief discussion. I will be referring chiefly to *Walden* and *Cape Cod*, that is, to the Thoreau whose thought has found a permanent place in the mainstream of American culture. Cf. Perry Miller, *Nature's Nation* (Cambridge, Massachusetts: Belknap Press, 1967), pp. 207ff.; and more generally, R. W. B. Lewis, *The American Adam: Innocence, Tragedy, and Tradition in the Nineteenth Century* (Chicago: University of Chicago Press, 1955), and Morton and Lucia White, *The Intellectual Versus the City: From Thomas Jefferson to Frank Lloyd Wright* (Cambridge, Massachusetts: Harvard University Press, 1962).
3. Henry David Thoreau, *Walden* (New York: W. W. Norton Company, 1951), pp. 350, 337f., 191, 90.
4. Thoreau, *Cape Cod* (New York: Thomas Y. Crowell Company, 1961), p. 319.
5. Thoreau, "Civil Disobedience," *The Works of Henry David Thoreau:*

Cape Cod and Miscellanies (New York: Houghton Mifflin Company, 1906), p. 358.

6. *Ibid.*, pp. 365, 368, 369. On the attitudes of the transcendentalists generally toward slavery, see Stanley M. Elkins, *Slavery: A Problem in American Institutional and Intellectual Life* (Chicago: University of Chicago Press, 1959), chap. IV.
7. Roderick Nash, *Wilderness and the American Mind* (New Haven: Yale University Press, 1967), chap. VIII.
8. John Muir, "My First Summer in the Sierra," in *The Works of John Muir*, Sierra ed. (Boston: Houghton Mifflin Company, 1917–18), p. 182. All the following references are to this edition.
9. Muir, "1000 Mile Walk," p. 415.
10. Muir, "Our National Parks," p. 3.
11. Muir, "My First Summer in the Sierra," p. 186f.
12. Muir, "1000 Mile Walk," p. 303.
13. Leo Marx, *The Machine in the Garden: Technology and the Pastoral Ideal in America* (New York: Oxford University Press, 1964), p. 191.
14. *Ibid.*, p. 202.
15. Lewis Mumford, *Technics and Civilization* (New York: Harcourt, Brace and Company, 1943), p. 25.
16. Miller, *Nature's Nation*, p. 205.
17. Irving Babbitt, *Rousseau and Romanticism* (Boston: Houghton Mifflin Company, 1930), p. 301.
18. Morton and Lucia White, *op. cit.*
19. Peter Michelson, "Pop Goes America," *New Republic*, CLVIII, 10 (2 September, 1967), pp. 26, 28.
20. Kenneth Keniston has studied this "new type" of American youth in his book *Young Radicals: Notes on Committed Youth* (New York: Harcourt, Brace and World, 1968).
21. Kenneth Keniston, *The Uncommitted: Alienated Youth in American Society* (New York: Harcourt, Brace, and World, 1960), pp. 93, 190.
22. *Ibid.*, p. 194.
23. *Ibid.*, p. 337.
24. David M. Gates, quoted in the *New York Times*, 11 August, 1968.
25. Paul Tillich, "The Struggle Between Time and Space," *Theology of Culture*, ed. Robert C. Kimball (New York: Oxford University Press, 1959).
26. Juergen Moltmann, *The Theology of Hope*, translated by James W. Leitch (New York: Harper and Row, 1967); Wolfhart Pannenberg, *Theology and the Kingdom of God* (Philadelphia: Westminster Press, 1969).
27. See Henri Frankfort, *Kingship and the Gods: A Study of Ancient Near Eastern Religion as the Integration of Society and Nature* (Chicago: University of Chicago Press, 1948), especially pp. 337–346.

7

PASTORAL IDEALS AND CITY TROUBLES
LEO MARX

> She told him about her childhood on a farm and of her love for animals, about country sounds and country smells and of how fresh and clean everything in the country is. She said that he ought to live there and that if he did, he would find that all his troubles were city troubles.

The woman whose opinions are being reported here is Betty, the robust, beautiful heroine of Nathanael West's macabre fable of modern American life, *Miss Lonelyhearts*. She is offering them to the protagonist, the writer of an advice-to-the-lovelorn column, Miss Lonelyhearts himself, who is neurotically obsessed with the anguish of his correspondents. And he momentarily assents, as many of us would, to Betty's plausible argument. She exaggerates, to be sure, yet who would deny that a great many of our troubles *are* city troubles? What does give us pause, however, is the notion that we can cope with them by retreating to the country. How shall we take this familiar idea? We know that it is deeply implanted in American culture, and especially in our literary culture. We know that American writers, from the beginning of a distinct national literature, have been fascinated by the theme of withdrawal from a complex, relatively 'advanced' civilization to a simpler, more natural environment. This movement in space typically has served to represent a movement of mind and spirit—a quest for a new and happier way of life. And even in the twentieth century, when the theme might be thought to have lost its relevance, it has in fact retained its hold upon the imagination of many of our leading writers.

Leo Marx is Professor of English and American Studies at Amherst College. His discussion of the attitudes toward nature and the city reflected in American literature is reprinted from *The Fitness of Man's Environment* (Smithsonian Annual II). Copyright 1968 by Smithsonian Institution.

Why? What does it signify? What bearing can it possibly have upon the problems of our urbanized society? My aim here is to answer these questions, and to suggest some ways in which the answers may be useful to those who plan the development of our physical environment.

But as a student of American culture, and one who has been concerned with the interplay between literary and extra-literary experience, I recognize that most attempts to trace the mundane consequences or implications of imaginative writing have been unsatisfactory. The crux of the difficulty is the need to make connections between two kinds of discourse. In poetry and fiction the controlling context is imagistic and metaphoric, and when we attempt to translate its meaning into everyday, practical language we all too often flatten the intricate, multidimensional structure of image, thought, and feeling; by reducing literary language to merely logical, discursive statements, we lose touch with precisely that affective power which is, after all, the distinctive property of literature—its reason for being.[1] To name this difficulty, however, is to suggest why the present enterprise could be worthwhile. Because imaginative literature remains one of our most delicate and accurate means of joining ideas with emotions, public with private experience, I believe that it can provide insights into the relations between mind and environment which are unavailable elsewhere. I want to show that the literary landscape, properly understood, could help us in planning the future of the actual landscape. I do not propose, of course, that literary works can be made to yield a blueprint or, for that matter, any specific, tangible features of a physical plan. But I do believe that they can help us sort out, clarify and reorder the principles which guide (or should guide) the planners.

No one needs to be reminded that imaginative writing, especially in the modern era, is a storehouse of ideas and emotions that men have attached to the landscape. In the American consciousness, as D. H. Lawrence observed long ago, the spirit of place is particularly strong.[2] I want to begin, therefore, with an ideal type of a familiar symbolic landscape—one that recurs everywhere in our native literature. This terrain characteristically has three sectors: a community (village, town, or city); a partly developed middle ground, neither urban nor wild; and a wilderness. But this imaginary countryside does not serve our writers merely as a backdrop or setting. In the best known American fables—I am thinking, for example, of Thoreau's *Walden*, Melville's *Moby Dick* and Mark Twain's *Huckleberry Finn*—the symbolic landscape is inseparable from the action or narrative structure, which may be divided into three movements: the retreat, the exploration of nature, and the return.[3]

First, then, the retreat. The action begins with the hero-narrator's withdrawal from a relatively complex, organized community from which he is alienated. Here life seems to be dominated by an oppressively mechanistic system of value, a preoccupation with the routine means of existence and an obliviousness of its meaning or purpose. Here, Thoreau says, men have become the tools of their tools. Unable to relate his inward experience to his environment, the narrator retreats in the direction of nature.

In the second, or central, movement he explores the possibilities of a simpler, more harmonious, way of life. At some point, invariably, there is an idyllic interlude when the beauty of the visible world inspires him with a sense of relatedness to the invisible order of the universe. During this episode, which can only be described as a moment of religious exaltation, he enjoys an unusual feeling of peace and harmony, free of anxiety, guilt, and conflict. But the possibilities of a life beyond the borders of ordinary society prove to be limited, and two characteristic kinds of episode help to define those limits.

In one, which may be called the interrupted idyll, the peace and harmony of the retreat into the middle landscape is shattered by the sudden, often violent intrusion of a machine, or of a force or person closely associated, in the figurative design, with the new industrial power. (Recall the scene in which the shriek of the locomotive destroys Thoreau's revery at Walden Pond; or when Ahab's violent declaration of purpose, which he associates with mechanized power, follows Ishmael's pantheistic masthead dream; or the decisive moment when the steamboat smashes into the raft in *Huckleberry Finn*.) The second characteristic limiting episode occurs when the narrator's retreat carries him close to or into untouched, untrammeled nature, and though his exposure to the wilderness often proves to be a spiritual tonic, evoking an exhilarating sense of psychic freedom, it also arouses his fear. For he soon comes to recognize that an unchecked recoil from civilization may destroy him—either in the sense of extinguishing his uniquely human traits or in the quite literal sense of killing him. He discovers, in short, that there are two hostile forces which impinge, from opposite sides of the symbolic landscape, upon the gardenlike scene of his retreat: one is the expanding power of civilization, and the other is the menacing anarchy of wild nature.

These insights lead, however indirectly, to the third and final phase of the action: the return. Having discovered the limited possibilities of withdrawal, above all its transience, the narrator now returns, or seems to be on the point of returning, to society. But the significance of this movement, which is also the ending of the work, is clouded by ambiguity. Has the hero been redeemed? Is he prepared to take up, once again, the common life? What is he able to bring back, as it were, from his exploration of the natural environment? Though he apparently acknowledges that society is inescapable, he usually remains a forlorn and lonely figure. Our most admired American fables seldom, if ever, depict a satisfying, wholehearted return, and in the closing sentences of one of them— *Huckleberry Finn*—the protagonist already has begun a new retreat, as if to suggest an unending cycle of withdrawal and return.

So much, then, for the design of the symbolic landscape. I propose to show that it is an embodiment of a more or less coherent view of life, a conception of the relations between imagination and reality, which may be called a peculiarly American version of romantic pastoralism. Before attempting to describe the viewpoint and its contemporary implications, let me briefly consider its specifically pastoral, its distinctively American, and its romantic components.

The "psychic root" of this thematic design, perhaps of all literary pastoralism, is the impulse to retreat from a complex society in search of happiness and virtue.[4] In Western literature the theme can be traced to the work of Theocritus and Virgil, but in fact we all know it at first hand. It is the familiar urge, in the face of civilization's growing complexity and power, to "get away"—to leave a complex world (traditionally associated with the royal court and city) and begin a new life in a simpler environment (traditionally associated with the actual rural landscape). The pastoral element of the design, then, lends expression to this centrifugal impulse; it turns upon the contrast between two styles of life, one sophisticated and the other simple, one identified with a relatively "advanced" society, the other with a life "closer to nature." The continuing appeal of pastoralism evidently derives from the universality of the conflict represented by the two physical environments, and if there is a single device which may be considered a constant feature of the mode, it is the symbolic landscape that has been used to figure forth that conflict from Virgil's time to that of Robert Frost, Ernest Hemingway and William Faulkner.

To appreciate the special affinity between the pastoral mode and the American consciousness, we have only to recall the symbolic topography invented by Virgil. We all remember Arcadia, the ideal site of harmony, beauty, and material sufficiency that chiefly engages Virgil's attention. But we tend to forget the extent to which this earthly paradise derived its charm from the two contrasting kinds of terrain upon its borders. In the first eclogue Virgil insists upon the encroaching presence both of Rome—locus of imperial power, authority, and repression—and of the bare rocks and marshland that epitomize unimproved, inhospitable, infertile, wild nature. Pastoralism may be regarded as an ecological literary mode, its purpose being to mediate between the claims of these two conflicting yet inescapable human environments: one associated with man's biological origins, the other a product of technological change and sociocultural evolution. When the pastoral ideal is pictured as a middle landscape located between the extremes of wildness and overcivilization, it is easy to see why it lent iself, beginning in the Age of Discovery, to interpretations of life in the New World. Here, in place of an imaginary Arcadia, was the utopian promise of the new colonies, with the old world to the east, realm of sophistication, power, and history, and the whole reach of the North American wilderness to the west. It is not surprising, under the circumstances, that the transit of Europeans to America often was conceived, like the good shepherd's retreat to an ideal, green pasture, as a symbolic movement toward a new, simpler, and happier way of life.

The crucial distinction, then, between American and traditional versions of pastoral, is the new realism that was imparted to the ideal by the new world situation. Before the Renaissance, poets had seldom if ever thought of Arcadia as anything but a dreamland. But in Shakespeare's time the symbolic landscape which had for so long been considered a mere poetic figure suddenly acquired a real geographic location. Now the pastoral ideal was taken seriously, with a novel literalness, as a social and political possibility, and its temporal location was shifted from the golden past to the utopian future. In America, by Jefferson's time, it had acquired political as well as geographical reality. When the authors of the Declaration of Independence rephrased John Locke's enumeration of the rights for whose protection government is instituted, replacing his "life, liberty and property" with "life, liberty and the pursuit of happiness," they in effect transferred the ancient pastoral dream of human possibilities from its conventional literary context to an actual political context. No wonder that the enemies of the third President of the United States called him a poet and dreamer! In formulating the goals of the Republic, Jefferson subordinated material well-being, national wealth, and power, to what nowadays would be called the general "quality of life."

That the American public responded favorably to the pastoral idiom of the Jeffersonians seems beyond dispute. During the nineteenth century the image of a green garden, a rural society of peace and contentment, became a dominant emblem of national aspirations. In the general culture the image of the garden served to blend the ideals derived from literary pastoralism and from Christianity. Only the most astute grasped the contradiction between the kind of society that Americans *said* they wanted and the kind they actually were creating. While the stock rhetoric affirmed a desire for a serene, contemplative life of pastoral felicity, the nation's industrial achievements were demonstrating to all the world its tacit commitment to the most rapid possible rate of technological progress, and to an unlimited buildup of wealth and power. This is the conflict of value dramatized by the interrupted idyll, the episode in which a machine suddenly destroys the tranquillity of an asylum in nature.

Before this time, however, the attitudes born of international romanticism also had been assimilated to the native version of the pastoral design. To elucidate the complicated and obscure relations between the romantic vision and the pastoral mode is beyond the scope of my subject. Suffice it to say, right here, that under the influence of the romantics the pastoral retreat into nature took on a far more explicitly metaphysical, quasireligious significance. By Wordsworth's time the natural landscape had become a repository for those ultimate values formerly attributed to the Christian deity. As Emerson puts it, nature (which he usually represented by landscape images), had become for his generation "the present expositor of the divine mind." At the same time in the "high culture," the machine was becoming a dominant symbol for the impersonal, squalid, and inhumane world of the new industrialism, so that the movement in the direction of nature now could be depicted as a melodramatic withdrawal from a cold, mechanized city into a warm, living, spiritually nurturing countryside. In the romantic era native pastoralism acquired new vitalistic sanctions. If the retreat to the countryside made possible a simpler, more harmonious worldly existence, it was because it provided closer access to divine sources of order, meaning, and purpose.

So much, then, for the classic, American version of the pastoral design. That it engaged the attention of our writers in a period when a vast population was moving into a prehistoric landscape hardly is surprising. But it is more difficult to account for its continuing hold upon the literary imagination in the twentieth century. Again and again, in the work of writers like Frost, Fitzgerald, Hemingway, and Faulkner (to name only a few well-known examples), we find a similar preoccupation with the pastoral impulse, that is, with a move- ment away from urban society toward nature as the outward expres- sion of a search for happiness, order, and meaning. Yet anyone familiar with the work of these writers would agree, I believe, that they are not sentimentalists; we cannot imagine them seriously entertaining the illusion, cherished by Nathanael West's Betty, that we can solve our city troubles by moving to the country. Their work does not, in other words, encourage us to believe that the recovery of a rural style of life is a genuine alternative to life in our intricately organized, urban, industrial society. But for what purpose, then, do they continue to employ the pastoral design? Why does it engage the attention of so many of our best writers and, presumably, the audience which admires their work? What significance, in short, does the design have?

To answer the question, I will consider a few examples from the work of Robert Frost and Ernest Hemingway.

Of all modern American writers, Robert Frost belongs most directly in the line from Virgil and the romantic pastoralism of Wordsworth and Emerson. It is significant that he placed, as the first poem in the *Complete Poems* a brief and deceptively slight invitational lyric, "The Pasture." There he invites us to leave the house of everyday life and move out toward nature.

> *I'm going out to clean the pasture spring;*
> *I'll only stop to rake the leaves away*
> *(And wait to watch the water clear, I may) :*
> *I shan't be gone long.— You come too.*
>
> *I'm going out to fetch the little calf*
> *That's standing by the mother. It's so young*
> *It totters when she licks it with her tongue.*
> *I shan't be gone long.— You come too.*★

Like most of Frost's work, the poem may be taken in two ways, either in the plainest sense, for the pleasure of reference, or for its extended meaning. In this case we are also being invited into a poetic world, an ideal pasture where the writer will clear a channel to a hidden source of renewal and creativity. Raking away the clutter of dead leaves and nurturing the just born calf are images that suggest how much—and how little—he expects of the retreat.

The landscape sketched here is the symbolic landscape of Frost's memorable lyrics.[5] As in earlier versions of the pastoral design, this topography is divided into three sectors: a community, a middle terrain or pasture, and beyond that the dark woods and desert places. When Frost occasionally looks directly at organized power, he too is likely to represent it by technological imagery (as in "A Brook in the City" or "The Egg and the Machine"), but the typical Frost lyric turns upon a moment after the speaker already has turned away from the urban-industrial environment. The poet's subject is retreat, and in the opening line of "Directive" he captures the root impulse of native pastoralism: "Back out of all this now too much for us." How many modern American novels and poems begin with variants of this statement! The theme is retreat—both what it promises and what it threatens, and it carries the speaker into a middle ground— for Frost it is likely to be a meadow with a brook at its center—where the water wells up from a savage source, offering the hope that we might "Drink and be whole again beyond confusion." But with-

---

★ From *The Poetry of Robert Frost* edited by Edward Connery Lathem. Copyright 1939, © 1967, 1969 by Holt, Rinehart and Winston, Inc. Reprinted by permission of Holt, Rinehart and Winston, Inc.

drawal into nature has specific limits in space and time, and Frost is careful to insist, always, that it must end with a return to the common life. "I shan't be gone long."

By now it should be evident that the pastoral motif as it is used by Frost is almost wholly drained of the literal meaning it had acquired in the Jeffersonian political tradition. Here the movement outward from society toward nature has little to do with the practical superiority of rural ways, and in a poem like "New Hampshire" Frost ends by mocking that idea. The concluding lines, where the speaker faces a choice between being "a prude afraid of nature" or a "puke," that is, between a prudish New England rustic or a New York (Freudian) alec, he says:

> *Well, if I have to choose one or the other,*
> *I choose to be a plain New Hampshire farmer*
> *With an income in cash of say a thousand*
> *(From, say, a publisher in New York City).*
> *It's restful to arrive at a decision,*
> *And restful just to think about New Hampshire.*
> *At present I am living in Vermont.*★

And in a letter to William S. Braithwaite,[6] Frost made clear his skeptical attitude toward sentimental pastoralism.

I kept a farm, so to speak, for nearly ten years but less as a farmer than as a fugitive from the world that seemed to me to "disallow me." It was all instinctive, but I can see now that I went away to save myself and fix myself before I measured my strength against all creation. I was never really out of the world for good and all.

The purpose of Frost's retreat, in short, is not social or political but rather psychological or metaphysical. Its value is inward. What impels the speaker is a yearning for an indefinable value, order, meaning—a sense of relatedness to that Wordsworthian "something" that is unavailable in the social environment. Following the romantics, Frost is tempted by the notion that natural facts, properly perceived, can be made to yield a surrogate for the moral or meta-

---

★ From "New Hampshire" from *The Poetry of Robert Frost,* edited by Edward Connery Lathem. Copyright 1923, © 1969 by Holt, Rinehart and Winston, Inc. Copyright 1951 by Robert Frost. Reprinted by permission of Holt, Rinehart and Winston, Inc.

physical coherence formerly expected from Christian revelation.
And so, again and again, in poems like "The Most of It" or "Mowing," he seizes upon a particular natural fact, suggesting the tantaliz-
ing possibility that he may be able to wrest from it a moral or
transcendent meaning. In "Mowing" the speaker is working in a
soundless pasture beside the wood, when it occurs to him that his
relation with nature, figured by the whispering sound of the scythe,
can be captured in a statement. "What was it it whispered?" he
asks, but in the end he characteristically retreats from that invasion
of the realm beyond the visible, where Nature is an embodiment of
ultimate value, to a mediating middle ground: "The fact *is* the
sweetest dream that labor knows."

Not only is the "content" of Frost's poetry controlled by the
pastoral design, but his explanation of the creative process, and of
the function of poetry, conforms to the same pattern. The inception
of a poem is an impulse similar to the retreat, or what Freud might
have called an enactment of the pleasure principle. "It begins in
delight," Frost says, "and ends in wisdom. The figure is the same
as for love." As he describes it, there is a similar reaching out for
gratification, a similar arrest of the centrifugal motion, checked in
this case by the requirements of form, and then a denouement
comparable to the hero's return:

It begins in delight, it inclines to the impulse, it assumes direction with the
first line laid down, it runs a course of lucky events, and ends in a clarification
of life—not necessarily a great clarification, such as sects and cults are founded
on, but in a momentary stay against confusion.[7]

With Frost, then, the pastoral design is more than a convenient
device for structuring a work of art. It figures the rhythm of consciousness itself; it is a landscape of mind. Moreover, Frost's
popularity—and he is beyond question the modern American poet
with authentic gifts who has the largest audience—would seem to
argue the universal appeal of the design. His most popular poem,
which has been subjected to endless critical explication, reprinted in
mass circulation magazines, and repeatedly anthologized, is "Stopping by Woods on a Snowy Evening." It would be difficult to
imagine a more complete statement of our theme, and familiar as
the lines are, it is useful to reconsider them with the pastoral design
in mind.

> *Whose woods these are I think I know*
> *His house is in the village, though;*
> *He will not see me stopping here*
> *To watch his woods fill up with snow.*

The complex institutional world has been left behind, and though we are made to feel how it impinges on the countryside, in the property owner's invisible presence, the speaker's attention is drawn to the landscape. The falling snow obliterates details, harmonizes the scene, and provides a receptive field for his meditation. (As in "Directive": "Back in a time made simple by loss of detail.") Yet his withdrawal is far from complete.

> *My little horse must think it queer*
> *To stop without a farmhouse near*
> *Between the woods and frozen lake*
> *The darkest evening of the year*
>
> *He gives his harness bells a shake*
> *To ask if there is some mistake.*
> *The only other sound's the sweep*
> *Of easy wind and downy flake.*

Now the sense of being in the precarious middle, having to mediate the claims of two environments, becomes acute. The horse, trained on a workaday routine, would pull the speaker back to the daily round. But he is transfixed by the serenity and beauty in the sphere of Not-Man, and the enticing, barely audible whisper of the snow, like the sound of the scythe in "Mowing," suggests some obscure fulfillment or possible transcendence. The temptation to keep going is strong. The poem ends:

> *The woods are lovely, dark and deep,*
> *But I have promises to keep,*
> *And miles to go before I sleep,*
> *And miles to go before I sleep.**

In spite of the lovely woods, with all that they imply of soothing release, the speaker turns away, as if aware that to continue his

---

* From *The Poetry of Robert Frost* edited by Edward Connery Lathem. Copyright 1923 by Holt, Rinehart and Winston, Inc. Copyright 1951 by Robert Frost. Reprinted by permission of Holt, Rinehart and Winston, Inc.

retreat is to court the ultimate simplification—a total merging into dark otherness, a deathlike loss of self. The repetition of the final line underscores the precariousness of this resolution, but in the end he has turned back to the obligations of the common life.

Turning now to the work of Ernest Hemingway, we often find a strikingly similar moral landscape. Organized society is identified with organized violence, often with a brutal war, with mechanical, meaningless killing. And the action originates in something like the pastoral impulse to get away; the hero has been wounded, physically or psychically or both, and he opts out—declares a separate peace—retreating from the impersonal cruelty toward a simpler life in a natural setting. The retreat may take the form of an African safari, a fishing trip in Michigan or Spain, but its true object, as in Emerson, Thoreau, or Frost, is psychic and moral renewal. But let me consider a specific example.

"Big Two-Hearted River," the final story in Hemingway's first book, *In Our Time,* has had a strange history.[8] At first many readers, including some who were intrigued by it, thought the story was pointless. Once F. Scott Fitzgerald and Dean Gauss taunted Hemingway for "having written a story in which nothing happens."

"Big Two-Hearted River" is an account of a two-day fishing trip that Nick Adams takes in Michigan. In the course of the story Nick leaves the train that has brought him to the country, hikes overland to a meadow where he pitches his tent, eats supper, and goes to sleep; the next day he goes fishing, catches some fish, and decides not to fish in a swamp. That's all. He meets no one, and there is no significant action. The whole tale is told in simple, declarative sentences, constructed with a fastidious attention to detail and in a seemingly calculated monotonous rhythm. Here is an example:

There was no underbrush in the island of pine trees. The trunks of the trees went straight up or slanted toward each other. The trunks were straight and brown without branches. The branches were high above. Some interlocked to make a solid shadow on the brown forest floor. Around the grove of trees was a bare space. It was brown and soft underfoot as Nick walked on it.

Since its publication, in 1925, a number of critics—notably Edmund Wilson, Malcolm Cowley and Philip Young—have uncovered certain of the story's unstated themes. They have noticed that it belongs to a chronological sequence of Nick Adams stories in the book, which has a degree of thematic unity. Nick has suffered a traumatic wound in the war, and now he has come back to Michigan to recuperate. On careful inspection, it becomes evident that the central action lies beneath the surface, in Nick's mind, and that the numbed, almost lobotomized prose is an index of his effort to repress his panicky emotions.

But the implications of "Big Two-Hearted River" become even more evident when we examine its symbolic landscape. Here is the way the story begins:

The train went on up the track out of sight, around one of the hills of burnt timber. Nick sat down on the bundle of canvas and bedding the baggage man had pitched out of the door of the baggage car. There was no town, nothing but rails and the burned-over country. The thirteen saloons that had lined the one street of Seney had not left a trace. The foundations of the Mansion House hotel stuck up above the ground. The stone was chipped and split by the fire. It was all that was left of the town of Seney. Even the surface had been burned off the ground.

The great world from which Nick has withdrawn is represented only by the train, moving out of sight, and by the unexplained fire that has obliterated this outpost of civilization. The surrounding country is a burned out wasteland. For a time, Nick walks over blackened earth with no green vegetation; even the grasshoppers have turned black. The idea that preoccupies him is getting away. "He felt he had left everything behind, the need for thinking, the need to write, other needs. It was all back of him." Or, in Frost's words, "Back out of all this now too much for us." Later he reaches the place where the fire ended, and the country turns green. He walks along the river in the hot sun. When he finally selects a spot to make camp, it is a meadow on the shore of the river, and on the other side there is a dark swamp. The train and the burned out town and war-decimated Europe are behind him. Like Thoreau at Walden, his aim is to reduce life to its simplest elements. He cooks his dinner, makes his bed, and gets ready for sleep.

Nick was happy as he crawled inside the tent. He had not been unhappy all day. This was different though. Now things were done. It had been a hard trip. He was very tired. That was done. He had made his camp. He was settled. Nothing could touch him. It was a good place to camp. He was there, in the good place. He was in his home where he had made it.

Nick's camp is a psychological middle landscape, and the next day, when he goes fishing, his mind starts to work. But he cannot stand too much emotion. When he loses a big fish he becomes over-excited, feels sick, and decides not to "rush his sensations." Throughout the detailed account of the fishing, Hemingway reminds us several times of the swamp across the river. Its presence makes Nick uneasy. Toward the end of the story it becomes his pre-occupation, like the dark woods that transfix the speaker of Frost's poem.

He did not feel like going on into the swamp. He looked down the river. A big cedar slanted all the way across the stream. Beyond that the river went into the swamp.

Nick did not want to go in there now. He felt a reaction against deep wading with the water deepening up under his armpits, to hook big trout in places impossible to land them. In the swamp the banks were bare, the big cedars came together overhead, the sun did not come through, except in patches; in the fast deep water, in the half light, the fishing would be tragic. In the swamp fishing was a tragic adventure. Nick did not want it. He did not want to go down the stream any further today.

And then, after Nick cleans his fish, and washes them, the story ends abruptly and, as many readers have testified, enigmatically.

Nick stood up on the log, holding his rod, the landing net hanging heavy, then stepped into the water and splashed ashore. He climbed the bank and cut up into the woods, toward the high ground. He was going back to camp. He looked back. The river just showed through the trees. There were plenty of days coming when he could fish the swamp.

And miles to go before I sleep! What is striking here, apart from the similarity to Frost's version of the design, is the close correlation between the external landscape and the pattern of Nick's inner life —the structure of his feelings. First, the burned-over land, identi-fied with machines and war, and with Nick's anxious sense of threatening, repressive, wounding forces; then the camp in the meadow, a good safe place midway between the world of collective imperatives and raw nature, represented by the third sector of the landscape, the swamp identified with darker, impulse-ridden, un-known life that is both attractive and frightening. Nature in Hem-ingway's world is at once benign and menacing—it is, like the river, two-hearted. Variations of this design recur elsewhere in his work, as they do in the work of other gifted American writers of our time. But here the story will suffice as a representative embodiment of a peculiarly American version of postindustrial romantic pastoralism.

With these examples from the work of Frost and Hemingway in view, it should be evident that the pastoral design does not embody an unqualified affirmation of the initial retreat toward nature. The movement in the direction of a simple, preindustrial setting does not reach an alternative, in any literal sense, to the complex world we inhabit. What it does offer, however, is a symbolic structure of thought and feeling, a landscape of mind in which the movement in physical space corresponds to a movement in consciousness. The literary topography is built, in other words, on a subjective model. The succession of contrasting spatial images (town, meadow, swamp) is a vocabulary for expressing a sequence of feelings—feelings which we ordinarily would regard as irreconcilable. A typical starting-point is our ambivalent attitude toward the urban-industrial environment. We are simultaneously repelled and captivated by it; we may feel a strong impulse to escape from it, but we recognize that it is finally inescapable. By deploying these contradictory feelings in literary space the pastoral design enables us to sort them out, and to impose a degree of order upon them. To indicate how this happens, I shall review the tripartite structure of the design: the retreat, the exploration of the limits of nature, and the return.

The retreat from the complex world has both a negative and a positive aspect. The negative aspect is escapist. It expresses a revulsion against the more unpleasant features of the urban-industrial landscape: the ugliness, the noise, the poisoned air, the chaotic overabundance of stimuli, the symptoms of social disorganization, and the general impression of incoherence and individual powerlessness. Since Carlyle's time this environment often has been represented in literature by the image of a vast machine. As Lewis Mumford explained recently, the word "machine" may be used to represent the dominant forces in the world today.

Most of the creative forces in our time have been canalized into the Machine, a systematic organization of scientific discovery and technical invention that, under the pressure of excessive pecuniary gains and exorbitant political power, has transformed the entire existence of the Western World. The insensate dynamism of this mechanical organization *with no goals but its own ceaseless expansion and inflation,* has broken down the continuities of history.[9]

Whether or not it accurately represents the state of the "Western World" in our time, the image of the Machine as an emblem for a system with "no goals but its own ceaseless expansion and inflation" does express an attitude toward industrial society that permeates modern literature. It implies that the course of contemporary history is largely, perhaps irresistibly, determined by the course of technological development. And however much we may disapprove of this fatalistic idea, it does *seem* to be confirmed by the fact that when technical skill makes possible a flight to the moon, the building of an H-bomb or a supersonic jet, our society seems invariably to follow the lead of technology.[10]   Given a world dominated by such a machine, in any case, the pastoral impulse to withdraw (or to "drop out," in the idiom of today's radical youth), is an impulse to recapture a human situation as it might be imagined to exist beyond, or to have existed anterior to, our intricate technological order.   The withdrawal of the pastoral hero in effect repudiates the assumption of Western culture that man is or can be wholly distinct from nature, and that the environment exists chiefly as a source of raw material for the satisfaction of our unique needs. At the outset, accordingly, the hero does seem to deny any possibility of locating worthy purpose, meaning, or value within the collective existence of which the machine is our cardinal symbol.

The positive aspect of the retreat, on the other hand, may be described as a tribute to the pleasure principle. It expresses a desire to achieve felicity through a simplification of living that restores priority to basic instinctual gratifications. It is a search for precisely those qualities of life which our urban environment allegedly fails to satisfy. It would be useful, therefore, as a way of understanding the shortcomings of urbanism, to make a careful study of the satisfactions that writers of pastoral continue to identify with retreat to the natural landscape. I shall return to that proposal. But the point here is that the impulse to escape from our complex environment may prove to be regressive or progressive, depending upon what happens during the next stage: the exploration of nature.

The first thing to be said about the "return to nature" in our sophisticated pastoralism is that it avoids, or at least masks, the conventional romantic claim for the superiority of a rural or wilderness life-style. If the retreat can be salutary, it is not because it provides access to a mysterious, divine, or absolute principle in-

herent in the natural landscape. Our best writers are in remarkable
agreement on this elusive metaphysical issue. Accordingly, they do
not provide much comfort for those who would have us deal with
city troubles by refurbishing preindustrial institutions. In other
words, they recognize the irreversibility of history. But this is not
to deny that they present the symbolic return to "nature" as a source
of real satisfactions. Their work indicates that it can be just that.
Again and again they show us that withdrawal from society in the
direction of nature makes possible moments of emotional release and
integration, a recovery of psychic equilibrium comparable to the
release of repressed feelings in dreams or psychotherapy."[11] This
fact, to which the record of Western religion and literature abundantly testifies, imparts a degree of authenticity to the idea of a
valuable "return to nature." At the same time, our sophisticated
writers of pastoral are virtually unanimous in their emphasis upon
the limited value of such withdrawals from the world. Retreat is
useful only if temporary. It does not, cannot, satisfy the hero's
longing for a permanent alternative to our social environment. What
it does provide, in Frost's well-known phrase, is a "momentary stay
against confusion." If unchecked, however, the pastoral impulse
can lead to disaster. It leads the protagonist into the dark woods, or
that swamp of instinct and uncontrolled feelings where, as Hemingway's hero senses, the fishing will be tragic.

What requires emphasis, then, is that while the first stage may
seem to sanction the impulse to escape the machine of modern
history, the second stage discloses the necessarily individualistic,
transient character of the satisfactions that such an escape provides.
Contrary to the connotations usually attached to the word, pastoralism reveals the inadequacy of the retreat to nature as a way of solving
social and political problems. (The fate of William Faulkner's
pastoral hero, Ike McCaslin, is perhaps our most eloquent testimony
on this point.) Thus the recurrent episode of the interrupted idyll
has served to convey our writers' sense of disenchantment, however
inchoate, with the promise of individual redemption that our literary
culture took over from the radical antinomian strain in native protestantism. The retreat to nature represents moments of integration
but, as Melville warned, "what plays the mischief with the truth is
that some men will insist upon the universal application of a temporary feeling or opinion."

Hence the return.   In the end, however equivocal the denouement may seem, the pastoral figure characteristically has turned back toward the world defined by the machine.   Having discovered that the retreat can provide only a "momentary stay," he seems to recognize that his true home is, after all, society.   If the endings of our pastoral fables generally are unsatisfactory, if they seem to place the protagonist in equivocal, self-contradictory postures, it is largely because of the seemingly insoluble dilemma in which he has been put.   How can he carry back into our complex social life the renewed sense of possibility and coherence that the pastoral interlude has given him?   None of our writers has been able to find a satisfactory answer to this question.

At the outset I suggested that our imaginative literature, and particularly those works which embody the pastoral design, might be of some use—at least as a source of guiding principles—to those who plan the development of the physical environment.   Yet there is a paradox here, for the significance of the design, as we have seen, is primarily subjective.   It refers chiefly to the inner, not the external, landscape.   The topographical imagery in our twentieth-century pastoral fables must be understood as a metaphoric vehicle for a landscape of consciousness.   It would be a serious mistake, however, to conclude that the design therefore is irrelevant to the problems of the actual landscape.   On the contrary, literary criticism insists that a powerful figurative relationship of this kind is never merely decorative or illustrative.   It is not a one-way channel of meaning.   If our writers consistently employ a pattern of landscape imagery, and if readers understand and lend assent to it—and, to repeat, the works which embody the pastoral design do seem to have a special appeal for a contemporary audience—then we must assume that the vehicle (in this case, the entire topographical design) is an indispensable feature of the total aesthetic result.   So far as the design is convincing, the landscape imagery contributes to that conviction.   Aesthetic success confers a kind of validity upon the pattern.   What valid principles, then, can planners derive from the view of life inherent in this body of literature?

The most obvious inference is that more attention be paid to the subjective and in large measure traditional, aesthetic, or symbolic significance that our culture attaches to images of the external landscape—urban, rural and wild.   (On first looking into the literature of planning, the cultural historian cannot help being impressed by the lack of allusion to the centuries-old accretion of meaning that clings to our dominant topographical images.) The continuing hold of pastoralism upon the literary imagination in this urban-industrial age is but one measure of the power of such images. A specific measure, already mentioned, is that we undertake a thorough, precise, analytic inventory of the satisfactions that men have derived, or have claimed to derive, from various features of the landscape. Such a survey ultimately would require the collaboration, in addition to planners and literary scholars, of art historians, urban and rural sociologists, and psychologists. One aim of the inventory would be to sort out the kinds of satisfaction, real and illusory, that are associated with the pastoral retreat. Decisive here is the sense of repose, renewal, and sensual gratification identified with withdrawal from the city to a more natural environment. We know that some of these pleasurable feelings derive as much from what is missing as from what is actually present in the extra-urban setting. In the literary retreat, the pastoral figure's mind is released from the nagging responsibilities of a complex social life, the flood of conflicting stimuli, and the painful omnipresence of history itself. Some of his satisfaction, however, actually derives from the natural landscape, either from its specific physical attributes (the fresh air, the greenness, the color of flowers, etc.), or from its psychological and associative attributes. A natural setting, if only because it is less cluttered with man-made objects, provides a more hospitable field for the projection of his feelings. It thereby enhances, if only momentarily, his sense of his own power and importance. But a vital element here is the residuum of teleological modes of thought—the tendency to identify the seeming orderliness of the natural landscape with the hypothetical design and purpose of the cosmos. Whether these ideas are objectively "true" or not, they do in some measure control our responses to the physical environment, and planners might profitably use more information about them.

Another principle suggested by literary pastoralism is the importance of diversity in physical settings—the need to preserve the distinctness of the three spheres of our environment: the city, the rural countryside, and the wilderness. Our literature supports the idea that each of these performs an important role in our psychic economy, and that quite apart from nostalgia, sentiment, or any narrow measures of utility, either economic or recreational, each offers indispensable satisfactions. Hence the prospect of the disappearance of any one of them, or of the irrevocable blurring of the boundaries between them, as in the spread of suburbia, would be an intolerable loss. The literary pastoral emphasizes the value of contrast as a mental resource, and seems to endorse the views of those ecologists who define the relation between the urban and extraurban environments as a form of symbiosis.

Our pastoralism would therefore seem to confirm the view, advanced by Paul Goodman and others, that our society requires rural as well as urban reconstruction. Indeed, urban renewal without rural renewal is self-defeating, if only because rural decay is driving an impossibly large population into our cities. To make our small towns and vast countryside economically viable and culturally interesting is an indispensable aspect of solving the urban problem. Besides, the countryside should be made available to our city dwellers, and not merely a select few, as a necessary retreat from the nerve-racking demands of our complex civilization. Here again we see the relevance of the symbiotic relation that the pastoral design tacitly establishes between the contrasting environments. In Western society the wealthy and aristocratic always have appreciated the advantages of periodic retreats from the world, of moral and physical holidays from complexity. Today, in the United States, when only a small fraction of the population can be classified as rural, enjoyment of the land itself is denied to most of the people. What is needed is not the extension of suburbia or the proliferation of commercial resorts, but the invention of means whereby city dwellers can temporarily enjoy the pleasures of an alternative way of life. To make such facilities available to a much larger segment of our population would seem to be a legitimate goal for planners in an affluent, democratic society.

My final suggestion brings us back to the realistic implications of the third stage of the pastoral design: the return. Our literary pastoralists, surprisingly enough, reinforce the inescapable lesson of common sense, namely, that the mainstream of contemporary history is to be found in the urban-industrial environment. If many people feel the urge to retreat, it is in some measure an effort to invest their lives with a sense of order and meaning that is lacking in the world of the machine. The curious tendency to find more significance in the seemingly haphazard dispersal of trees, animals, and hills than in the relatively deliberate patterning of streets, buildings, and parks, cannot be wholly attributed to the actual physical character of the two settings. The flight to suburbia, which might after all be described as a debased and doomed version of the pastoral retreat, is in part at least a gesture of revulsion at the chaos, contradiction and nonmeaning that we associate with our cities. It is, by the same token, an effort somehow to recapture certain social and political attributes of smaller communities.

In arguing for the importance of the social and political as well as psychological motives for the effort to escape the city, I do not mean to discount the importance of "real" physical discomfort, ethnic prejudices, and sheer ugliness. But there is reason to believe that the almost universal preference for the suburban "country" over the city (and however foolish the idea may seem, the commuter on his way to Levittown does say that he is on his way to the "country"), also derives from the symbolic significance of the two settings. That is why it would be useful to learn more about the values that men attach to various forms of pastoral retreat, and to distinguish between those aspects of rural or wilderness living which are capable of fulfillment, and those which are illusory. For it is possible that our planners could find ways to provide some of those satisfactions within the city. They could accomplish this purpose both in the traditional manner, by reproducing certain physical conditions of rural life (parks, playgrounds, open spaces), but also by taking into consideration the need for social and political surrogates for rural and small town institutions.[12] Our literary pastoralism suggests that physical planning without political (to use the word in its broadest sense) planning is futile. What I am saying, in short, is that today the planner finds himself in a position analogous to that of the pastoral figure at the conclusion of an American fable. His problem is to find ways of creating, within the urban environment, that sense of belonging to an orderly pattern of life which has for so long been associated with the relatively unspoiled, natural landscape.

NOTES

1. A relevant example of this reductive method is Morton and Lucia White's book, *The Intellectual Versus the City* (1962). In effect the book

is an attack upon the great American writers—indeed, upon the entire intellectual community—from Jefferson's time to that of Frank Lloyd Wright, for idealizing rural and other preindustrial ways of life and thereby creating what the Whites call an "antiurban roar." I would not deny that an antiurban bias is to be found in our literature, but I would contend that the Whites, by neglecting the conventional, metaphoric character of the urban-rural contrast, its long history in Western thought, miss the subtle ways in which that bias often is qualified, and most important, they miss its deeper meaning. For the apparent animus usually is directed not against the city itself, i.e., the city as an actual physical environment, but rather against the system of value which the city, within a specific historical and cultural context, has come to represent. The model for this distinction is the metaphor: it is a distinction between the city as a *vehicle* or *secondary subject* (which it so often is for the literary imagination) and the city as the *primary subject*.

2. *Studies in Classic American Literature* (1923).
3. In the section that follows I summarize, in simplified form, material developed in greater detail in *The Machine in the Garden: Technology and the Pastoral Ideal in America* (1964).
4. Renato Poggiolo, "The Oaten Flute," *Harvard Library Bulletin*, vol. XI, pp. 147–148, 1957. I am paraphrasing his definition.
5. I have in mind a group of the well-known short poems such as "Mowing," "The Oven Bird," "The Last Moving," "A Time to Talk," "The Tuft of Flowers," "A Brook in the City," "The Need of Being Versed in Country Things," "Spring Pools," "Desert Places," "Design," "The Most of It," and probably the most detailed and complex version of the design, "Directive."
6. L. Thompson, editor, *Selected Letters*, p. 158. Letter of 22 March, 1915.
7. From "The Figure a Poem Makes" from *Selected Prose of Robert Frost* edited by Hyde Cox and Edward Connery Lathem. Copyright 1939, (c) 1967 by Holt, Rinehart and Winston, Inc. Reprinted by permission of Holt, Rinehart and Winston, Inc.
8. Ernest Hemingway, "Big Two-Hearted River" in *In Our Time*. Quoted herein by permission of the publisher, Charles Scribner's Sons.
9. "Constancy and Change," *The New Yorker*, p. 162, 6 March, 1965. My italics.
10. The seemingly universal appeal of this theme, and especially the tendency to regard Western culture as technologically determined, is nowhere more tellingly revealed than in the notorious 1965 statement of the Chinese Minister of Defence, Marshall Lin Piao, in which he defined the present world power struggle as in essence a conflict between the big cities of the West and the revolutionary spirit of the people of the Asian,

African, and Latin American countryside. "Taking the entire globe," he said, "if North America and Western Europe can be called the 'cities of the world,' then Asia, Africa and Latin America constitute the 'rural areas of the world.' " And, most interesting in the present context, his argument turns upon the association of the superior inner resources ("courage and spirit of sacrifice") of the revolutionists with their rural lives, and the relative weakness of Westerners with their urban, industrial environment. "The spiritual atom bomb that the revolutionary people possess is a far more powerful and useful weapon than the physical atom bomb." And the current spectacle of huge American bombers attacking a peasant nation in Southeast Asia may well seem to lend credence to this melodramatic image of world conflict. *New York Times*, p. 2, 4 September, 1965.

11. There is a striking analogy between the symbolic landscape that recurs in our modern pastoral fables and the theory of ego autonomy held by certain Freudian psychiatrists, notably Anna Freud, Erik Erikson, Heinz Hartmann, and David Rapaport. Running through this literature is a tacit spatial metaphor, in which the ego appears as a psychic middle ground between the claims of the unconscious id and external (social) reality. To maintain the health of the ego is to maintain a precarious equilibrium, and in Rapaport's formulation, which is comparable to the idea implicit in the examples I have cited from Frost and Hemingway, when the ego achieves maximum autonomy from one side, it risks increasing impairment from the other side. Experiments in sensory deprivation have shown that when the subject is given virtually total autonomy from the external environment, for example, he quickly becomes vulnerable to inward, instinctual drives. Similarly, when Nick Adams cuts himself off from the social environment identified with war, fire, and machines, he becomes prey to attack from his inner drives identified with the swamp. For a concise example, see David Rapaport's "The Theory of Ego Autonomy: a Generalization," in *Bulletin of the Menninger Clinic*, vol. 22, pp. 13–35, 1958.

12. For a convincing account of the degree to which the loss of certain features of community determines attitudes toward urbanization, see Maurice R. Stein, *The Eclipse of Community : an Interpretation of American Studies* (1960).

8

ECOLOGY AND THEOLOGY
GABRIEL FACKRE

"Earth Sunday!" So read the flier from church headquarters that clergy received a few weeks before the April, 1970, teach-in. The national conscience had been stung awake to the ecological crisis. And now the churches were being urged to action.

The reaction to both the general interest in ecology and the church's new zeal for the environment is mixed. Those deeply caught up in the struggles for racial justice or peace wonder if the pollution fever is a diversionary tactic on the part of those in power. Others despair at the ecclesiastical trumpet call, for it seems once again that the church is the "tail light rather than the headlight."

Why should the church turn its attention to the environmental issue? There is, of course, the obvious reason that we have to do with the survival of the planet itself, if the somber prophecies of Ehrlich and Commoner are correct. But there are other reasons. One is this temptation to thrust the "crisis in Eden" forward to the exclusion of social anguishes that are as clamant as ever.[1] As partisans in the battles of the 60s—race, peace, poverty—we have a special responsibility to see that these do not get lost from view, and to lobby for full-orbed mission. Yet another reason for the church's urgent attention is the allegation by some of the most dedicated pollution crusaders that the debasing of the environment is traceable to an attitude toward nature rooted in the Judeo-Christian tradition itself. Thus Lynn White, whose comments appear in *The Environmental Handbook* used in conjunction with the teach-in, charges that the biblical mandate that man should have

Gabriel Fackre is professor of theology at Andover Newton Theological Seminary. The selection is reprinted from *Religion in Life*, Vol. 40, p. 210–224 (Summer, 1971). Copyright © 1971 by Abingdon Press.

"dominion over" nature and "subdue the earth" lies back of Western society's exploitation of its natural resources.[2] In contrast to this "anthropocentric" view of the world, more than a few ecological activists recommend a nature-affirming reverence for all of life, and look to the religions of the East to sustain it. In particular, the "counter culture," which sets itself against the technocracy and goes back to the land in primitive communes, experiments with native Indian and non-Western religious options.[3] See how these tendencies come together (with a few exceptions) in the Berkeley Ecological Revolutionary Organization's statement:

> It seems evident that there are throughout the world certain social and religious forces which have worked through history toward an ecologically and culturally enlightened state of affairs. Let these be encouraged: Gnostics, hip Marxists, Teilhard de Chardin Catholics, Druids, Taoists, Biologists, Witches, Yogins, Bhikkus, Quakers, Sufis, Tibetans, Zens, Shamans, Bushmen, American Indians, Polynesians, Anarchists, Alchemists . . . the list is long. All primitive cultures, all communal and ashram movements.[4]

There are no Jews or Protestants in that list. The Christians mentioned are a select group. The rest of us are the culprits.

If the charges are true, we have a massive job of reforming our teaching and ourselves. If they are not true, then we have an equally massive job of interpretation, to our own constituencies as well as to others. One way or the other, serious religious reflection on the environment is an absolute must. The ecological problem is a theological problem.

THE DOCTRINE OF CREATION: ITS USE AND ABUSE

An environmental theology, in the context of the pollution question, must confront head-on the allegations that the biblical doctrine of creation espouses an anthropocentricism which shows respect for man at the price of disrespect for the environment. Lynn White is indeed correct when he says that the biblical story places man above nature. Man is the crown of creation, made in the very image of God. This Old Testament premise is confirmed in the New Testament. God chooses to enter his world in the form of man: "the Word became flesh and dwelt among us." As Karl Barth has put it, "God did not become a stone or a star, or even an angel. He became man. Man, therefore, enjoys an unique status within creation. He is the 'apple of God's eye'."

Embedded deeply in the cultures influenced by this conviction is the belief in human dignity, honored far better in its charters, of course, than in practice. But it is there. The life of a starving child takes precedence over a sacred cow. A tree is not worshipped but felled to provide shelter for a pioneer family. (Not only that, for a Joyce Kilmer or Martin Buber can commune with the tree as well, a dimension of Judeo-Christian sensitivity we shall subsequently explore.)

Nature, in this perspective, undergoes a "disenchantment," as it is described by Harvey Cox, following Max Weber.[5] This matter-of-fact relationship to the environment is grounded in the biblical idea of creation itself, specifically the doctine of *creatio ex nihilo*. To affirm that God brings the world to be "out of nothing" means that the created order is not cut from the same cloth as deity, but rather "invented" by God. Tribal man, on the other hand, associates divinity so intimately with the natural world—all, or parts of it—that awe, incantation, imprecation, worship, become the ways of relating to it. The overagainstness of God and the world in the biblical teaching forbids the divinizing of anything finite. It therefore frees creation for use to the glory of God, and man is enjoined to steward it to that end. As Whitehead, Butterfield, and White himself have pointed out, the rise of science and technology in the West are directly related to this fundamental assumption.

But that is just the point, say the critics. This teaching encouraged the rape of Mother Earth. Standing alone, such a belief can do just that. That is what, in fact, happened with the rise of modern commerce and industrialization. The mechanization of nature in the Cartesian world view provided further ideological cover for the ruthless exploitation of natural resources. And now we are suffering the consequences. But the reason is that a society hellbent on profit and/or technological salvation tore loose from a larger context the assumption that nature was a thing only to be used (the Marxists are no better than the capitalists, for both ideologies were born in the womb of the technological revolution, accredited nature's despoliation, and continue to do so—this in spite of fugitive references in the early Marx to the dignity of nature). That larger context is the *full* biblical doctrine of creation, basic notes of which were censored in the era of feverish industrial expansion currently expressing itself in the phenomenon of "technocracy."

A group of contemporary writers with quite varying perspectives (Theodore Roszak, Robert Theobald, Jacques Ellul, Alvin Toffler, Paul Goodman, Kenneth Boulding) are sharpening our understanding of that complex of institutions, methodologies, cultural premises and passions that constitutes technocracy. In describing the character of this phenomenon it seems appropriate to speak of its "components."

1. The belief that the methods and momentum of science-technology can and will create a viable society.

2. "Econocentrism" (Toffler)—a confident faith in economic growth as the polestar of that society.

3. Present-orientation, the focus upon and drive toward immediate achievements, with little or no attention to the long-range effects of *now* activity.

4. The rule of elites—on the one hand, managerial generalists, and on the other, highly specialized "experts."

5. The lust for political, economic, and social power—a day-to-day "anthropocentrism" that finds easy the choice "between God and mammon."

It is this technocratic juggernaut that has rolled over the helpless in man and nature. Its victims include the young, the poor, the women, the black, brown, and red, and in less obvious ways the blue-collar white. Now in our time of ecological sensitivity we become aware that it has ravaged the air, the water, and the soil. And among the fabrics it has shredded are the tender things of human relationship and inner feeling.

Technocracy's steamroller has produced responses that run from the bizarre to the explosive. Chemical fantasy and neomystical reverie in the counter culture of the young represent both protest against and flight from the rational-empirical techniques whose fruits seem to be the hardware of war and blight. The quest for the community ruptured by the mechanisms and individualisms of technocracy casts about for the utopian commune or the togetherness of an encounter group. The ritual flaggery and superpatriotism of middle America are themselves distress signals of dehumanization. And for the lowest levels of the under class whose lives have been most seriously wounded there is always heroin, hooch, and holy rolling.

Alongside these symptoms of anguish, there is the more aggressive feedback, the clenched fist and the midnight bomb of the terrorist.

To get beyond the first screams of pain and anger will involve building a strategy of ideas and actions that loosen the grip of technocracy on our future. It will mean taming technology, not disdaining it, and harnessing it to the purposes of personal, social, and environmental healing. It is the latter which here engages us, particularly the quest for a Christian interpretation of nature consistent with the biblical perspective and preparing the church for both the human and ecological struggles of the 70s.

The doctrine of creation out of nothing had a twin development. It served to refute, on the one hand, the divinizing and romanticizing of nature. But, on the other, it fought the degradation of nature. Strangely enough, one of the very movements in history approved by the Ecological Revolutionary Organization actually denigrated nature—Gnosticism. (It is probably the astrological interests of Gnosticism which prompted ERO to list it in the approved category of nature-affirming religions.) For that reason Gnosticism was attacked by patristic writers who fought for the significance of the finite, earthly terrain. Gnosticism, of course, was not a monolithic religious system, but rather the ideological atmosphere breathed by large segments of the ancient world. Variegated it was—but for all that, consistent in its estimate of the natural order. The world was second-class stuff. The earth was of inferior material, made either by a lieutenant deity, an emanation many times removed down the scale of being from the True God, or by a rebel "aeon" alienated from the source of all things. The purpose of religion was to extract from the mire of materiality the souls of men, helping them to escape from the burdens of their fleshly existence and its defiled visibilities into the realm of pure spirit.

Other ancient philosophical commitments also had their doubts about the importance of nature in the scheme of things. Modern ecologists bewail the denuding of Greece, the stripping away of the forests in the interest of building navies and engines of war. The rationalist tendencies of the Greek schools of thought gave little aid and comfort to Mother Earth. Goodness was located in reason, the purpose of which was to order the recalcitrant vitalities of life. God himself was conceived as Mind that gave form, and therefore significance, to a low-grade pre-existent stuff.

It was against this demeaning of the earth, in both the Gnostic and rationalistic temper of the times, that the fathers of the first centuries laid out the Christian doctrine of creation. The world was not the product of a lower divinity, an estranged emanation. Nor was it a pre-existent stuff of dubious parentage. "I believe in God the Father almighty, Maker of heaven and earth," read the early rule of faith that came to be the present Apostles' Creed. It asserted that the world was made by God himself. As such, it bore his stamp, and enjoys a derived dignity. "God saw everything that he had made, and behold, it was very good." Or as someone put it, "God invented matter, therefore he must like it."

The Genesis affirmation of the earth is echoed in a thousand biblical passages that celebrate the intrinsic worth, beauty, and order of the natural environment. Thus the psalmist repeats a familiar refrain: "Thou [God] art clothed with honor and majesty, who coverest thyself with light as with a garment; who has stretched out the heavens as a tent, who hast laid the beams of they chambers on the waters, who makest the clouds thy chariot, who ridest on the wings of the wind" (*Psalm* 104: 1–3). And the One who preaches the love of neighbor can also say, "Consider the lilies of the field, how they grow; they neither toil nor spin; yet I tell you, even Solomon in all his glory was not arrayed like one of these" (*Matt.* 6: 28–29). The biblical love of neighbor extends to our neighbor the earth, as St. Francis so clearly understood.

To struggle to defend the dignity of man does not mean one has to denigrate the earth. In fact, one requires the other, as the very struggle against pollution demonstrates. What has given the environmental crisis its special urgency is the threat to the survival of man. Those who are most concerned about the welfare of man on earth will be those moved most passionately to restore a healthy environment.

Responsible Christian participation in that struggle requires, therefore, the rediscovery of the forgotton aspects of the doctrine of creation, the respect for and rapport with nature. One does not have to worship or romanticize nature in order to treat it as precious, any more than one has to worship or romanticize man in order to affirm his dignity. Both naturalists and humanists have propagated those theses. We have paid a heavy price for those kinds of absolutizations of the finite. The romantic naturalism of the Nazi era that deified blood and soil is a particularly demonic expression of the tendency.   The Judeo-Christian tradition affirms, in the case of both man and nature, a *derived* dignity, and accords each a respect commensurate with its source in God.   It is the *relationship* in which creation stands to its Creator that confers upon it value, not any presumed virtues or vitalities whose claims outrun the facts.

MAN, CREATOR OUT OF SOMETHING

The Genesis saga has yet more light to shed on ecological issues. Theologians of the secular have underscored the call to man to take responsibility for the future in the mandate to "name the animals" and "subdue the earth," the challenge to be co-creators with God. Again ecological critics of Christian tradition can find grist for their mills in what sounds like a thoughtless subservience of nature to man's machinations.   And again they would be right if only one side of this passage's meaning were stressed.   It is no accident that Harvey Cox has become a target of environmentalists, for he has stressed only one facet of the divine-human partnership.[6]   There is another dimension to co-creatorship.

To take responsibility for "naming the animals" is to work with givens.   Man does not do his creating *de novo;* he works over what he has inherited.   He is not God, who creates out of nothing; he creates out of something already present.   God is infinite, man is finite.   And as such he works within the limits of a created order with its own pre-existing character.   "While men, indeed, cannot make anything out of nothing but only out of matter already existing, yet God is in this point pre-eminently superior to man.   That He Himself called into being the substance of His creation, when previously it had no existence."[7]

A related premise of co-creatorship is that man's mandate comes from a Source outside himself.   His management of creation is not one of absolute control.   Rather it is stewardship of the earth before a higher Claimant.   To "have dominion over" means to hold in trusteeship.   Man is called to tend the earth in responsibility to its Creator.

These convictions have profound implications for the ecological crisis.   Because man creates within the framework of givens, he must honor the integrity of the pre-existing material.   Responsible human creativity takes into account the balances and harmonies of the natural world. Man cannot do anything he wants, but has to abide by the rules of the game. Humility is, therefore, a virtue appropriate to his secondary role in creation. And that modesty is underscored by his trusteeship. He is accountable to Another.

Our present environmental plight is traceable to man's failure to acknowledge the limitations attendant to his subsidiary creatorship. He has acted as if he were the Creator, rather than a creator, in defiance of the givens and their Giver. In fact, he has played out the role of Adam in the Genesis saga, claiming prerogatives reserved to God alone. He has sought to create out of nothing, when he in fact can only create out of something, in harmony with the rhythm of the created order. For overreaching his finitude, he must suffer the consequences. In the Genesis story man is cast out of paradise and nature itself falls. Man's relation to nature becomes one of contest with creation. He is set against nature and nature responds in kind. Red in tooth and claw, spawning the terrors of earthquake, fire, flood, disease, and destruction, groaning "the whole creation has been in travail together until now." Sophisticated moderns smile at this ancient imagery, and dismiss it as an old wives' tale, or at best, as the anthropomorphism of a primitive society fearful of natural disaster. But the ecologically sensitive today recognize in this saga some very accurate reporting of the terrors that nature has in store for a technological society that tries to play God, ignoring the limitations placed on man's dominion. Existing in symbiotic relationship, nature does fall when man violates the built-in balances. And further, the earth takes its toll on man when such anthropocentrism runs riot, whether it be in the form of the London smog that killed four thousand people, or a Colorado earthquake provoked by army engineers who poured chemical wastes into deep wells, or the threat to the planet's oxygen supply by the DDT destruction of ocean plankton. It may well be that we shall rediscover the meaning of that line in the insurance policy which describes natural havoc as an "act of God." Such calamities as they happen in a society of indiscriminate human technology are just that, the delicate harmonies that sustain life in the cosmos fighting back against the thoughtless intrusions of man. Those exquisite networks of order and rhythm bear the imprint of deity itself. Whether we take a leaf from a Whiteheadian philosophy which sees these mutualities as the work of the divine vision and creativity, or from the biblical testimony itself which lies behind such an insight—that the divine nature, love, has left its mark on its creation in the order of nature —we know that man cannot violate cosmic interrelationships without suffering the consequences. Where profit and self-aggrandizement exploit nature, the "wrath of God," the anger of Mother Nature, manifests itself in the coming of the four horsemen themselves: plague, pestilence, famine, and death.

CREATION'S COMPANION THEMES

While we have focused on the Christian doctrine of beginnings to provide a framework for an environmental theology, the dignity of nature is honored all around the circle of Christian teaching. For example, we might have spoken about sacramental theology which finds in bread, water, and wine a dignity that enables them to be vehicles of the divine life. Or we could have explored the doctrine of the incarnation that lies behind this sacramental affirmation of nature, and proved to be the most important bulwark of the early church against the gnosticisms that threatened to derogate the world of time and space, nature and man. We might also have examined the doctrine of the end, which works in tandem with the doctrine of the beginning in affirming the goodness of the whole created order, especially the key vision of shalom. Thus shalom is God's dream and promise for the fulfillment of his creation, the knitting together of all the brokenness in the cosmos, in the relations between man and man, a man and himself, man and nature, within nature, and between man-nature and God. At one or another time we have been sensitized to one or another of these rifts. Thus the peace movement with its shalom symbol has underscored the biblical vision of a time when men shall beat their swords into plowshares. The human potential movement is currently exposing the sham in interpersonal relations and the deep psychic cleavages in selves, and working for the transformation of those spears into pruning hooks. It is time now to recover other elements in the biblical vision that have to do with the reconciliation of man and nature, and nature with itself— the child putting her hand over the asp's hole, the lying down of the wolf and the lamb, and the stilling of the sea's turbulence.

The eschatological horizon not only drives us to set up signposts in the present to a healed earth, but it charges us to keep the environmental crusade in company with other visionary movements. How can the child play with the snake if it must be forever in flight from the sword and the spear? The Christian vision is a big picture, a tapestry of many scenes, all interrelated. Its seers are multi-visionaries, neglecting no dimension of mission—race, peace, poverty, pollution. One of their particular mandates in a time of parochial crusades is to stretch the spectrum of the mono-visionary to its full range.

THEOLOGY AND THE STRATEGIES OF ENVIRONMENTAL MISSION

Theology and ecology are mated not only in ends but also means. Our basic premises about the nature and destiny of the cosmos shape the way we go about our environmental mission. Insights in the Christian faith do not provide blueprints, but they do offer guidelines for action.

Human nature: incurvature and creatureliness. Man's self-regarding impulses overwhelm his unselfish ones. He is always looking out for Number One. In the code language of Christian tradition, man is a sinner. In Luther's language, each one of us is curved inward.

To take this "Christian realism" seriously is to expect that those whose manifest self-interest is at stake will be the most likely prospects as change agents in the pollution struggle. "Manifest" is an important qualification, for one's personal welfare may indeed be jeopardized, but one might not be aware of it. Those whose are in fact threatened, and whose social location or aroused sensitivity alerts them to the peril, may be our most aggressive prophets. Presupposed here as a secondary motif is another biblical premise about man— his finitude. He is immersed in the contingencies and vicissitudes of time and space. The self is not a free-floating balloon of mind or spirit, as it is portrayed in some other religious and philosophical options. Man is a creature of his time and place. His ability to perceive reality is conditioned by where he lives, how he feels, who he knows, and what he sees.

It is no accident that some of the most fervent pollution crusaders are the West Coast wealthy. From Sierra Club outdoorsmen to activist movie stars Eddie Albert and Arthur Godfrey, people who have the leisure to enjoy the horizons of the earth and the sky (see Godfrey's comments on flying his plane over the country's smog blanket, Albert's account of the death of bird and animal life, or the Sierra Club's aggressive *Ecotactics* handbook[8]) are positioned sociologically and physically to feel the weight of the environmental crisis. Further, the peculiar combination of accelerating population and technology on a collision course with a vast and virginal nature, and a geographic vulnerability to massive catastrophe (the Santa Barbara oil catastrophe and the atmospheric dangers in Los Angeles) have a way of producing ecological revolutionaries.

Ideologues have no place for the affluent in their designs for social change, except to consign them to hell. A biblical perspective, on the other hand, takes creatureliness and sin seriously, and harnesses them to healing. Rich men have to breathe too. In the quest for their own survival, they may prove to be significant allies in the struggle for the earthly shalom of us all.

Some may, but others may not. Again an appreciation of sin and finitude gives us some programmatic clues. Where self-interest is crystallized into the inertia and short-range vision of immense collectivities, the life and breath of even the individuals who sit atop them become secondary to corporate aggrandizement. Given sin, power, particularly structural power, seeks to perpetuate itself and expand its orbit. From the "principalities and powers" of our time that pollute the air, water, and soil we can expect the charge that the ecological drive is exaggerated, that what is needed is education, that we must not do anything hastily, that it is the hippies and the Communists who are behind it all, that jobs will be lost if drastic action is taken, that the problem is really the individual polluter and not the corporation, that the people must bear the burden anyway by increasing the price of the product to pay for anti-pollution measures. One of these claims does deserve careful consideration—the loss of jobs—and we shall address ourselves to it. But this catalog of industrial argumentation is essentially a rhetorical smokescreen and one that can be anticipated within a biblical framework. Sin regularly clothes itself in the garments of righteousness. The fog of pious rhetoric is calculated to obscure the smoke from the furnaces.

Given "immoral society,"[9] the expectation that vested interest will not divest itself of its poisons on its own initiative, then it is clear that the impulses for change must comes from another direction. As other movements learned about the intransigence of collective power and organized to resist it—woman power, labor power, black power, student power—so an aroused citizenry must aggregate anti-pollution power to challenge the powers that be. In addition to frontal assaults by Nader's Raiders and the like, there must be a bringing to self-consciousness of those within the population who suffer the most from pollution. The citizen of the city, be he white collar, blue collar, black, or poor, pays a big price for his habitat and style of life. Middle American and minority groups may well find themselves aligned against the same entrenched interests since they suffer from the same urban maladies.

Human nature: the social bundle. "God setteth the solitary in families," declares the psalmist. "The fathers have eaten sour grapes, and the children's teeth are set on edge," intones Jeremiah. We are all part of the interdependent bundle of life, affected by our contemporaries and predecessors, affecting our contemporaries and our successors. The ecological threat has underscored this mutuality among men as well as our interrelationship with nature. Thus the two airline passengers in adjacent seats, one smoking a cigarette and the other chewing gum. The latter offers the former his well-masticated wad. The former expresses shock, "Chew your used-up gum!" The reply: "Well, I'm smoking your cigarette!"

What is true in space is also true in time. The acids of worked-out mines in the northern tier of Pennsylvania seep into the water supply of succeeding generations in the lower regions.

A free-wheeling technocracy has for decades operated in azure isolation, without taking into account the disastrous effect on human life of its effluents. How many steelworkers I buried in a decade of ministry in Pittsburgh who died from silicosis and other lung disorders! Industry is no more free to go its way with such destruction than is the rugged individualist permitted to cry "Fire" in a crowded theater. To affirm human interdependence is to demand responsibility from those whose wastes contaminate other humans. Further, it is to insist that the costs of this self-control be borne by the offender and not the offended. The absorption of these expenses are but small reparations that can be paid for the lives and health lost by years of thoughtlessness.

Human nature: the tragic options. All that has been said points to ecological action. The healing of a wounded environment is an imperative. Yet the mission cannot be executed in a vacuum. There are other crises. And there are circumstances when we are faced with tragic choices among legitimate ethical claimants. The reserve and sometimes suspicion of the human rights and peace movements about the pollution crusade is rooted in this ambiguity. Will passion for the environment draw attention from the struggles against other injustices?

Yet another dimension of this ambiguity was unfurled in the NBC white paper on the plight of a depressed Maine coastal town. Environmentalists were campaigning against a proposed seaport to berth giant cargo ships because of the pollution and destruction of a spot of natural beauty. Local workers and unemployed persons took offense at the affluent who were leading the drive because a new industry would have meant jobs for the poor.

In a world of competing claims, where there are no simple moral choices, it is necessary to establish priorities in particular situations based on what constitutes the maximum welfare both to those affected by the choices and to posterity. It is possible, therefore, that in a given context where justice for the poor and black are overwhelming needs, and a technology with as-yet-unconquered environmental hazards is required to implement that justice (a factory with its thousands of jobs and equal employment practices), the ecological values may have to take second place. Or, if it could be demonstrated that the urban poisons have such a malignant effect on these very same persons and the citizens of the region, then the tragic choice of long-term ecological life rather than short-term economic life must be made. Ideally, those struggling on both the ecological and economic fronts should band together and seek complementary solutions. But, until such alliances can be formed, and nonpollutant technology developed, we shall be faced with such ambiguous options and must be prepared to make tragic choices, in "fear and trembling" and in penitence.

THE BIRTH OF A NEW STYLE OF LIFE
In, with, and under the press for social controls and institutional restructuring for environmental health, there must be a quest for a new commitment and style of life. The best laws in the world are useless if there is no will to enforce them. Just social structures can also be corrupted if those that inhabit them espouse inimical values.

The classic Christian virtue of neighbor love is no pious luxury in a society whose ethic of self-aggrandizement bears within it the seeds of self-destruction. When men exploit other men and nature in the interest of personal profit, we pull our own social and natural house down about our ears. Lust for private gain and its attendant ravages must be replaced by care for our neighbor the earth, and his neighbor, mankind. This means a transvaluation of some of the values considered so basic to "success" in our society. So vocal a barker of modern products as Arthur Godfrey has been moved to observe, "Prosperity means progress, means people—the more people, the more progress, the more prosperity. Too late we have seen that it also means more pollution, more filth, more death."[10] We must call into question the shibboleth that sustained another age with its seemingly limitless resources and reach: "Growth equals progress." We need new goals: "life," "the quality of life," "cooperation," "mutuality," and behind them all the neighbor love of the Jericho road.

New values mean a new mode of personal conduct. Virtues long scorned by an affluent society will have to be woven into the new style of life. For example, thrift and frugality. Instead of consuming rapaciously and throwing away thoughtlessly, we must conserve, recycle, be scrupulous in our acquisition. Thus, on the "Activists' Check List" of the Sierra Club, it is proposed that we not only put a brick in our toilet tank (the back!), question the value of electric carving knives, can openers, and tooth brushes, but use only biodegradable materials, and even "save six packs of empty one-way containers and ship them back to the board of directors of the company that manufactured the product."[11] Through it all, we ponder the sin of the United States consuming 40 percent of the world's food supply.

Parsimony extends to production as well as consumption. Since the population explosion is integrally related to the environmental catastrophe, self-control and frugality in life style will mean the limitation of family size. It may mean not only a norm of two children to attain ZPG, but also a willingness (in a time of women's liberation) for the male to choose a vasectomy after the limit is reached.

Learning to live with much less, the control of the obscene affluence of our age of glut will contribute to a fairer distribution of the world's goods. It may even prevent us from being smothered in our own wastes. And the habit of restraint might teach us as well some of the joys of self-abnegation about which the ascetic tradition has known for millennia.

CONCLUSION

"It is one minute to midnight on the ecological clock." Some wonder whether it will be the sounds of nuclear explosion or the silent spring that will end it all—the bang or the whimper. There can be another future. To the extent the Christian community has contributed to the bleak prospect rather than a promising one, we need a fresh penitence, a reformation of our bad theology, and zealous action toward shalom. We have good guidelines deep in our tradition. Two guides, both priestly custodians of that much misunderstood and ignored heritage, set the pace. One of them sent out an early warning signal at the outset of a burgeoning nineteenth-century technocracy:

> *Generations have trod, have trod, have trod;*
> *And all is seared with trade; bleared, smeared with toil;*
> *And wears man's smudge and shares man's smell: the soil*
> *Is bare now, nor can foot feel, being shod.*
>
> *And for all this nature is never spent;*
> *There lives the dearest freshness deep down things.*[12]

Do they still live? Can they? Another poet of the Christian community, a century later, less sanguine about the present but lighting still one candle, pleads for the future:

> *Dear World:*
> *I've got a feeling*
> *you're gonna be.*
> *Maybe not for me,*
> *but I don't mind.*
> *Go pass me by.*
> *It's just*
> *the children,*
> *take them for*
> *a happy ride,*
> *let them have*

*a little fun
just don't go too
close to the
sun . . . Oh yeah,
You've got the
Whole Sky.*[13]

NOTES

1. See Frederick Elder, *Crisis in Eden* (Nashville: Abingdon Press, 1970)—one of the pioneering religious works in the current environmental crusade.

2. White, "The Historical Roots of Our Ecologic Crisis," in *The Environmental Handbook*, ed. Garrett De Bell (New York: Ballantine Books, 1970).

3. See Theodore Roszak, *The Making of a Counter Culture* (Garden City, New York: Doubleday, 1969). It is often forgotten that Judaism and Christianity are also religions of the East.

4. *The Lancaster Independent Press*, 14 February, 1970. For a much more critical assessment of environmental conditions in societies influenced by religions of the Far East, see Yi-Fu Tuan, "Our Treatment of the Environment in Ideal and Actuality," *American Scientist*, May–June, 1970.

5. *The Secular City* (New York: Macmillan, 1965), pp. 21–24.

6. See Elder, *Crisis in Eden*, pp. 73–80.

7. Irenaeus, *Against Heresies; Ante-Nicene Fathers*, I (Buffalo: Christian Literature Publishing Company, 1886), 370.

8. Godfrey, "Crud Ho!" *Journal* (Division of Higher Education, United Church of Christ), April–May, 1970; Albert, "God Help Us, Man Won't," *Lancaster Independent Press*, 28 March, 1970; *Ecotactics*, the Sierra Club Handbook for Environmental Activists (New York: Pocket Books, 1970).

9. See Reinhold Niebuhr's classic portrayal of collective egoism, *Moral Man and Immoral Society* (New York: Scribner's, 1932, 1937).

10. "Crud Ho!" p. 5.

11. *Ecotactics*, p. 255.

12. Gerard Manley Hopkins, "God's Grandeur."

13. From *One Circus, 3 Rings, Forever and Ever, Hooray* by Joseph Pintauro. Copyright © 1968 by Joseph Pintauro. Used by permission of Harper and Row, Publishers.

9

A SECULAR PILGRIMAGE
WENDELL BERRY

One of the most exciting and vital kinds of poetry being written now in this country is nature poetry. There is some danger of over-simplification in saying so, for you will not find many poets, if any, who are writing only about nature; those who are writing the best nature poems are also writing well on other subjects: the city, love, marriage, politics, war, history, art, and so on. But running through the work of such poets as Gary Snyder, Denise Levertov, and A. R. Ammons,[1] there is a sustained attentiveness to nature and to the relation between man and nature.

"Nature poetry" is a clumsy term, and it presents immediate difficulties, for there is a sense in which most poetry is nature poetry; most poets, even those least interested in nature, have found in the natural world an abundant stock of symbols and metaphors. But I will use the term here to refer only to those poets who seem to me to have turned to the natural world, not as a source of imagery, but as subject and inspiration—as Marvell and Wordsworth and Thoreau (in his prose) turned to it. With those men nature was of primary interest; by seeing into its life they sensed the presence of a shaping and sustaining spirit within it. With poets such as Donne or Pope or Shelley the particulars of nature were only of secondary interest insofar as they "stood for" an abstraction that interested the poet primarily and that he had in mind before he turned to nature for an image.

The nature poets of our own time characteristically approach their subject with an openness of spirit and imagination, allowing

Wendell Berry, poet, essayist and novelist, is Professor of English at the University of Kentucky. Copyright © 1970 by Wendell Berry. First published in *The Hudson Review*, Vol. XXIII, No. 3 (Autumn, 1970).

the meaning and the movement of the poem to suggest themselves out of the facts. Their art has an implicit and essential humility, a reluctance to impose on things as they are, a willingness to relate to the world as student and servant, a wish to be included in the natural order rather than to conquer nature, a wish to discover the natural form rather than to create new forms that would be exclusively human. To create is to involve oneself as fully, as consciously and imaginatively, as possible in the Creation, to be immersed in the world. In "Some Notes on Organic Form" Denise Levertov has said: "For me, back of the idea of organic form is the concept that there is a form in all things (and in our experience) which the poet can discover and reveal." "Form," she says, "is never more than the *revelation* of content." And she speaks of "A religious devotion to the truth, to the splendor of the authentic. . . ."

As I have already made clear, this poetry arises out of a state of mind that could very accurately be described as religious. I am probably giving that adjective a broader application than it usually has. My use of it might, I suppose, be defined as primitive. I would apply it, for instance, to the sense of the presence of mystery or divinity in the world, or even to the attitudes of wonder or awe or humility before the works of the Creation. And I will not use the word here to refer to any of those revealed certainties that are so large a part of the lore of the various churches. A better term than religious might be worshipful, in the sense of *valuing* what one does not entirely understand, or aspiring beyond what may be known. There is a passage in John Stewart Collis's book *The Triumph of the Tree* that will serve perfectly as a definition of the state of mind I am talking about; he is speaking of primitive man:

Having become aware of objects and begun to name them, this Earliest Man became aware of something else. It is a remarkable fact that no sooner had he looked closely at the phenomena of Nature than he began to concern himself with, not the visible object in front of him which he could clearly see, but with an invisible object which he could not see at all. He looked at the trees, the rocks, the rivers, the animals, and having looked at them he at once began to talk about something *in them* which he had never seen and never heard of. This thing inside the objective appearance was called a god. No one forced man at this time to think about gods, there was no tradition imposing it upon him—and yet his first thoughts seem to have turned towards a Thing behind the thing, a Force behind or within the appearance. Thus *worship* . . .

The peculiar thrust and aspiration of the contemporary nature poetry might be fairly accurately suggested by calling it a secular pilgrimage—at least that is a phrase that has begun to accompany it in my own thinking. It is secular because it takes place outside of, or without reference to, the institutions of religion, and it does not seek any institutional shrine or holy place; it is in search of the world. But it is a pilgrimage nevertheless because it is a religious quest. It does not seek the world of inert materiality that is postulated both by the Heaven-oriented churches and by the exploitive industries; it seeks the world of the Creation, the created world in which the Creator, the formative and quickening spirit, is still immanent and at work. This sense of immanence is given memorably in two lines of "Flowers and Leaves," Guy Davenport's long poem: ". . . the ghost who wears out inert rock/ is fanatic with metamorphosis. . ."

I begin, then, with the assumption that perhaps the great disaster of human history is one that happened to or within religion: that is the conceptual division between the holy and the world, the excerpting of the Creator from the Creation. Collis is worth quoting again in this connection; though perhaps it may be argued that he is wrong about the cause, I think he is correct in his description of what happened:

> . . . whereas under polytheism the gods were intimately connected with the earth, and stimulated veneration for it, under monotheism deity was extracted from the earth. God was promoted to higher regions. He went completely out of sight. It became possible to fear God without fearing Nature—nay, to love God (whatever was meant) and to hate his creations.

If God was not in the world, then obviously the world was a thing of inferior importance, or of no importance at all. Those who were disposed to exploit it were thus free to do so. And this split in public attitudes was inevitably mirrored in the lives of individuals: a man could aspire to Heaven with his mind and his heart while destroying the earth, and his fellow men, with his hands.

The human or earthly problem has always been one of behavior, or morality: How should a man live in this world? Our institutional Christianity has usually tended to give a non-answer to this question: He should live for the next world. Which completely ignores the *fact* that the here is antecedent to the hereafter, and that, indeed, the Gospels would seem to make one's fate in the hereafter dependent on one's behavior here. Some varieties of Christianity have held that one should despise the things of this world—which made it all but mandatory that they should be neglected as well. In that way men of conscience—or men who might reasonably have been expected to be men of conscience—have been led to abandon the world, and their own posterity, to the exploiters and ruiners. So, exclusively focused on the hereafter, they have been neither here nor there.

This schism in man's sense of himself was protested at the end of the eighteenth century by William Blake, who wrote (of the time when "the whole creation will be consumed and appear infinite and holy"): "But first the notion that man has a body distinct from his soul is to be expunged. . . ." It was protested by Henry David Thoreau, who wrote in his journal on 21 June, 1840: "The body is the first proselyte the Soul makes. Our life is but the Soul made known by its fruits, the body. The whole duty of man may be expressed in one line—Make to yourself a perfect body." And it has been protested in our own time by the Welsh clergyman, R. S. Thomas, in his poem, "The Minister":

> *Is there no passion in Wales? There is none*
> *Except in the racked hearts of men like Morgan,*
> *Condemned to wither and starve in the cramped cell*
> *Of thought their fathers made them.*
> *Protestantism—the adroit castrator*
> *Of art; the bitter negation*
> *Of song and dance and the heart's innocent joy—*
> *You have botched our flesh and left us only the soul's*
> *Terrible impotence in a warm world.*

The contempt for the world or the hatred of it, that is exemplified both by the wish to exploit it for the sake of cash and by the willingness to despise it for the sake of "salvation," has reached a terrifying climax in our own time. The rift between soul and body, the Creator and the Creation, has admitted the entrance into the world of the machinery of the world's doom. We no longer feel ourselves threatened by the God-made doomsday of Revelation, or by the natural world's-end foreseen by science. We face an apocalypse of *our own* making—a man-made cosmic terror. The old-fashioned doomsdays of religion and nature were terrifying enough for mere humans, perhaps, but looking back from the perspective of our own time, we can see that their meanings were not entirely negative. The Doomsday of God, as described in the Bible, in spite of the terror and the destruction, was at the same time to be the triumph of divinity, of virtue, of spiritual value. In the doomsday of nature, the burning out of the sun or whatever, the life of the world would presumably be survived by natural law, the cosmic forces that brought it into being in the first place, and might bring into being another of the same kind or a better. But the doomsday of man is creation in reverse. Should we accomplish the destruction we are now capable of, we will destroy not only ourselves and the world, but also whatever right we may once have had to live. Perhaps many men have come, like Job, to wish that they had never been born. But until ours, no generation ever had to face the possibility that its extinction at birth might have been a benefit to the world. Such is the drastic and fearful change we have made in our life and in our sense of ourselves. How did it happen? It could only have happened by our failure to care enough for the world, to be humble enough before it, to think competently enough of its welfare. Rather than to be ruled by the thought of the world's good, which is identical with our own most meaningful good, we have set up the false standards of national interest, power, production, personal comfort or pride or greed—or the desire to get to Heaven, which, if it involves neglect of the life of the world, becomes only a rarefied form of gluttony.

Do we really hate the world? Are we really contemptuous of it? Have we really ignored its nature and its needs and the problems of its health? The evidence against us is everywhere. It is in our wanton and thoughtless misuse of the land and the other natural resources, in our wholesale pollution of the water and air, in strip mining, in our massive use and misuse of residual poisons in agriculture and elsewhere, in our willingness to destroy whole landscapes in the course of what we call "construction" and "progress," in the earth-destroying and population-destroying weapons we use in our wars, in the planet-destroying weapons now ready for use in the arsenals of the most powerful and violent nations of the world. It is in our hatred of races and nations. It is in our willingness to honor profit above everything except victory. It is in our willingness to spend more on war than on everything else. It is in our unappeasable restlessness, our nomadism, our anxiousness to get to another place or to "the top" or "somewhere" or to Heaven or to the moon.

Our hatred of the world is most insidiously and dangerously present in the constantly widening discrepancy between our power and our needs, our means and our ends. This is because of machinery and what we call efficiency. In order to build a road we destroy several thousand acres of farmland forever, all in perfect optimism, without regret, believing that we have gained much and lost nothing. In order to build a dam, which like all human things will be temporary, we destroy a virgin stream forever, believing that we have conquered nature and added significantly to our stature. In order to burn cheap coal we destroy a mountain forever, believing, in the way of lovers of progress, that what is of immediate advantage to us must be a permanent benefit to the universe. Fighting in Vietnam in the interest, as we say and would have ourselves believe, of the Vietnamese people, we have destroyed their villages, their croplands, their forests, herded the people into concentration camps, and in every way diminished the possibility of life in that country; and the civilian casualties are vastly greater than the military. In order to protect ourselves against Russia or China, or whoever our enemy will be in ten years, we have prepared weapons the use of which will, we know, involve our own destruction and the destruction of the world as well. Great power has always been blinding to those who wield it. Those who follow blindly in the wake of their own power practice hypocrisy by reflex; it is their natural camouflage. And in this age of super machines and super weapons hypocrisy is not only sinful, it is probably suicidal.

A man cannot hate the world and hate his own kind without hating himself. The familiar idea that a man's governing religious obligation is to "save" himself, procure *for himself* an eternal life, is based on a concept of individualism that is both vicious and absurd. And this religious concept is the counterpart, and to a considerable extent the cause, of the vicious secular individualism that suggests that a man's governing obligation is to enrich himself in this world. But man cannot live alone—he cannot have values alone, religious or otherwise, any more than he can live by bread alone. Such desires can live only at the world's expense, and at the expense of one's own earthly life which one inevitably devalues in devaluing the earth. So when a man seeks to live on the earth only for the eternal perpetuation, or only for the economic enrichment, of a life that he has devalued and despised, he is involved not only in absurdity but in perversion—a perversion that has now become the deadly disease of the world.

In *The Triumph of the Tree*, Collis outlines a most useful and clarifying historical scheme. First, he says, there was the "Era of Mythology," when men believed that they should venerate the world because it was inhabited by spirits and gods; they were frugal and considerate in their use of the world for fear of offending the resident divinities. Next came the "Era of Economics" when the Creation began to be valued in terms of cash; the sacred groves were cut down and since the gods took no direct revenge, the trees were sawed into lumber and put up for sale. This era built into an orgy of exploitation which has now "brought us to the edge of disaster." At this point we may, *if* we are able to make ourselves wise enough and humble enough, enter an "Era of Ecology," when we will utilize "the science of achieving an equilibrium with the environment." We will be as protective of the natural world as our primitive forebears, but this time for reasons that are knowledgeable and conscious rather than superstitious. We will realize and live in the realization that nature is not inexhaustible and that, in fact, we have already used up more than our share of its wealth. We will realize that we do not live *on* the earth, but with and within its life. We will realize that the earth is not dead, like the concept of property, but as vividly and intricately alive as a man or a woman, and that there is a delicate interdependence between its life and our own. We will take for granted what our farmers have had to learn with surprise and pain and to their cost, and what most politicians and business-men have never learned yet: it is not the area of a country that makes its value or its most meaningful strength, but its life, the depth and richness of its topsoil.

But Collis's vision of this last era, this future in which man may live in harmony with the world, is not merely scientific, though science will provide many of the necessary insights and methods; his vision is also religious. He accepts the contemporary decline of the organized religions, and finds hope in it:

Both polytheism and monotheism have done their work. The images are broken, the idols are all overthrown. This is now regarded as a very irreligious age. But perhaps it only means that the mind is moving from one state to another. The next stage is not a belief in many gods. It is not a belief in one god. It is not a belief at all—not a conception in the intellect. It is an extension of consciousness so that we may *feel* God, or, if you will, an experience of harmony, an intimation of the Divine, which will link us again with *animism*, the experience of unity lost at the in-break of self-consciousness. This will atone for our sin (which means *separation*); it will be our at-one-ment.

And here I can go back to the subject of poetry, for it is clear that if such an era is to be achieved—and it is either that or the apocalypse of technology—it will not be by the mechanical obedience of most men to new rules set up by a few. In the first place, men do not often obey mechanically; they tend to be good only in so far as they understand goodness. Much of our present destructiveness, for instance, is in defiance of rules that have been in existence for many years, but whose applicability to present lives has been blurred by new circumstances or obscured by old rhetoric. If the rules are to apply and be observed they must not only be written and publicized and learned, but understood, *felt*, accommodated to the particularities of the lives of particular people. If it is well to consider the needs of the earth as one's own needs, that must be carried beyond abstraction into the specific relation between each man and his place in the world. There must be new contact between men and the earth; the earth must be newly seen and heard and felt and smelled and tasted; there must be a renewal of the wisdom that comes with knowing clearly the pain and the pleasure and the risk and the responsibility of being alive in this world. This is only to say that such an era, like all eras, will arrive and remain by the means of a new speech—a speech that will cause the world to live and thrive in men's minds.

"Poetry," Thoreau said, "is nothing but healthy speech. . . ." By which he meant, I suppose, speech that is not only healthy in itself but conducive to the health of the speaker, giving him a true and vigorous relation to the world.

In the first of his books on haiku, R. H. Blyth says: "Poetry is that excess, that over-abundance which makes morality bearable and virtue alive. . . ." Also: "Poetry is a return to nature: to our own nature, to that of each thing, and to that of all things." Also: "Poetry is interpenetration"—and he quotes Marcus Aurelius, a passage that could have been written by an ecologist in our own day: "All things are interwoven each with [the] other: the tie is sacred, and nothing, or next to nothing is alien to aught else." And poetry, Blyth says, is that sacred tie. To complete his thought, he is emphatic in refusing to account for poetry in purely literary terms: "Poetry is not the words written in a book, but the mode of activity of the mind of the poet." In other words, it is not only a technique and a medium, but a power as well, a power to apprehend the unity, the sacred tie, that holds life together.

The poetry of this century, like the world in this century, has suffered from the schism in the modern consciousness. It has been turned back upon itself, fragmented, obscured in its sense of its function. Like all other human pursuits, it has had to suffer, and to some extent enact, the modern crisis: the failure of the past to teach us to deal with the present, or to envision and prepare for a desirable future. It has often seemed to lack wholeness and wisdom. One is tempted to say that some poets have grown too civilized, have become hive poets. In his book, *Spring in Washington*, Louis J. Halle expresses some strong reservations about the hive mentality:

It is curious how the preoccupations of the hive fill us, driving out all memory of the universe into which we were born. Perhaps the whole human race may be said to suffer from amnesia, not knowing whence it came or why it finds itself here. But we inhabitants of the hive suffer from double amnesia, one case within another, and are removed one stage further from the ultimate reality in which we have our beginning and our end. We have forgotten that we live in the universe, and that our civilization itself is merely an elaboration of the palm-leaf hat that one of our ancestors tried on ten thousand years ago to ward off the sun, a more complicated and ample version that now not only wards off the sun but shuts out the view. We have lost ourselves within it.

Thomas Merton wrote that "The new consciousness which isolates man in his own knowing mind and separates him from the world around him (which he does not know as it is in itself but only as it is in his mind) makes wisdom impossible because it severs the communion between subject and object, man and nature, upon which wisdom depends." But he says in the same essay that in Greek tragedy, "The catharsis of pity and terror delivers the participant from *hubris* and restores him to an awareness of his place in the scheme of things. ..." I think that this is to a considerable degree true also of the best nature poetry, which seeks expressly the power to deepen our insight into the very relationship Merton is talking about. It seeks to give us a sense of our proper place in the scheme of things. Its impulse is toward the realization of the presence of other life. Man, it keeps reminding us, is the center of the universe only in the sense that wherever he is it *seems* to him that he is at the center of his own horizon; the truth is that he is only a part of a vast complex of life, on the totality and the order of which he is blindly dependent. Since that totality and order have never yet come within the rational competence of our race, and even now do not seem likely ever to do so, the natural effect of such poetry is the religious one of humility and awe. It does not seem farfetched to assume that this religious effect might, in turn, produce the moral effect of care and competence and frugality in the use of the world.

As I have already suggested, I think that there is a considerable body of contemporary nature poetry in existence in this country that incorporates the essential double awareness of the physical presence of the natural world and of the immanence of mystery or divinity in the physical presence. This poetry, of course, did not materialize solely out of the awareness of nature. It has an extensive poetical ancestry of which it is conscious, and I think one may go far toward saying what this new poetry is like by hypothesizing at some length about its ancestry. It will necessarily be hypothesizing, because the ancestors I will speak of are the ones that I happen to be most aware of myself; I think that they are likely ones, but I cannot guarantee that they are the ones best known to other poets.

Though English poetry is full of nature *imagery*, and though it has had a constant interest in one or another of the *concepts* of nature, it seems to me surprisingly seldom that the immediate and particular manifestations of nature are acknowledged and looked at for their own sake. The natural world does impinge powerfully and unforgettably upon the consciousness of Geoffrey Chaucer at the beginning of his Prologue to the *Canterbury Tales;* though he is setting off on a pilgrimage, he cannot resist the attraction of the flowers, the birdsong, the damp earth and fresh sunlight of the April morning. But so far as I know, nature was not so openly turned to again until, in the seventeenth century, Andrew Marvell wrote such poems as "The Garden" and "Upon Appleton House." In the latter, his most ambitious poem, there is a clear gradation or ascent from the purely human context of the house and its family heritage, to the domesticated nature of the fields along the river, to the forest. The poem is notable, for one reason among many others, because it shows clearly that Marvell was thoughtful of wild nature and valued it in a way that was rare in English poetry before the romantic period. As the poem moves from house to forest, his imagination quickens and he becomes more and more exuberant both in mood and imagery. In the stanza where he turns from the house to the fields, he makes a stunning acknowledgment of the wildness and mystery in nature; at this point the wildness is not so much in the scene as in an awesome power to change and transform that Marvell senses *in* the scene, suddenly, and apparently to his surprise, and which his imagination seizes upon and emulates:

> *And now to the Abbyss I pass*
> *Of that unfathomable Grass,*
> *Where Men like Grashoppers appear,*
> *But Grashoppers are Gyants there . . .*

And then, the fields having been mowed and grazed, the river floods, and Marvell takes "Sanctuary in the Wood," which he calls "this yet green, yet growing Ark." The wood he describes as a natural temple, where one may read "Natures mystick Book." And the poet emerges as a priest in another striking passage that is almost Whitmanian:

> *The Oak-Leaves me embroyder all,*
> *Between which Caterpillars crawl:*
> *And Ivy, with familiar trails,*
> *Me licks, and clasps, and curles, and hales.*
> *Under this* antick Cope *I move*
> *Like some great* Prelate of the Grove . . .

And there is at last complete submergence into this wild place; he becomes one with it, in a kind of baptism or planting or crucifixion:

> *Bind me ye* Woodbines *in your 'twines,*
> *Curle me about ye gadding* Vines,
> *And Oh so close your Circles lace,*
> *That I may never leave this Place:*
> *But, lest your Fetters prove too weak,*
> *Ere I your Silken Bondage break,*
> *Do you,* O Brambles, *chain me too,*
> *And courteous* Briars *nail me through.*

In the same century Henry Vaughan wrote poems that acknowledge, like the thirty-third Psalm, that "the earth is full of the goodness of the Lord." He apparently took to heart the exultant spirit of
Psalm 104 where it is said that the Lord created the world "in
wisdom" and that he rejoices in his work. It is as though he read
literally Christ's admonition to "Consider the lilies of the field, how
they grow . . ." In his poem "The Bird" he says that "All things that
be praise Him, and had/Their lesson taught them when first made.
//So hills and valleys into singing break . . ." The very stones "are
deep in admiration." And Thomas Traherne wrote in one of his
prose meditations:

Suppose a river, or a drop of water, an apple or a sand, an ear of corn, or an
herb: God knoweth infinite excellencies in it more than we: he seeth how it
relateth to angels and men; how it proceedeth from the most perfect Lover
to the most perfectly beloved; how it representeth all his attributes; how it
conduceth in its place, by the best of means to the best of ends: and for this
cause it cannot be beloved too much. God the Author and God the End is
to be beloved in it; angels and men are to be beloved in it; and it is highly
to be esteemed for all their sakes.

Later there came Blake's well-known formula:

> To see a World in a Grain of Sand
> And a Heaven in a Wild Flower,
> Hold Infinity in the palm of your hand
> And Eternity in an hour.

Wordsworth virtually made this his life's work—this reaching
into the life of nature toward its informing spirit—

> a dark
> Inscrutable workmanship that reconciles
> Discordant elements, makes them cling together
> In one society.

This led him, in *The Prelude*, to an affirmation that is epic both in
scale and statement:

> Should the whole frame of earth by inward throes
> Be wrenched, or fire come down from far to scorch
> Her pleasant habitations, and dry up
> Old Ocean, in his bed left singed and bare,

Yet would the Living Presence still subsist
Victorious, and composure would ensue,
And kindlings like the morning . . .

But though Wordsworth was preoccupied with the experience of
nature, there is remarkably little in the way of particular observation
to be found in him.   What absorbed him was that Presence that
loomed behind created things and was manifested in them. He was
apparently able to "see into the life of things" without having to
scrutinize very closely the things themselves.

Gerard Manley Hopkins, more conventionally religious than
Wordsworth, had the same eagerness to thrust through appearances
toward a realization of the divine. With Hopkins, this was not the
anonymous Presence of Wordsworth's poems, but God, Jehovah,
who broods over his creation in which his glory is manifest. But
Hopkins was nevertheless a keener observer than Wordsworth; he
loved the physical facts of nature, and took pains to capture their
look and feel and movement.   In the accuracy of his observation,
and in the onomatopoeia of his diction and rhythms, his is clearly a
forebear of the contemporary nature poets.   "God's Grandeur" not
only gives a sense of his technique but also of his critical values
with respect to nature and civilization:

The world is charged with the grandeur of God.
It will flame out like shining from shook foil;
It gathers to a greatness like the ooze of oil
Crushed. Why do men then now not reck his rod?
Generations have trod, have trod, have trod;
And all is seared with trade; bleared, smeared with toil;
And wears man's smudge and shares man's smell: the soil
Is bare now, nor can foot feel, being shod.

The earliest American ancestor, among the poets, is Whitman.
I think that some of our poets are very close in attitude and affinity,
though not often in manner, to these passages from "Song of
Myself":

My tread scares the wood-drake and wood-duck, on my distant
*   and day-long ramble;*
They rise together—they slowly circle around.
I believe in those wing'd purposes,

And acknowledge red, yellow, white, playing within me,
And consider green and violet, and the tufted crown,
*   intentional . . .*

★

All truths wait in all things;
They neither hasten their own delivery, nor resist it . . .

★

I believe a leaf of grass is no less than the journey-work of the
*   stars,*
And that the pismire is equally perfect, and a grain of sand,
*   and the egg of the wren . . .*

★

I find I incorporate gneiss, coal, long-threaded moss, fruits, grains,
*   esculent roots,*
And am stucco'd with quadrupeds and birds all over . . .

Among the American poets who began writing early in our own century, there was a prevalent distrust of abstractions, especially those abstractions that had begun to be credited automatically by the society. They felt that men and the world had been poorly served by these abstractions, and it is clearer now than in their own time how right they were. But they also realized that men's minds were insulated and benumbed by their platitudes and clichés—blinded and deafened, exiled from the world. There is a memorable poem on this subject by Wallace Stevens; it is called "On the Road Home":

> *It was when I said,*
> *"There is no such thing as the truth,"*
> *That the grapes seemed fatter.*
> *The fox ran out of his hole.*[2]

William Carlos Williams, in *Paterson*, said emphatically that man must turn to the world to learn whatever he would know:

> *—Say it, no ideas but in things—*
> *nothing but the blank faces of the houses*
> *and cylindrical trees*
> *bent, forked by preconception and accident—*
> *split, furrowed, creased, mottled, stained—*
> *secret—into the body of the light!*[3]

In Canto LXXXI, Ezra Pound wrote some lines that could serve as the epigraph of the science of ecology. Again the message is to escape the abstractions; man will have to break out of the context of his own assumptions and measure himself by the truer measure of "the green world":

> *The ant's a centaur in his dragon world.*
> *Pull down thy vanity, it is not man*
> *Made courage, or made order, or made grace,*
> *Pull down thy vanity, I say pull down.*
> *Learn of the green world what can be thy place . . .*[4]

And in a late poem entitled "Directive," Robert Frost wrote both a proposal and an enactment of a secular pilgrimage—a return to the wilderness in order to be restored, made whole, made one with nature. The poem is explicitly religious, bearing allusions to the tenth chapter of *Matthew* ("he that loseth his life . . . shall find it"), to the eighteenth chapter of *Matthew* ("become as little children"), to the healing water of Bethesda, to the communion and the Holy Grail. The poet appears frankly in the role of priest, howbeit a slyly humorous one. Though it is hardly a typical Frost poem, I think it is his best.

> *Back out of all this now too much for us,*
> *Back in a time made simple by the loss*
> *Of detail, burned, dissolved, and broken off*
> *Like graveyard marble sculpture in the weather,*
> *There is a house that is no more a house . . .*
> . . . .
> *Your destination and your destiny's*
> *A brook that was the water of the house,*
> *Cold as a spring as yet so near its source,*
> *Too lofty and original to rage.*
> *(We know the valley streams that when aroused*
> *Will leave their tatters hung on barb and thorn.)*
> *I have kept hidden in the instep arch*
> *Of an old cedar at the waterside*
> *A broken drinking goblet like the Grail*
> *Under a spell so the wrong ones can't find it,*
> *So can't get saved, as Saint Mark says they mustn't.*

(I stole the goblet from the children's playhouse.)
Here are your waters and your watering place.
Drink and be whole again beyond confusion.*

A more innately religious man than any of the four Americans I have just named, D. H. Lawrence was, I think, one of the best nature poets. He seems to have come very naturally to the role of priest-poet, and unlike most of the poets of his generation he could speak of spirit or mystery without embarrassment. I will quote his poem "Shadows," one of the *Last Poems*, written when he knew he was dying:

And if tonight my soul may find her peace
in sleep, and sink in good oblivion,
and in the morning wake like a new-opened flower
then I have been dipped again in God, and new-created.

And if, as weeks go round, in the dark of the moon
my spirit darkens and goes out, and soft strange gloom
pervades my movements and my thoughts and words
then I shall know that I am walking still
with God, we are close together now the moon's in shadow.

And if, as autumn deepens and darkens
I feel the pain of falling leaves, and stems that break in storms
and trouble and dissolution and distress
and then the softness of deep shadows folding, folding
round my soul and spirit, around my lips
so sweet, like a swoon, or more like the drowse of a low, sad song

singing darker than the nightingale, on, on to the solstice
and the silence of short days, the silence of the year, the shadow,
then I shall know that my life is moving still
with the dark earth, and drenched
with the deep oblivion of earth's lapse and renewal.

---

* From "Directive" from *The Poetry of Robert Frost*, edited by Edward Connery Lathem. Copyright 1947, © 1969 by Holt, Rinehart and Winston, Inc.

And if, in the changing phases of man's life
I fall in sickness and in misery
my wrists seem broken and my heart seems dead
and strength is gone, and my life
is only the leavings of a life:

and still, among it all, snatches of lovely oblivion, and snatches of
     renewal
odd, wintry flowers upon the withered stem, yet new, strange
     flowers
such as my life has not brought forth before, new blossoms of me—

then I must know that still
I am in the hands [of] the unknown God,
he is breaking me down to his own oblivion
to send me forth on a new morning, a new man.[5]

Nearer to us, there was Theodore Roethke who wrote, toward the end of his life, poems of visionary peace-making with the world. This is the ending of one called "Journey to the Interior":

As a blind man, lifting a curtain, knows it is morning,
I know this change:
On one side of silence there is no smile;
But when I breathe with the birds,
The spirit of wrath becomes the spirit of blessing,
And the dead begin from their dark to sing in my sleep.[6]

That gives a possible line of descent through the history of poetry in England and America. But before speaking of my contemporaries, I want to suggest two other influences that I think have come to be strongly felt.

The first is that of Oriental poetry—its directness and brevity, its involvement with the life of things, its sense that the poem does not create the poetry but is the revelation of a poetry that is in the world. Here is a poem "Written on the Wall at Chang's Hermitage" by Tu Fu, a Chinese poet of the eighth century; the translation is by Kenneth Rexroth, who has written excellent nature poems of his own:

It is Spring in the mountains.
I come alone seeking you.

The sound of chopping wood echoes
Between the silent peaks.
The streams are still icy.
There is snow on the trail.
At sunset I reach your grove
In the stony mountain pass.
You want nothing, although at night
You can see the aura of gold
And silver ore all around you.
You have learned to be gentle
As the mountain deer you have tamed.
The way back forgotten, hidden
Away, I become like you,
An empty boat, floating, adrift.

These qualities perhaps reach their height of refinement in haiku, an art that developed both out of and into a complex awareness of nature:

> I am one
> Who eats his breakfast,
>   Gazing at the morning-glories.
>
>   *Basho*

>   Over my legs,
> Stretched out at ease,
>   The billowing clouds.
>
>   *Issa*

>   Spring departs,
> Trembling, in the grasses
>   Of the fields.
>
>   *Issa*

"A Haiku," Blyth says, "is not a poem, it is not literature; it is a hand beckoning, a door half-opened, a mirror wiped clean. It is a way of returning to nature.... It is a way in which the cold winter rain, the swallows of evening, even the very day in its hotness, and the length of the night become truly alive, share in our humanity, speak their own silent and expressive language."

The second influence is that of the prose writings of Henry David Thoreau. In his poems, Thoreau usually seems weighted and bound by the vagueness and inflated diction of most romantic nature poetry. It was only in prose that he could break free into the presence of the life around him and become a poet. In his prose we see, maybe for the first time, the poet-as-American, speaking out of the life of an American place—a new place, relatively speaking, the life of which had not been much spoken of by white poets or writers of any kind, and which therefore demanded a clear direct vision. We find this clarity and directness in his prose. We also find a painstaking accuracy of observation, a most unsolemn and refreshing reverence, a sense of being involved in nature, and a rare exuberance and wit. These are samples from his *Journal*:

You tell of active labors, of works of art, and wars the past summer; meanwhile the tortoise eggs underlie this turmoil.

The air over these fields is a foundry full of moulds for casting bluebirds' warbles. Any sound uttered now would take that form. . . .

The fishes are going up the brooks as they open. They are dispersing themselves through the fields and woods, imparting new life into them. They are taking their places under the shelving banks and in the dark swamps. The water running down meets the fishes running up. They hear the latest news. Spring-aroused fishes are running up our veins too.

Now, to give some idea of the contemporary work, I will quote from the three poets I mentioned at the beginning. Very different from each other, they are all alike in seeking a new awareness of nature and their own place in it.

Denise Levertov is a poet deeply interested in myth, as many modern poets have been. With her this is not an antiquarian interest. She has, I think, no wish merely to reconstruct old myths and observances in homage to the past or in opposition to the present; she is interested in them as clues to the meaning and nature of our deepest needs. In her poems, myth never leads inward to a purely imaginative or purely human interior, but outward toward the world. To imagine is to realize, to sense the authentic. The myth is the acceptance and the enactment of the bond between mankind and the world—as in "The Novices," a poem very different from Frost's "Directive," but closely parallel to it:

> They enter the bare wood, drawn
> by a clear-obscure summons they fear
> and have no choice but to heed.

A rustling underfoot, a
long trail to go, the thornbushes grow
across the dwindling paths.

Until the small clearing, where they
anticipate violence, knowing some rite
to be performed, and compelled to it.

The man moves forward, the boy
sees what he means to do : from an oaktree
a chain runs at an angle into earth

and they pit themselves to uproot it,
dogged and frightened, to pull the iron
out of the earth's heart.

But from the further depths of the wood
as they strain and weigh on the great chain
appears the spirit,

the wood-demon who summoned them.
And he is not bestial, not fierce
but an old woodsman,

gnarled, shabby, smelling of smoke and sweat,
of a bear's height and shambling like a bear.
Yet his presence is a spirit's presence

and awe takes their breath.
Gentle and rough, laughing a little,
he makes his will known :

not for an act of force he called them,
for no rite of obscure violence
but that they might look about them

and see the intricate branch and bark,
stars of moss and the old scars
left by dead men's saws,

and not ask what the chain was.
To leave the open fields
and enter the forest,

> *that was the rite.*
> *Knowing there was mystery, they could go.*
> *Go back now! And he receded*
>
> *among the multitude of forms,*
> *the twists and shadows they saw now, listening*
> *to the hum of the world's wood.*[7]

A. R. Ammons studied science when he was in college, and his poems have managed to incorporate the viewpoint, the curiosity and even the vocabulary of the biologist. He tends to be a poet, not of natural objects, but of natural processes, and so his language seeks to particularize movement and relationship rather than appearance. But if his vision is scientific, it is also mystical: "I admit to mystery/in the obvious . . ." If he is fascinated by the study of the interweavings of energies into the ecology, he is also fascinated and awe-struck by the unexplainable: "mind rising/from the physical chemistries . . ." If he finds grounds for affirmation in his comprehension of the world, he finds the possibility of even greater affirmation in the limits of his comprehension: "I know nothing;/still, I cannot help singing . . ." If all that a man can understand were all there is, if there were no mystery, then the mind would be trapped and damned within its limits; one should rejoice in understanding, but rejoice also in failing to understand, for in that failure the mind is set free.

Some of Ammons' poems involve an explicit worshipfulness, which consists in the understanding of the failure to understand, the mind's graceful, and grateful, sense of its boundaries:

> *I will show you*
> *the underlying that takes no image to itself,*
> *cannot be shown or said,*
> *but weaves in and out of moons and bladderweeds,*
> *is all and*
> *beyond destruction*
> *because created fully in no*
> *particular form   . .*[8]

It should be emphasized that the divinity here is sensed as "underlying" rather than overlooking—not the withdrawn author of forms and substances, but one of their properties. His worship is secular, speculative, curious, meditative, studious.

It is one of the obligations of his religious vision to refuse the presumption of the closed forms of a humanistic art. Form, he believes, is in all things, but the forms comprehended in nature or achieved in art are necessarily partial forms, fragments, inferior to the form of the whole creation which can be neither comprehended nor imagined:

> *I see narrow orders, limited tightness, but will*
> *not run to that easy victory:*
> > *still around the looser, wider forces work:*
> > *I will try*
> > *to fasten into order enlarging grasps of disorder, widening*
> *scope, but enjoying the freedom that*
> *Scope eludes my grasp, that there is no finality of vision,*
> *that I have perceived nothing completely*
> > *that tomorrow a new walk is a new walk.*[9]

Of these three poets, Gary Snyder is the most austere, the one willing to venture farthest from the human assumptions and enclosures. His poem "Piute Creek" is a spiritual discipline in which he confronts the non-human time and space of the Sierra Nevada. His realization of the smallness and shortness of his life in relation to the world's life is of such intensity as to make him virtually absent from the place and from his own sense of things. He is present in the poem finally only as another creature, along with moon and rock and juniper and the wild animals. And in proportion as he withdraws himself and his human claims, his sense of it grows whole and grand. He is a worshipper only in the sense that in his clarified consciousness of it the Creation is seen to be awesome and mysterious, deserving worship:

> *One granite ridge*
> *A tree, would be enough*
> *Or even a rock, a small creek,*
> *A bark shred in a pool.*
> *Hill beyond hill, folded and twisted*
> *Tough trees crammed*
> *In thin stone fractures*
> *A huge moon on it all, is too much.*
> *The mind wanders. A million*
> *Summers, night air still and the rocks*
> *Warm. Sky over endless mountains.*

All the junk that goes with being human
Drops away, hard rock wavers
Even the heavy present seems to fail
This bubble of a heart.
Words and books
Like a small creek off a high ledge
Gone in the dry air.

A clear, attentive mind
Has no meaning but that
Which sees is truly seen.
No one loves rock, yet we are here.
Night chills. A flick
In the moonlight
Slips into Juniper shadow ·
Back there unseen
Cold proud eyes
Of Cougar or Coyote
Watch me rise and go.[10]

It is necessary for me to say, ending, that this collection of quotations and comments is not meant to be taken as a definitive statement. Like most things said about poetry by poets, it is personal and somewhat arbitrary. It is an effort to suggest that there is in our poetry an impulse of reverence moving toward the world, toward a new pertinence of speech and a new sense of possibility.

NOTES

1. These poets are representative of the sort of interest in nature that I am talking about. I don't mean to imply either that they are our only nature poets or that they are the only ones whose work I value.
2. From "On the Road Home," by Wallace Stevens, from *Collected Poems of Wallace Stevens*. Copyright 1954 by Alfred A. Knopf. Used by permission of Alfred A. Knopf.
3. William Carlos Williams, *Paterson*. Copyright 1946 by William Carlos Williams. Reprinted by permission of New Directions Publishing Corporation.
4. Ezra Pound, *The Cantos*. Copyright 1948 by Ezra Pound. Reprinted by permission of New Directions Publishing Corporation.
5. From *The Complete Poems of D. H. Lawrence*, edited by Vivian de Sola

10

ALL ABOUT ECOLOGY
WILLIAM MURDOCH AND JOSEPH CONNELL

The public's awakening to the environmental crisis over the past few years has been remarkable. A recent Gallup Poll showed that every other American was concerned about the population problem. A questionnaire sent to about five hundred University of California freshmen asked which of twenty-five topics should be included in a general biology course for non-majors. The top four positions were: Human Population Problems (85%), Pollution (79%), Genetics (71.3%), and Ecology (66%).

The average citizen is at least getting to know the word ecology, even though his basic understanding of it may not be significantly increased. Not more than five years ago, we had to explain at length what an ecologist was. Recently when we have described ourselves as ecologists, we have been met with respectful nods of recognition.

A change has also occurred among ecologists themselves. Until recently the meetings of ecologists we attended were concerned with the esoterica of a "pure science," but now ecologists are haranguing each other on the necessity for ecologists to become involved in the "real world." We can expect that peripatetic "ecological experts" will soon join the ranks of governmental consultants jetting back and forth to the Capitol—thereby adding their quota to the pollution of the atmosphere. However, that will be a small price to pay if they succeed in clearing the air of the political verbiage that still passes for an environmental policy in Washington.

Concern about environment, of course, is not limited to the

The authors are members of the Biology Department at the University of California at Santa Barbara. Their article is reprinted, with permission, from the January 1970 issue of *The Center Magazine*, a publication of the Center for the Study of Democratic Institutions in Santa Barbara, California.

United States. The ecological crisis, by its nature, is basically an international problem, so it seems likely that the ecologist as "expert" is here to stay. To some extent the present commotion about ecology arises from people climbing on the newest bandwagon. When the limits of ecological expertise become apparent, we must expect to lose a few passengers. But, if only because there is no alternative, the ecologist and the policymakers appear to be stuck with each other for some time to come.

While a growing awareness of the relevance of ecology must be welcomed, there are already misconceptions about it. Further, the traditional role of the expert in Washington predisposes the nation to a misuse of its ecologists. Take an example. A common lament of the socially conscious citizen is that though we have enough science and technology to put a man on the moon we cannot maintain a decent environment in the United States. The implicit premise here seems clear: the solution to our ecological crisis is technological. A logical extension of this argument is that, in this particular case, the ecologist is the appropriate "engineer" to resolve the crisis. This reflects the dominant American philosophy (which is sure to come up after every lecture on the environment) that the answer to most of our problems is technology and, in particular, that the answer to the problems raised by technology is more technology. Perhaps the most astounding example of this blind faith is the recent assurance issued by the government that the SST will not fly over the United States until the sonic boom problem is solved. The sonic boom "problem," of course, cannot be "solved." One job of the ecologist is to dispel this faith in technology.

To illustrate the environmental crisis, let us take two examples of how the growth of population, combined with the increasing sophistication of technology, has caused serious problems which planning and foresight could have prevented. Unfortunately, the fact is that no technological solutions applied to problems caused by increased population have ever taken into consideration the consequences to the environment.

The first example is the building of the Aswan High Dam on the upper Nile. Its purposes were laudable—to provide a regular supply of water for irrigation, to prevent disastrous floods, and to provide electrical power for a primitive society. Other effects, however, were simply not taken into account. The annual flood of the Nile had brought a supply of rich nutrients to the eastern Mediterranean Sea, renewing its fertility; fishermen had long depended upon this annual cycle. Since the Aswan Dam put an end to the annual flood with its load of nutrients, the annual bloom of phytoplankton in the eastern Mediterranean no longer occurs. Thus the food chain from phytoplankton to zooplankton to fish has been broken; and the sardine fishery, once producing eighteen thousand tons per year (about half of the total fish catch), has dropped to about five hundred tons per year.

Another ecological effect of the dam has been the replacement of an intermittent flowing stream with a permanent stable lake. This has allowed aquatic snails to maintain large populations, whereas before the dam was built they had been reduced each year during the dry season. Because irrigation supports larger human populations, there are now many more people living close to these stable bodies of water. The problem here is that the snails serve as intermediate hosts of the larvae of a blood fluke. The larvae leave the snail and bore into humans, infecting the liver and other organs. This causes the disease called schistosomiasis. The species of snail which lives in stable water harbors a more virulent species of fluke than that found in another species of snail in running water. Thus the lake behind the Aswan Dam has increased both the incidence and virulence of schistosomiasis among the people of the upper Nile.

A second example we might cite is the effect of DDT on the environment. DDT is only slightly soluble in water, so is carried mainly on particles in the water for short distances until these settle out. But on tiny particles in the atmosphere it is carried great distances; it may even fall out more heavily in distant places than close to where it was sprayed. DDT is not readily broken down by microorganisms; it therefore persists in the environment for many years. It is very soluble in fats so that it is quickly taken up by organisms. Herbivores eat many times their own weight of plants; the DDT is not broken down but is accumulated in their bodies and becomes further concentrated when the herbivores are eaten by the carnivores. The result is that the species at the top of the food chain end up with high doses of it in their tissues. Evidence is beginning to show that certain species of predators, such as ospreys, are being wiped out as a result of physiological debilities which lead to reproductive failure, all caused by accumulations of DDT.

The reproduction of top carnivores such as ospreys and pelicans is being reduced to negligible amounts, which will cause their extinction. No amount of technological ingenuity can reconstruct a species of osprey once it is extinct.

The tendency of DDT to kill both the herbivorous pest as well as its predators has produced some unpredicted consequences. In natural circumstances, herbivores are often kept at rather low numbers by their predators, with occasional "outbreaks" when there is a decrease in these enemies. Once spraying is started, and both the pests and their natural enemies are killed, the surviving pests, which have higher rates of increase than their predators, can then increase explosively between applications.

Before pesticides were applied to North American spruce and balsam forests, pest populations exploded once every thirty years or so, ate all the leaves, and then their numbers plummeted. Since spraying began, the pests, in the absence of a balancing force of predators, are continually able to increase between sprayings. In two instances, in cotton fields in Peru and in cocoa plantations in Malaysia, the situation became so bad that spraying was stopped. The predators returned and the damage by pests was diminished to the former tolerable levels. Another consequence of spraying has been that any member of the pest population which happens to be physiologically resistant to an insecticide survives and leaves off-spring; thus resistant strains are evolved. Several hundred of these resistant strains have evolved in the last twenty years.

Because DDT is not present in concentrated form in the environment, it does not represent an energy resource common enough to support microorganisms. None has yet evolved the ability to break it down, even though it has been used as a pesticide for twenty-five years. Chlorinated hydrocarbons may even reduce drastically the plant productivity of the oceans. These plants are not only the base of the ocean food chain but also help maintain the oxygen supply of the atmosphere.

In sum, the indiscriminate use of DDT throughout the world, its dispersal by the atmosphere, its property of killing both pests and their enemies, and the evolution of resistant strains, have combined to create a crisis in the environment. The reaction has been to stop spraying some crops and to ban the use of DDT in some countries. Probably the correct solution, though, is to use pesticides carefully, applying them very locally (by hand if possible) to places where pest outbreaks are threatening and to introduce or encourage enemies of the pests. This is called "integrated control." It is the hope of the future.

Since this article concerns pure ecology, it is probably worth distinguishing between pure and applied ecology. Applied ecologists are concerned with such problems as controlling pests and maximizing the yield from populations. Pure ecologists study interactions among individuals in a population of organisms, among populations, and between populations and their environments. (A population is a more or less defined group of organisms that belong to the same species.)

A brief indication of how some ecologists spend their time may be in order here. One of us (Connell) became interested in discovering what determines the distribution on the rocky seashore of a species of barnacle. He made frequent visits to the shore, photographed the positions of barnacles, counted their numbers at different levels on the shore at different life stages, noted the density and positions of predators, other barnacle species, and so forth. He developed hypotheses (in one area, that the limit to distribution is set by the presence of another barnacle species; in another, that beyond a certain height on the seashore a snail species eats them all) and tested the ideas by various experiments such as placing cages on the shore to exclude predators or removing the competing species. This work went on for several years and has now firmly established the two hypotheses.

Murdoch spent the past three years in the laboratory examining an idea about predators. The idea was that predators keep the numbers of their various prey species stable by attacking very heavily whichever species is most abundant. (The idea is a bit more complicated than that, but that is approximately it.) This entailed setting up experiments where different predators were offered different mixtures of two prey species at a variety of densities, and then counting the number eaten of each species. These experiments led to others, in order to test different sub-hypotheses. The conclusion was that predators would "switch" only under very particular conditions.

Other ecologists spend long periods in the field trying to measure what happens to the vegetable material in a field. How much is produced and what percentage goes to rabbits, mice, insects? What percentage of the total weight of mice produced (biomass) is eaten by weasels and how efficient are weasels at converting mouse biomass to weasel biomass? Such work takes a great deal of time, estimates are rough, shaky assumptions have to be made, and in the end we have only approximate answers.

Other ecologists try to build mathematical models which might suggest how a community or some subset of a community comes to have the structure which our rough measurements tell us it may have. In pursuing all these activities they hope to build models of how nature works. The models, while not being copies of nature, should catch the essence of some process in nature and serve as a basis for explaining the phenomena that have been observed. They hope these models will be generally, though not necessarily universally, applicable. They study particular systems in the hope that these systems are not in all respects, or even in their major aspects, unique. Thus the aspirations of ecologists are not different from those of any other scientists.

Ecologists face problems which make their task difficult and at times apparently insurmountable. It is a young science, probably not older than forty years; consequently, much of it is still descriptive. It deals with systems which are depressingly complex, affected by dozens of variables which may all interact in a very large number of ways. Rather than taking a census of them, these systems must be sampled. Ecology is one of the few disciplines in biology in which it is not clear that removing portions of the problem to the laboratory for experimentation is an appropriate technique. It may be that the necessary simplification this involves removes exactly the elements from the system which determine how it functions. Yet field experiments are difficult to do and usually hard to interpret. Ecology, moreover, is the only field of biology which is not simply a matter of applied physics and chemistry. The great advances in molecular biology resulted from physicists looking at biological systems (such as DNA), whose basic configuration is explicable in terms of the positions of atoms. But the individual or the population is the basic unit in ecology. It seems certain, then, that a direct extension of physics and chemistry will not help ecologists.

Finally, there is the problem that each ecological situation is different from every other one, with a history all its own; ecological systems, to use a mathematical analogy, are non-Markovian, which is to say that a knowledge of both the past and the present is necessary in order to predict the future. Unlike a great deal of physics, ecology is not independent of time or place. As a consequence, the discipline does not cast up broad generalizations. All this is not a complete list of the general problems ecologists face, but it may be enough to provide a feeling for the difficulty of the subject.

Ecologists, though, do have something to show for forty years' work. These are some of the general conclusions they have reached. (Not all ecologists, by any means, would agree that they are generally applicable—and those who do agree would admit that exceptions occur—but they are the kind of basic conclusions that many ecologists would hope to be able to establish.)

1. Populations of most species have negative feedback processes which keep their numbers within relatively narrow limits. If the species itself does not possess such features, or even if it does, the community in which it exists acts to regulate numbers, for example, through the action of predators. (Such a statement obviously is not precise, e.g. how narrow are "relatively narrow limits"? A measure of ecology's success, or lack of it, is that, in forty years, there are no more than a half-dozen populations in which regulation has been adequately demonstrated; and the basis for belief in regulation is either faith or very general observations, such as the fact that most species are not so abundant that they are considered pests.)

2. The laws of physics lead to derivative statements in ecology. For example, the law that matter cycles through the ecosystem, to be used again and again. Or the law that energy from the sun is trapped by plants through photosynthesis, moves up the food chain to herbivores and then to carnivores as matter, losing energy at each successive conversion so that there is generally less energy and biomass in higher food levels than in lower ones. Ecologists have tried to take such truths from physics and construct more truly ecological generalities from them. Thus, to stay with the same example, it appears likely that there are never more than five links in any one chain of conversions from plant to top predator.

3. It is probably true, on a given piece of the earth and provided

that the climate doesn't change, that a "climax" ecosystem will develop which is characteristic of the area's particular features and that places with similar features will develop similar ecosystems if left undisturbed.   Characteristically, a "succession" from rather simple and short-lived communities to more complex and more persistent communities will occur, though there may be a reduction in the complexity of the final community.   We use "final" to mean that a characteristic community will be found there for many generations.   We might go further and say that during the period of development disturbances of the community will result in its complexity being reduced.   (Again, such statements will certainly arouse the dissent of some ecologists.)

4. Finally, most ecologists would agree that complex communities are more stable than simple communities.   This statement illustrates the difficulties faced by theoretical ecologists.   Take some of its implications: What is complexity and what is stability in an ecological setting?   Charles Elton embodied the idea in a simple, practical, and easily understood way.   He argued that England should maintain the hedgerows between its fields because these were complex islands in a simple agricultural sea and contained a reservoir of insect and other predators which helped to keep down pest populations.   The idea here seems quite clear.   Ecologists, though, want a more precise exposition of the implications of the statement.   What kind of complexity?   What is stability?

Physical complexity, by providing hiding places for prey, may increase stability.   Certainly biological complexity in general is thought to lead to stability—more species or more interspecific interactions, more stability.   But we may ask, more species of what sort?   Here a variety of answers is available.   It has been suggested that complex communities are stable, i.e. able to resist invasion by species new to the area, by having all the "niches" filled.   Thus sheer numbers of kinds of organisms in all food levels were considered the appropriate sort of complexity.   To keep the numbers of prey stable, the most likely candidates are predators.   Now other questions arise: Do we just want more species of predators?   Do we want more species of predators which are very specific in the prey they eat, implying that prey are stabilized by having many species feed on them?   Do we want predators which are very general and attack many prey species, so that we still have a large number of interspecific interactions which are made up in a different way? The answer is not obvious, and indeed there is disagreement on it. Furthermore, if one studies the way some predators react to changes in the numbers of their prey, their short-term responses are such as to cause *instability*.   Thus only some types of biological complexity may produce stability.

What do we mean by stability? In the examples cited, we have meant numerical constancy through time, but this is by no means the only meaning. It has even been suggested that numerical *in*constancy is a criterion for stability. Stability might also mean that the same species persist in the same area over long periods, showing the same sort of interspecific interactions (community stability). A community or population might be considered stable because it does not change in response to a great deal of environmental pressure, or because it changes but quickly returns to its original state when the disturbing force is removed. It is worth noting that if a population or community is observed merely not to change, we cannot tell whether this is owing to its ability to resist perturbing factors or merely to the absence of such factors. If we want to know about the *mechanisms* which might lead to the truth of our original statement, "complexity leads to stability," all the above points are important.

This general statement about complexity and stability rests upon the kind of observation readily apparent to most intelligent laymen. Thus simple agricultural systems seem to be much more subject to outbreaks of herbivores than the surrounding countryside. Ecosystems in the tropics appear to be more stable than in the simpler temperate zone. In turn the temperate zone seems to be more stable than the Arctic. This seems to be mainly an article of faith. However, even this classic sort of evidence is questioned—for example, small mammals may actually be more unstable numerically in the United States than in the much simpler Arctic environment. Other evidence comes from the laboratory. If one takes small species of prey and predator—for example, two single-celled animals or two small mites—and begins culturing them together, the numbers of prey and predators fluctuate wildly and then both become extinct quickly, for the predators exhaust their food source. "Simple" predator-prey systems tend to be unstable. There is some evidence that if physical complexity is added the system may become more stable.

From these examples of the generalizations ecologists have arrived at, an important question emerges. Even if we dispense with the idea that ecologists are some sort of environmental engineers and compare them to the pure physicists who provide scientific rules for engineers, do the tentative understandings we have outlined provide a sound basis for action by those who would manage the environment? It is self-evident that they do not.

This conclusion seems to be implied in a quotation from an article published in *Time* on the environment, which underlines the point that application of the ecologist's work is not the solution to the environmental crisis. According to *Time :* "Crawford S. Holling was once immersed in rather abstract research at the University of British Columbia—mathematical models of the relationship between predators and their prey. 'Three years ago, I got stark terrified at what was going on in the world and gave it up.' Now he heads the university's interdepartmental studies of land and water use, which involve agriculture, economics, forestry, geography, and regional planning. 'What got me started on this,' says Holling, 'were the profound and striking similarities between ecological systems and the activities of man: between predators and land speculators; between animal-population growth and economic growth; between plant dispersal and the diffusion of people, ideas, and money'."

The "rather abstract research" was ecology. Holling's testimony is that it would not provide a solution. Yet, by and large, ecologists are concerned and probably have the best understanding of the problem.

We submit that ecology as such probably cannot do what many people expect it to do; it cannot provide a set of "rules" of the kind needed to manage the environment. Nevertheless, ecologists have a great responsibility to help solve the crisis; the solution they offer should be founded on a basic "ecological attitude." Ecologists are likely to be aware of the consequences of environmental manipulation; possibly most important, they are ready to deal with the environmental problem since their basic ecological attitude is itself the solution to the problem. Interestingly enough, the supporting data do not generally come from our "abstract research" but from massive uncontrolled "experiments" done in the name of development.

These attitudes and data, plus obvious manifestations of physical laws, determine what the ecologist has to say on the problem and constitute what might be called environmental knowledge. Some examples of this knowledge follow, though this is not to be taken as an encapsulation of the ecologist's wisdom.

1. Whatever is done to the environment is likely to have repercussions in other places and at other times. Because of the characteristic problems of ecology some of the effects are bound to be unpredictable in practice, if not in principle. Furthermore, because of the characteristic time-dependence problem, the effects may not be measurable for years—possibly not for decades.

2. If man's actions are massive enough, drastic enough, or of the right sort, they will cause changes which are irreversible since the genetic material of extinct species cannot be reconstituted. Even if species are not driven to extinction, changes may occur in the ecosystem which prevent a recurrence of the events which produced the community. Such irreversible changes will almost always produce a simplification of the environment.

3. The environment is finite and our non-renewable resources are finite. When the stocks run out we will have to recycle what we have used.

4. The capacity of the environment to act as a sink for our total waste, to absorb it and recycle it so that it does not accumulate as pollution, is limited. In many instances, that limit has already been passed. It seems clear that when limits are passed, fairly gross effects occur, some of which are predictable, some of which are not. These effects result in significant alterations in environmental conditions (global weather, ocean productivity). Such changes are almost always bad since organisms have evolved and ecosystems have developed for existing conditions. We impose rates of change on the environment which are too great for biological systems to cope with.

5. In such a finite world and under present conditions, an increasing population can only worsen matters. For a stationary population, an increase in standard of living can only mean an increase in the use of limited resources, the destruction of the environment, and the choking of the environmental sinks.

There are two ways of attacking the environmental crisis. The first approach is technology; the second is to reverse the trends which got us into the crisis in the first place and to alter the structure of our society so that an equilibrium between human population and the capacities of the environment can be established.

There are three main dangers in a technological approach to the environmental crisis. The first threatens the environment in the short term, the second concerns ecologists themselves, and the third, which concerns the general public attitude, is a threat to the environment in the long term.

Our basic premise is that, by its nature, technology is a system for manufacturing the need for more technology. When this is combined with an economic system whose major goal is growth, the result is a society in which conspicuous production of garbage is the highest social virtue. If our premise is correct, it is unlikely we can solve our present problems by using technology. As an example, we might consider nuclear power plants as a "clean" alternative to which we can increasingly turn. But nuclear power plants inevitably produce radioactive waste; this problem will grow at an enormous rate, and we are not competent to handle it safely. In addition, a whole new set of problems arises when all these plants produce thermal pollution. Technology merely substitutes one sort of pollution for another.

There is a more subtle danger inherent in the technological approach. The automobile is a blight on Southern California's landscape. It might be thought that ecologists should concern themselves with encouraging the development of technology to cut down the emission of pollutants from the internal combustion engine. Yet that might only serve to give the public the impression that something is being done about the problem and that it can therefore confidently await its solution. Nothing significant could be accomplished in any case because the increasing number of cars ensures an undiminishing smog problem.

Tinkering with technology is essentially equivalent to oiling its wheels. The very act of making minor alterations, in order to placate the public, actually allows the general development of technology to proceed unhindered, only increasing the environmental problems it causes. This is what sociologists have called a "pseudo-event." That is, activities go on which give the appearance of tackling the problem; they will not, of course, solve it but only remove public pressure for a solution.

Tinkering also distracts the ecologist from his real job. It is the ecologist's job, as a general rule, to oppose growth and "progress." He cannot set about convincing the public of the correctness of this position if in the meantime he is putting his shoulder behind the wheel of technology. The political power system has a long tradition of buying off its critics, and the ecologist is liable to wind up perennially compromising his position, thereby merely slowing down slightly or redirecting the onslaught of technology.

The pressures on the ecologist to provide "tinkering" solutions will continue to be quite strong. Pleas for a change of values, for a change to a non-growth, equilibrium economy seem naive. The government, expecting sophistication from its "experts," will probably receive such advice coolly. Furthermore, ecologists themselves are painfully aware of how immature their science is and generally take every opportunity to cover up this fact with a cloud of obfuscating pseudo-sophistication. They delight in turning prosaic facts and ideas into esoteric jargon. Where possible, they embroider the structure with mathematics and the language of cybernetics and systems analysis, which is sometimes useful but frequently is merely confusing. Such sophistication is easily come by in suggesting technological solutions.

Finally, there is always the danger that in becoming a governmental consultant, the ecologist will aim his sights at the wrong target. The history of the Washington "expert" is that he is called in to make alterations in the model already decided upon by the policymakers. It would be interesting to know what proportion of scientific advice has ever produced a change in ends rather than in means. We suspect it is minute. But the ecologist ought not to concern himself with less than such a change; he must change the model itself.

We should point out that we are not, for example, against substituting a steam-driven car for a gas-driven car. Our contention is that by changing public attitudes the ecologist can do something much more fundamental. In addition, by changing these attitudes he may even make it easier to force the introduction of "cleaner" technology, since this also is largely a *political* decision. This certainly seems to be so in the example of the steam-driven car.

We do not believe that the ecologist has anything really new to say. His task, rather, is to inculcate in the government and the people basic ecological attitudes. The population must come, and very soon, to appreciate certain basic notions. For example: a finite world cannot support or withstand a continually expanding population and technology; there are limits to the capacity of environmental sinks; ecosystems are sets of interacting entities and there is no "treatment" which does not have "side effects" (e.g., the Aswan Dam); we cannot continually simplify systems and expect them to remain stable, and once they do become unstable there is a tendency for instability to increase with time. Each child should grow up knowing and understanding his place in the environment and the possible consequences of his interaction with it.

In short, the ecologist must convince the population that the only solution to the problem of growth is not to grow. This applies to population and, unless the population is declining, to its standard of living. It should be clear by now that "standard of living" is probably beginning to have an inverse relationship to the quality of life. An increase in the gross national product must be construed, from the ecological point of view, as disastrous. (The case of underdeveloped countries, of course, is different.)

We do not minimize the difficulties in changing the main driving force in life. The point of view of the ecologist, however, should be subversive; it has to be subversive or the ecologist will become merely subservient. Such a change in values and structure will have profound consequences. For example, economists, with a few notable exceptions, do not seem to have given any thought to the possibility or desirability of a stationary economy. Businessmen, and most economists, think that growth is good, stagnation or regression is bad. Can an equilibrium be set up with the environment in a system having this philosophy? The problem of converting to non-growth is present in socialist countries too, of course, but we must ask if corporate capitalism, by its nature, can accommodate such a change and still retain its major features. By contrast, if there are any ecological laws at all, we believe the ecologists' notion of the inevitability of an equilibrium between man and the environment is such a law.

We would like to modify some details of this general stand. Especially after the necessary basic changes are put in motion, there *are* things ecologists as "experts" can do: some of them are sophisticated and others, in a very broad sense, may even be techno-logical. Certainly, determining the "optimum" U.S. population will require sophisticated techniques. Ecologists, willy-nilly, will have to take a central role in advising on the management of the environment. They already are beginning to do this. The character-istics of ecology here determine that this advice, to be good, will be to some extent sophisticated to fit particular cases. Thus, good management will depend on long-term studies of *particular* areas, since ecological situations are both time-dependent and locale-dependent. These two features also ensure that there will be a sizable time-lag between posing the question and receiving the ecological advice, and a major job of the ecologists will be to make the existence of such lags known to policymakers.

Ecologists sometimes will have to apply technology. As one instance, integrated pest control (that is, basically biological control with occasional small-scale use of pesticides) will surely replace chemical control, and integrated pest control can be considered biological technology. In this area there is some promise that sophisticated computer modeling techniques applied to strategies of pest control may help us design better techniques. The banning of DDT, for example, could no doubt be a laudable victory in the war to save the environment, but it would be disastrous to mistake a symbolic victory like this for winning the war itself.

11

THE PLACE OF NATURE IN THE CITY OF MAN
IAN L. McHARG

"Before we convert our rocks and rills and templed hills into one spreading mass of low grade urban tissue under the delusion that because we accomplish this degradation with the aid of bulldozers, atomic piles and electronic computers we are advancing civilization, we might ask what all this implies in terms of the historic nature of man. . . ."—Lewis Mumford.[1]

The subject of this essay is an inquiry into the place of nature in the city of man. The inquiry is neither ironic nor facetious but of the utmost urgency and seriousness. Today it is necessary to justify the presence of nature in the city of man; the burden of proof lies with nature, or so it seems. Look at the modern city, that most human of all environments, observe what image of nature exists there— precious little indeed and that beleaguered, succumbing to slow attrition.

William Penn effectively said, Let us build a fair city between two noble rivers; let there be five noble squares, let each house have a fine garden, and let us reserve territories for farming. But that was before rivers were discovered to be convenient repositories for sewage, parks the best locus for expressways, squares the appropriate sites for public monuments, farm land best suited for buildings, and small parks best transformed into asphalted, fenced playgrounds.

Charles Eliot once said, in essence, This is our city, these are our hills, these are our rivers, these our beaches, these our farms and forests; I will make a plan to cherish this beauty and wealth for all

Ian McHarg is Chairman of the Department of Landscape Architecture and Regional Planning at the University of Pennsylvania. The article was published in *Annals of the American Academy of Political and Social Science,* Vol. 352, p. 2–12 (March, 1964). Copyright 1964 by the American Academy of Political and Social Science.

those who do or will live here. And the plan was good but largely disdained. So here, as elsewhere, man assaulted nature disinterestedly, man assaulted man with the city; nature in the city remains precariously as residues of accident, rare acts of personal conscience, or rarer testimony to municipal wisdom, the subject of continuous assault and attrition while the countryside recedes before the annular rings of suburbanization, unresponsive to any perception beyond simple economic determinism.

Once upon a time, nature lay outside the city gates a fair prospect from the city walls, but no longer. Climb the highest office tower in the city, when atmospheric pollution is only normal, and nature may be seen as a green rim on the horizon. But this is hardly a common condition and so nature lies outside of workaday experience for most urban people.

Long ago, homes were built in the country and remained rural during the lives of persons and generations. Not so today, when a country house of yesterday is within the rural-urban fringe today, in a suburb tomorrow, and in a renewal area of the not-too-distant future.

When the basis for wealth lay in the heart of the land and the farms upon it, then the valleys were verdant and beautiful, the farmer steward of the landscape, but that was before the American dream of a single house on a quarter acre, the automobile, crop surpluses, and the discovery that a farmer could profit more by selling land than crops.

Once men in simple cabins saw only wild nature, silent, implacable, lonely. They cut down the forests to banish Indians, animals, and shadows. Today, Indians, animals, and forests have gone and wild nature, silence, and loneliness are hard to find.

When a man's experience was limited by his home, village, and environs, he lived with his handiworks. Today, the automobile permits temporary escapes from urban squalor, and suburbanization gives the illusion of permanent escape.

Once upon a time, when primeval forests covered Pennsylvania, its original inhabitants experienced a North Temperate climate, but, when the forests were felled, the climate became, in summer, intemperately hot and humid.

Long ago, floods were described as Acts of God. Today, these are known quite often to be consequences of the acts of man.

As long ago, droughts were thought to be Acts of God, too, but these, it is now known, are exacerbated by the acts of man.

In times past, pure air and clean abundant water were commonplaces. Today, "pollution" is the word most often associated with the word "atmosphere," drinking water is often a dilute soup of dead bacteria in a chlorine solution, and the only peoples who enjoy pure air and clean water are rural societies who do not recognize these for the luxuries they are.

Not more than two hundred years ago, the city existed in a surround of farm land, the sustenance of the city. The farmers tended the lands which were the garden of the city. Now, the finest crops are abject fruits compared to the land values created by the most scabrous housing, and the farms are defenseless.

In days gone by, marshes were lonely and wild, habitat of duck and goose, heron and egret, muskrat and beaver, but that was before marshes became the prime sites for incinerator wastes, rubbish, and garbage—marshes are made to be filled, it is said.

When growth was slow and people spent a lifetime on a single place, the flood plains were known and left unbuilt. But, now, who knows the flood plain? *Caveat emptor.*

Forests and woodlands once had their own justification as sources of timber and game, but second-growth timber has little value today, and the game has long fled. Who will defend forests and woods?

Once upon a time, the shad in hundreds of thousands ran strong up the river to the city. But, today, when they do so, there is no oxygen, and their bodies are cast upon the shores.

THE MODERN METROPOLIS

Today, the modern metropolis covers thousands of square miles, much of the land is sterilized and waterproofed, the original animals have long gone, as have primeval plants, rivers are foul, the atmosphere is polluted, climate and microclimate have retrogressed to increased violence, a million acres of land are transformed annually from farm land to hot-dog stand, diner, gas station, rancher and split level, asphalt and concrete, billboards and sagging wire, parking lots and car cemeteries, yet slums accrue faster than new buildings, which seek to replace them. The epidemiologist can speak of urban epidemics—heart and arterial disease, renal disease, cancer, and, not least, neuroses and psychoses. A serious proposition has been advanced to the effect that the modern city would be in serious jeopardy without the safeguards of modern medicine and social legislation. Lewis Mumford can describe cities as dysgenic. There has arisen the recent specter, described as "pathological togetherness," under which density and social pressure are being linked to the distribution of disease and limitations upon reproduction. We record stress from sensory overload and the response of negative hallucination to urban anarchy. When one considers that New York may well add 1,500 square miles of new "low-grade tissue" to its perimeter in the next twenty years, then one recalls Loren Eiseley's image and sees the cities of man as gray, black, and brown blemishes upon the green earth with dynamic tentacles extending from them and asks: "Are these the evidence of man, the planetary disease?"

WESTERN VIEWS: MAN AND NATURE

Yet how can nature be justified in the city? Does one invoke dappled sunlight filtered through trees of ecosystems, the shad run or water treatment, the garden in the city or negative entropy? Although at first glance an unthinkable necessity, the task of justifying nature in the city of man is, with prevailing values and process, both necessary and difficult. The realities of cities now and the plans for their renewal and extension offer incontrovertible evidence of the absence of nature present and future. Should Philadelphia realize the Comprehensive Plan, then $20 billion and twenty years later there will be less open space than there is today. Cities are artifacts becoming ever more artificial—as though medieval views prevailed that nature was defiled, that living systems shared original sin with man, that only the artifice was free of sin. The motto for the city of man seems to be: salvation by stone alone.

Of course, the medieval view of nature as rotten and rotting is only an aspect of the historic Western anthropocentric-anthropomorphic tradition in which nature is relegated to inconsequence. Judaism and Christianity have been long concerned with justice and compassion for the acts of man to man but have traditionally assumed nature to be a mere backdrop for the human play. Apparently, the literal interpretation of the creation in Genesis is the tacit text for Jews and Christians alike—man exclusively divine, man given dominion over all life and nonlife, enjoined to subdue the earth. The cosmos is thought to be a pyramid erected to support man upon its pinnacle;

reality exists only because man can perceive it; indeed, God is made in the image of man. From origins in Judaism, extension into classicism, reinforcement in Christianity, inflation in the Renaissance, and absorption into nineteenth- and twentieth-century thought, the anthropocentic-anthropomorphic view has become the tacit Western posture of man versus nature. The nineteenth- and twentieth-century city is the most complete expression of this view. Within the Western tradition exists a contrary view of man and nature which has a close correspondence to the Oriental attitude of an aspiration to harmony of man in nature, a sense of a unitary and encompassing natural order within which man exists. Among others, the naturalist tradition in the West includes Duns Scotus, Joannes Scotus Erigena, Francis of Assisi, Wordsworth, Goethe, Thoreau, Gerard Manley Hopkins, and the nineteenth- and twentieth-century naturalists. Their insistence upon nature being at least the sensible order within which man exists or a Manifestation of God demanding deference and reverence is persuasive to many but not to the city builders.

Are the statements of scientists likely to be more persuasive?

David R. Goddard:[2]

No organism lives without an environment. As all organisms are depletive, no organism can survive in an environment of its exclusive creation.

F. R. Fosberg:[3]

An ecosystem is a functioning, interacting system composed of one or more organisms and their effective environment, both physical and biological. All ecosystems are open systems. Ecosystems may be stable or unstable. The stable system is in a steady state. The entropy in an unstable system is more likely to increase than decrease. There is a tendency towards diversity in natural ecosystems. There is a tendency towards uniformity in artificial ecosystems or those strongly influenced by man.

Paul Sears:[4]

Any species survives by virtue of its niche, the opportunity afforded it by environment. But in occupying this niche, it also assumes a role in relation to its surroundings. For further survival it is necessary that its role at least be not a disruptive one. Thus, one generally finds in nature that each component of a highly organized community serves a constructive or at any rate, a stabilizing role. The habitat furnishes the niche, and if any species breaks up the habitat, the niche goes with it. . . . To persist, organic systems must be able to utilize radiant energy not merely to perform work, but to maintain the working system in reasonably good order. This requires the presence of organisms adjusted to the habitat and to each other so organized to make the fullest use of the influent radiation and to conserve for use and reuse the materials which the system requires.

Complex creatures consist of billions of cells, each of which, like any single-celled creature, is unique, experiences life, metabolism, reproduction, and death. The complex animal exists through the operation of symbiotic relationships between cells as tissues and organs integrated as a single organism. Hans Selyé describes this symbiosis as intercellular altruism, the situation under which the cell concedes some part of its autonomy towards the operation of the organism and the organism responds to cellular processes.

Aldo Leopold has been concerned with the ethical content of symbiosis:[5]

Ethics so far studied by philosophers are actually a process in ecological as well as philosophical terms. They are also a process in ecological evolution. An ethic, ecologically, is a limitation on freedom of action in the struggle for existence. An ethic, philosophically, is a differentiation of social from anti-social conduct. These are two definitions of one thing which has its origin in the tendency of interdependent individuals and groups to evolve modes of cooperation. The ecologist calls these symbioses. There is as yet no ethic dealing with man's relation to the environment and the animals and plants which grow upon it. The extension of ethics to include man's relation to environment is, if I read the evidence correctly, an evolutionary possibility and an ecological necessity. All ethics so far evolved rest upon a single premise that the individual is a member of a community of interdependent parts. His instincts prompt him to compete for his place in the community, but his ethics prompt him to cooperate, perhaps in order that there may be a place to compete for.

The most important inference from this body of information is that interdependence, not independence, characterizes natural systems. Thus, man-nature interdependence presumably holds true for urban man as for his rural contemporaries. We await the discovery of an appropriate physical and symbolic form for the urban man-nature relationship.

NATURAL AND ARTIFICIAL ENVIRONMENTS
From the foregoing statements by natural scientists, we can examine certain extreme positions. First, there can be no conception of a

completely "natural" environment. Wild nature, save a few exceptions, is not a satisfactory physical environment. Yet the certainty that man must adapt nature and himself does not diminish his dependence upon natural, nonhuman processes. These two observations set limits upon conceptions of man and nature. Man must adapt through both biological and cultural innovation, but these adaptations occur within a context of natural, nonhuman processes. It is not inevitable that adapting nature to support human congregations must of necessity diminish the quality of the physical environment. Indeed, all of preindustrial urbanism was based upon the opposite premise, that only in the city could the best conjunction of social and physical environment be achieved. This major exercise of power to adapt nature for human ends, the city, need not be a diminution of physiological, psychological, and aesthetic experience.

While there can be no completely natural environments inhabited by man, completely artificial environments are equally unlikely. Man in common with all organisms is a persistent configuration of matter through which the environment ebbs and flows continuously. Mechanically, he exchanges his substance at a very rapid rate while, additionally, his conceptions of reality are dependent upon the attribution of meaning to myriads of environmental stimuli which impinge upon him continuously. The materials of his being are natural, as are many of the stimuli which he perceives; his utilization of the materials and of many stimuli is involuntary. Man makes artifices, but galactic and solar energy, gases of hydrosphere and atmosphere, the substance of the lithosphere, and all organic systems remain elusive of human artificers.

Yet the necessity to adapt natural environments to sustain life is common to many organisms other than man. Creation of a physical environment by organisms as individuals and as communities is not exclusively a human skill. The chambered nautilus, the beehive, the coral formation, to select but a few examples, are all efforts by organisms to take inert materials and dispose them to create a physical environment. In these examples, the environments created are complementary to the organisms. They are constructed with great economy of means; they are expressive, they have, in human eyes, great beauty, and they have survived periods of evolutionary time vastly longer than the human span.

Simple organisms utilize inert materials to create physical

environments which sustain life. Man also confronts this necessity. Man, too, is natural in that he responds to the same laws as do all physical and biological systems. He is a plant parasite, dependent upon the plant kingdom and its associated microorganisms, insects, birds, and animals for all atmospheric oxygen, all food, all fossil fuel, natural fibres and cellulose, for the stability of the water cycle and amelioration of climate and microclimate. His dependence upon the plant and photosynthesis establishes his dependence upon the microorganisms of the soil, particularly the decomposers which are essential to the recycling of essential nutrients, the insects, birds, and animals which are in turn linked to survival of plant systems. He is equally dependent upon the natural process of water purification by microorganisms. The operation of these nonhuman physical and biological processes is essential for human survival.

Having concluded that there can be neither a completely artificial nor a completely natural environment, our attention is directed to some determinants of optimal proportions. Some indication may be inferred from man's evolutionary history. His physiology and some significant part of his psychology derive from the billions of years of his biological history. During the most recent human phase of a million or so years, he has been preponderantly food gatherer, hunter, and, only recently, farmer. His urban experience is very recent indeed. Thus, the overwhelming proportion of his biological history has involved experience in vastly more natural environments than he now experiences. It is to these that he is physiologically adapted.

According to F. R. Fosberg:[6]

It is entirely possible that man will not survive the changed environment that he is creating, either because of failure of resources, war over their dwindling supply, or failure of his nervous system to evolve as rapidly as the change in environment will require. Or he may only survive in small numbers, suffering the drastic reduction that is periodically the lot of pioneer species, or he may change beyond our recognition. . . . Management and utilization of the environment on a true sustaining yield basis must be achieved. And all this must be accomplished without altering the environment beyond the capacity of the human organism, as we know it, to live in it.

HUMAN ECOSYSTEMS
There are several examples where ecosystems, dominated by man, have endured for long periods of time; the example of traditional

Japanese agriculture is perhaps the most spectacular. Here an agriculture of unequaled intensity and productivity has been sustained for over a thousand years, the land is not impoverished but enriched by human intervention, the ecosystem, wild lands, and farm lands are complex, stable, highly productive, and beautiful. The pervasive effect of this harmony of man-nature is reflected in a language remarkable in its descriptive power of nature, a poetry succinct yet capable of the finest shades of meaning, a superb painting tradition in which nature is the icon, an architecture and town building of astonishing skill and beauty, and, not least, an unparalleled garden art in which nature and the garden are the final metaphysical symbol.

In the Western tradition, farming in Denmark and England has sustained high productivity for two or more centuries, appears stable, and is very beautiful; in the United States, comparable examples exist in Amish, Mennonite, and Pennsylvania Dutch farming.

Understanding of the relationship of man to nature is more pervasive and operative among farmers than any other laymen. The farmer perceives the source of his food in his crops of cereal, vegetables, roots, beef, fish, or game. He understands that, given a soil fertility, his crop is directly related to inputs of organic material, fertilizer, water, and sunlight. If he grows cotton or flax or tends sheep, he is likely to know the source of the fibers of his clothes. He recognizes timber, peat, and hydroelectric power as sources of fuel; he may well know of the organic source of coal and petroleum. Experience has taught him to ensure a functional separation between septic tank and well, to recognize the process of erosion, runoff, flood and drought, the differences of altitude and orientation. As a consequence of this acuity, the farmer has developed a formal expression which reflects an understanding of the major natural processes. Characteristically, high ground and steep slopes are given over to forest and woodland as a source of timber, habitat for game, element in erosion control, and water supply. The more gently sloping meadows below are planted to orchards, above the spring frost line, or in pasture. Here a seep, spring, or well is often the source of water supply. In the valley bottom, where floods have deposited rich alluvium over time, is the area of intensive cultivation. The farm buildings are related to conditions of climate and microclimate, above the flood plain, sheltered and shaded by the farm woodland. The septic tank is located in soils suitable for this purpose and below the elevation of the water source.

Here, at the level of the farm, can be observed the operation of certain simple, empirical rules and a formal expression which derives from them. The land is rich, and we find it beautiful.

Clearly, a comparable set of simple rules is urgently required for the city and the metropolis. The city dweller is commonly unaware of these natural processes, ignorant of his dependence upon them. Yet the problem of the place of nature in the city is more difficult than that of the farmer. Nature, as modified in farming, is intrinsic to the place. The plant community is relatively immobile, sunlight falls upon the site as does water, nutrients are cycled through the system in place. Animals in ecosystems have circumscribed territories, and the conjunction of plants and animals involves a utilization and cycling of energy and materials in quite limited areas. The modern city is, in this respect, profoundly different in that major natural processes which sustain the city, provide food, raw materials for industry, commerce, and construction, resources of water, and pure air are drawn not from the city or even its metropolitan area but from a national and even international hinterland. The major natural processes are not intrinsic to the locus of the city and cannot be.

NATURE IN THE METROPOLIS

In the process of examining the place of nature in the city of man, it might be fruitful to consider the role of nature in the metropolitan area initially, as here, in the more rural fringes, can still be found analogies to the empiricism of the farmer. Here the operative principle might be that natural processes which perform work or offer protection in their natural form without human effort should have a presumption in their favor. Planning should recognize the values of these processes in decision-making for prospective land uses.

A more complete understanding of natural processes and their interactions must await the development of an ecological model of the metropolis. Such a model would identify the regional inventory of material in atmosphere, hydrosphere, lithosphere, and biosphere, identify inputs and outputs, and both describe and quantify the cycling and recycling of materials in the system. Such a model would facilitate recognition of the vital natural processes and their interdependence which is denied today. Lacking such a model, it is necessary to proceed with available knowledge. On a simpler basis, we can say that the major inputs in biological systems are sunlight, oxygen-carbon dioxide, food (including nutrients), and water. The first three are not limiting in the metropolis; water may well be limiting both as to quantity and quality. In addition, there are many other reasons for isolating and examining water in process. Water is the single most specific determinant of a large number of physical processes and is indispensible to all biological processes. Water, as the agent of erosion and sedimentation, is causal to geological evolution, the realities of physiography. Mountains, hills, valleys, and plains experience variety of climate and microclimate consequent upon their physiography; the twin combination of physiography and climate determines the incidence and distribution of plants and animals, their niches, and habitats. Thus, using water as the point of departure, we can recognize its impact on the making of mountains and lakes, ridges and plains, forests and deserts, rivers, streams and marshes, the distribution of plants and animals. Lacking an ecological model, we may well select water as the best indicator of natural process. In any watershed, the uplands represent the majority of the watershed area. Assuming equal distribution of precipitation and ground conditions over the watershed, the maximum area will produce the maximum runoff. The profile of watersheds tends to produce the steeper slopes in the uplands with the slope diminishing toward the outlet. The steeper the slope, the greater is the water velocity. This combination of maximum runoff links maximum volume to maximum velocity—the two primary conditions of flood and drought. These two factors in turn exacerbate erosion, with the consequence of depositing silt in stream beds, raising flood plains, and increasing intensity and incidence of floods in piedmont and estuary.

The natural restraints to flooding and drought are mainly the presence and distribution of vegetation, particularly on the uplands and their steep slopes. Vegetation absorbs and utilizes considerable quantities of water; the surface roots, trunks of trees, stems of shrubs and plants, the litter of forest floor mechanically retard the movement of water, facilitating percolation, increasing evaporation opportunity.

A certain amount of water is removed temporarily from the system by absorption into plants, and mechanical retardation facilitates percolation, reduces velocity, and thus diminishes erosion. In fact vegetation and their soils act as a sponge restraining extreme runoff, releasing water slowly over longer periods, diminishing erosion and sedimentation; in short, diminishing the frequency and intensity of oscillation between flood and drought.

Below the uplands of the watershed are characteristically the more shallow slopes and broad plains of the piedmont. Here is the land most often developed for agriculture. These lands, too, tend to be favored locations for villages, towns, and cities. Here, forests are residues or the products of regeneration on abandoned farms. Steep slopes in the piedmont are associated with streams and rivers. The agricultural piedmont does not control its own defenses. It is defended from flood and drought by the vegetation of the uplands. The vegetation cover and conservation practices in the agricultural piedmont can either exacerbate or diminish flood and drought potential; the piedmont is particularly vulnerable to both.

The incidence of flood and drought is not alone consequent upon the upland sponge but also upon estuarine marshes, particularly where these are tidal. Here at the mouth of the watershed at the confluence of important rivers or of river and sea, the flood component of confluent streams or the tidal component of floods assumes great importance. In the Philadelphia metropolitan area, the ocean and the estuary are of prime importance as factors in flood. A condition of intense precipitation over the region, combined with high tides, full estuary, and strong onshore winds, combines the elements of potential flood. The relation of environmental factors of the upland component and the agricultural piedmont to flood and drought has been discussed. The estuarine marshes and their vegetation constitute the major defense against the tidal components of floods. These areas act as enormous storage reservoirs absorbing mile-feet of potentially destructive waters, reducing flood potential.

This gross description of water-related processes offers determinism for the place of nature in the metropolis. From this description can be isolated several discrete and critical phases in the process. Surface water as rivers, streams, creeks, lakes, reservoirs, and ponds would be primary; the particular form of surface water in marshes would be another phase; the flood plain as the area temporarily occupied by water would be yet another. Two critical aspects of ground water, the aquifer and its recharge areas, could be identified. Agricultural land has been seen to be a product of alluvial deposition, while steep slopes and forests play important roles in the process of runoff. If we could identify the proscriptions and permissiveness of these parameters to other land use, we would have an effective device for discriminating the relative importance of different roles of metropolitan lands. Moreover, if the major divisions of upland, piedmont, and estuary and the processes enumerated could be afforded planning recognition and legislative protection, the metropolitan area would derive its form from a recognition of natural process. The place of nature in the metropolis would be reflected in the distribution of water and flood plain, marshes, ridges, forests, and farm land, a matrix of natural lands performing work or offering protection and recreational opportunity distributed throughout the metropolis.

This conception is still too bald; it should be elaborated to include areas of important scenic value, recreational potential, areas of ecological, botanical, geological, or historic interest. Yet, clearly, the conception, analogous to the empiricism of the farmer, offers opportunity for determining the place of nature in the metropolis.

NATURE IN THE CITY

The conception advocated for the metropolitan area has considerable relevance to the problem of the place of nature in the city of man. Indeed, in several cities, the fairest image of nature exists in these rare occasions where river, flood plain, steep slopes and woodlands have been retained in their natural condition—the Hudson and Palisades in New York, the Schuylkill and Wissahickon in Philadelphia, the Charles River in Boston and Cambridge. If rivers, flood plains, marshes, steep slopes, and woodlands in the city were accorded protection to remain in their natural condition or were retrieved and returned to such a condition where possible, this single device, as an aspect of water quality, quantity, flood and drought control, would ensure for many cities an immeasurable improvement in the aspect of nature in the city, in addition to the specific benefits of a planned watershed. No other device has such an ameliorative power. Quite obviously, in addition to benefits of flood control and water supply, the benefits of amenity and recreational opportunity would be considerable. As evidence of this, the city of Philadelphia has a twenty-two mile water front on the Delaware. The most grandiose requirements for port facilities and water-related industries require only eight miles of water front. This entire water front lies in a flood plain. Levees and other flood protection devices have been dismissed as exorbitant. Should this land be transformed into park, it would represent an amelioration in Philadelphia of incomparable scale.

Should this conception of planning for water and water-related parameters be effectuated, it would provide the major framework for the role of nature in the city of man. The smaller elements of the face of nature are more difficult to justify. The garden and park, unlike house, shop, or factory, have little "functional" content. They are, indeed, more metaphysical symbol than utilitarian function. As such, they are not amenable to quantification or the attribution of value. Yet it is frequently the aggregation of these gardens and spaces which determines the humanity of a city. Values they do have. This is apparent in the flight to the suburbs for more natural environments—a self-defeating process of which the motives are clear. Equally, the selection of salubrious housing location in cities is closely linked to major open spaces, which reflects the same impulse. The image of nature at this level is most important, the cell of the home, the street, and neighborhood. In the city slum, nature exists in the backyard ailanthus, sumac, in lice, cockroach, rat, cat, and mouse; in luxury highrise, there are potted trees over parking garages, poodles, and tropical fish. In the first case, nature reflects "disturbance" to the ecologist; it is somewhat analogous to the scab on a wound, the first step of regeneration towards equilibrium, a sere arrested at the most primitive level. In the case of the luxury highrise, nature is a canary in a cage, surrogate, an artifice, forbidden even the prospect of an arrested sere.

Three considerations seem operative at this level of concern. The first is that the response which nature induces, tranquillity, calm, introspection, openness to order, meaning and purpose, the place of values in the world of facts, is similar to the evocation from works of art. Yet nature is, or was, abundant; art and genius are rare.

The second consideration of some importance is that nature in the city is very tender. Woodlands, plants, and animals are very vulnerable to human erosion. Only expansive dimensions will support self-perpetuating and self-cleansing nature. There is a profound change between such a natural scene and a created and maintained landscape.

The final point is related to the preceding. If the dimensions are appropriate, a landscape will perpetuate itself. Yet, where a site has been sterilized, built upon, and buildings demolished, the problem of creating a landscape, quite apart from creating a self-perpetuating one, is very considerable and the costs are high. The problems of sustaining a landscape, once made, are also considerable; the pressure of human erosion on open space in urban housing and the inevitable vandalism ensure that only a small vocabulary of primitive and hardy plants can survive. These factors, with abnormal conditions of ground water, soil, air, atmospheric pollution, stripping, and girdling, limit nature to a very constricted image.

THE FUTURE

Perhaps, in the future, analysis of those factors which contribute to stress disease will induce inquiry into the values of privacy, shade, silence, the positive stimulus of natural materials, and the presence of comprehensible order, indeed natural beauty. When young babies lack fondling and mother love, they sometimes succumb to moronity and death. The dramatic reversal of this pattern has followed simple maternal solicitude. Is the absence of nature—its trees, water, rocks, and herbs, sun, moon, stars, and changing seasons—a similar type of deprivation? The solicitude of nature, its essence if not its image, may be seen to be vital.

Some day, in the future, we may be able to quantify plant photosynthesis in the city and the oxygen in the atmosphere, the insulation of plants by lead from automobile exhausts, the role of diatoms in water purification, the amelioration of climate and microclimate by city trees and parks, the insurance of negative ionization by fountains, the reservoirs of air which, free of combustion, are necessary to relieve inversion pollution, the nature-space which a biological inheritance still requires, the stages in land regeneration and the plant and animal indicators of such regeneration, indeed, perhaps, even the plant and animal indicators of a healthy environment. We will then be able to quantify the necessities of a minimum environment to support physiological man. Perhaps we may also learn what forms of nature are necessary to satisfy the psychological memory of a biological ancestry.

Today, that place where man and nature are in closest harmony in the city is the cemetery. Can we hope for a city of man, an eco-system in dynamic equilibrium, stable and complex? Can we hope for a city of man, an ecosystem with man dominant, reflecting natural processes, human and non-human, in which artifice and nature conjoin as art and nature, in a natural urban environment speaking to man as a natural being and nature as the environment of man? When we find the place of nature in the city of man, we may return to that enduring and ancient inquiry—the place of man in nature.

NOTES

1. Lewis Mumford, *Man's Role in Changing the Face of the Earth* (Chicago: University of Chicago Press, 1956), p. 1142.
2. Transcript, WCAU-TV, "The House We Live In."
3. F. R. Fosberg, "The Preservation of Man's Environment," *Proceedings of the Ninth Pacific Science Congress, 1957,* Vol. 20, 1958, p. 160.
4. Paul B. Sears, "The Process of Environmental Change by Man," in *Man's Role in Changing the Face of the Earth,* ed. W. L. Thomas, Jr. (Chicago: University of Chicago Press, 1956).
5. Aldo Leopold, *A Sand County Almanac* (Oxford: Oxford University Press, 1949), pp. 202, 203.
6. See (3) above.

Part Three

TECHNOLOGY AND ECOLOGY

12

ECOLOGICAL RESPONSIBILITY
AND ECONOMIC JUSTICE
NORMAN J. FARAMELLI

According to ecologists, we are threatened with extinction within 50 years if current pollution trends are allowed to continue. Despite some overstatements by a few "prophets of doom," an increasing number of reasonable people recognize that the ecological problem has reached a crisis stage. All during 1970, leading magazines, newspapers, radio, and TV announced that we are entering an "age of ecology."[1] Although its popularity reached a zenith on Earth Day (22 April, 1970), ecology is still very much before the public. But despite the widespread rhetoric, the environmental problems are becoming more critical, as summer smog along the East coast has amply illustrated.

In theory, everyone wants a clean environment. But the real questions are: "How serious is the ecology problem in light of our other pressing needs?" and "Who is going to pay for pollution control?". With regard to the latter, we must heed the cry of both the ecologist and the economist: "There are no free lunches"; someone will pay for a clean environment. It is the belief of this writer that *ecology is a profoundly serious matter, yet most of the solutions suggested for environmental quality will have, directly or indirectly, adverse effects on the poor and lower income groups.* Hence, economic or distributive justice must become an active component in all ecology debates.

The Lord has entrusted man with the created order; he is to be a responsible steward of God's creation. Although the development

This article by Norman Faramelli, associate director of the Boston Industrial Mission, is reprinted with the permission of the *Andover Newton Quarterly* from Vol. 11, p. 81–93 (November, 1970).

of an environmental ethic is essential and long overdue, it should not overlook nor underplay the special role that man (particularly the poor and the oppressed) plays in the Judeo-Christian tradition.[2] Now that an environmental ethic is being shaped, it is imperative that it be in harmony with concerns for economic justice.

As a prolegomenon to the central concerns of ecology and justice, we should first establish the seriousness of the so-called ecological crisis. For the problems of relating justice and ecology are real only if the environmental issues are truly significant. If environmental damage is not as bad as publicized, then we are suffering from grand delusions.

A Worsening Problem

One can recite a litany of woes concerning land, air, water, and noise pollution:

Timber forests in the West are fast disappearing because we refuse to reuse paper. One of the wonders of creation, the Redwoods in California, is reducing in number. On the East Coast, the valuable salt marshes are being dredged and filled in by real estate and land developers. a move which is destroying some of our most productive land and damaging chains of marine life. In Appalachia, strip mining has ravaged several states, and after the coal has been removed and the landscape destroyed, some states pass laws curbing strip mining. Add to these the cluttering of the countryside with billboards and junk. A U.N. report released in 1969 noted that each year in the U.S. we discard 26 billion bottles, 7 million automobiles, and 48 billion cans.[3] It is no surprise that rubbish disposal is a mounting problem.

That same report noted that the U.S. emits 148 million tons of pollutants into the air each year, mostly from automobiles and power generators. The air pollution that used to be limited to central cities has now spread well beyond the suburbs. For example, the trees in the Sierra Nevada mountains, 100 miles from Los Angeles, are dying from air pollutants. The same holds true for other urban areas. Emphysema and other respiratory disorders are on the increase. Also, some studies have shown the links between air pollution and cancer growth.

Water pollution worsens each day. Lake Erie is undergoing a nonreversible biological decay, and many experts believe it might

soon be a sewer. The Cuyahoga River in Cleveland, rich in con-
taminants, actually caught on fire, but it was not the first! In certain
areas in the mid-West the "nitrogen run-offs" from fertilizers are
the principal causes of water pollution. The phosphates from
detergents are creating magnificent algae blooms in our waterways
which upset the ecological balance, and pesticides are poisoning our
oceans. In addition, oil spills, such as the ones by Union Oil off
Santa Barbara, Chevron off the Gulf, and oil tankers regularly, are
polluting our oceans and beaches.

To this litany we can add the problems of noise pollution.
Studies have shown that it influences arterial and neurological disorders. The noise near jet ports is already unbearable, yet the jets
get bigger, faster, and noisier.

If the items listed above represented the worst levels of pollution
to which man will be subjected, we could all breathe a sigh of relief.
But conditions are getting worse, because current trends are being
exacerbated. The effects of newly installed pollution control devices
are more than offset by expanding the pollution base via increased
production. For instance, Detroit has endowed us with 9 million
new internal combustion engines per year and now anticipates that
within 10 years it will be manufacturing 12–13 million automobiles
per year.[4] Power consumption is slated to double every ten years,
which may lead to an enormous production of pollutants. Our
President and others marvel at the U.S. Gross National Product,
which will reach 1 trillion dollars in 1970 and will increase to 1.5
trillion within 10 years. If a substantial amount of this growth is in
the material sector, pollution will significantly increase. And, of
course, all of these problems are made worse by rapid population
increases. By the year 2000, the American population will increase
from 200 to 300 million. Thus, one can see that the problems are
serious, and necessitate a new ethic for the environment and a new
look at our consumption of material resources.

The Two Revolutions
In the midst of the burgeoning interest for ecology, a few voices
have warned that ecology is becoming a new cop-out, a way to re-
focus the enthusiasm of the young (especially college students) away
from the war, urban problems, and poverty. One can rationalize
that the young are frustrated over Vietnam, almost completely

alienated from poverty and the ghettos, so ecology buffs are now in vogue. In many ways, ecology is a logical successor to the middle-class concerns of conservation. But that explanation is too simplistic and misses entirely the seriousness of the ecological crisis.

The ecology rage must be understood in light of the two cultural, social, and political revolutions occurring in our society today. They can be termed the "pre-affluent" and "post-affluent" revolutions. The first is dominated by the poor and the black communities. Their primary focus is on social and economic justice as well as freedom and self-determination. The quest of the powerless and the alienated is primarily for human dignity and the restructuring of power relationships. Some in this revolution, however, want to move beyond "getting a fair piece of the pie" to new life styles where "soul" or spontaniety is an essential ingredient. But most want a redistribution of power—political, economic, and social. For the alienated youth in the "post-affluent" revolution, however, the emphasis is not on power, but on new life-styles. There is a flat rejection of the values of over-consumption, technical efficiency, and economic growth that has dominated American society.[5] The ecology movement is closely linked with the "post-affluent" revolution. Only those who have been reared in affluent suburbs can rebel against over-consumption and the banality of materialism. It is no surprise that ecologists like Barry Commoner, Lamont Cole, Paul Ehrlich, and Eugene Odum receive their biggest ovations in jammed college auditoriums. The differences between the two movements were vividly expressed by a welfare rights organizer to a group of young ecology radicals. He said: "We will have some problems understanding one another for our welfare mothers want what you are rejecting."[6]

Those who have been involved with urban and poverty problems have often distrusted the "ecology fad." On the other hand, most ecology enthusiasts, and especially the old-line conservationists who are becoming attuned to ecology, almost completely ignore the problems of the ghettos and the poor. Ecology, for them, has more to do with saving a certain marine species than eradicating rats from infested ghetto apartments! To the ghetto resident, air pollution is clearly not at the top of his priority list. As one black community organizer in Chicago said recently: "The one thing I don't look forward to is living in a pollution-free, unjust and repressive society."

Distrust of the Ecology Movement: Is It Really a "Cop-Out"?

Distrust for the ecology movement is increasing on all sides. *Time* magazine (3 August, 1970) reports a burgeoning anti-ecology movement. Some critics believe that the environment cannot be as bad as many scientists say. Others sense the profound changes in the industrial system and life styles that the quest for environmental quality will demand; hence, they are "bugging out" by ignoring the issue. Others believe that the ecology movement has been characterized by too much radical pessimism and alarmism.

The anti-ecology sentiment among the poor, especially the blacks, is still prevalent. For example, one Black Panther leader in Roxbury said: "It is a sick society that can beat and murder black people on the streets, butcher thousands of children in Vietnam, spend billions in arms to destroy mankind, and then come to the conclusion that air pollution is America's number one problem."[7]

Why do the poor distrust the ecology movement? First, a clean environment is not on their priority list, at least not in terms of air and water pollution. The poor are part of a different revolution; their focus is on justice. Also, the ecology groups have almost totally ignored the needs of the poor. Most of the images of environmental quality refer to improved life styles for suburban dwellers—cleaner air, more trees, better hiking, boating, and swimming, etc. There is almost no emphasis on urban ecology.

Another reason the poor distrust ecology is related to the priorities of the nation stated in President Nixon's State of the Union Message. In a speech replete with many references to the environment, he said, "Restoring nature to its natural state is a cause beyond party and beyond factions. It has become a common cause of all the people of this country." The President also noted that Americans have to make "some very hard decisions" on priorities, which meant "rejecting pending programs which would benefit some of the people when their net effect would result in price increases for all the people."[8] In other words, urban spending, which benefits the white and black poor, is inflationary!

The lack of any references in the address to black America, the sparse references to poverty and urban blight, and the copious references to "law and order" illustrated the current concerns facing American society. It is not too surprising that many black citizens felt alienated by the President's address, saw in it the omens of repression, and from it, deduced that interest in ecology is a "cop-out." To the poor it was more than an isolated speech; it articulated a growing national mood. Hence, one can understand their charges that "ecology is a club over our heads; it's a cop-out; it's a middle-class issue."

But will funds actually be diverted from poverty to ecology? As of now, the funds spent on either ecology or poverty are pitifully small. This year the federal government approved 800 million dollars for water pollution programs, although far more is needed. Expenditures on poverty are also grossly inadequate. To choose ecology instead of poverty, or vice versa, is to make a bad choice. We should not be asked to select between schools and homes for urban dwellers, on the one hand, and a clean environment on the other, while the ABM is expanded, the supersonic transport is developed, and Vietnam continues almost untouched by sanity. Despite the deceptive Defense Department cuts, new weapons systems are still top priority items on the national agenda and devour a substantial part of the federal budget. Today over 60¢ of every federal tax dollar is used to pay off past or current wars or to plan new ones. An apt metaphor to describe the competing concerns of ecology and poverty is two people arguing over the crumbs from a loaf of bread while others run away with the slices! From the standpoint of resources expended, the issue of "ecology as a cop-out on the poor" is largely academic since both ecology and poverty are being starved. Given the pittances that are now spent on ecology, the "war on pollution" proposed by the current administration will probably be as ineffective as the "war on poverty" was in dealing with the problems of the poor.

Both ecology and poverty have to be seen in light of other national priorities. Dr. George Wiley, Executive Director of the National Welfare Rights Organization, summarized the problem of national priorities when he spoke at the Harvard Teach-In. After acknowledging the seriousness of the ecological crisis, he addressed a challenge to the environmentalists:

It is going to be necessary to have substantial governmental expenditures for the programs of environmental control—that means you will be directly competing with poor people for very scarce government dollars. And if you are not in a position to mount a confrontation with the military-industrial complex, if you are not prepared to join with poor people in saying that the war in Vietnam has got to end, that we've got to stop military imperialism around the world, that we've got to cut out the wasteful military expenditures . . . quite clearly poor people will pay the cost of your ecology program.[9]

But let us suppose that ecology is taken seriously. Have we properly assessed the impact of the proposed remedies on low-income households? This is necessary from two standpoints: (a) someone has to pay for pollution control and the poor will be asked to pay disproportionately, and (b) some of the remedies proposed to halt pollution, such as curbing economic growth, will have severe repercussions on the poor.

Who Pays for Pollution Control?

The idea posed by *Life* magazine and others that "Ecology is everybody's issue" is misleading. There is a widespread illusion that at last we have found a real national issue that is non-controversial, and thus, we act as if a clean environment can be obtained without cost. If, for example, the managers of a chemical or power plant install expensive pollution control equipment, they can do one of three things to cover expenditures: (1) raise the price of the product, (2) appeal for a government subsidy, or (3) reduce corporate profits.

Capital expenditure in pollution control equipment is basically an investment in non-productive devices. Given our current accounting procedures, such a venture increases the cost of production. We have for years assumed that disposal of waste into the air or waterways is free! The ecological costs have seldom been calculated, let alone included in the costs of production. To do any of the three items will tend to slow down consumption and attack our cherished sacred cow—an increasing "standard of living." Raising the price of a product will surely reduce the amount that a family can buy. The price increase is tantamount to a sales tax—a regressive form of taxation that hurts the poor most severely when imposed on necessities. Each person will pay the same increased amount per item, but some can pay it easily and others cannot.

The federal subsidy also does not come free of charge because the tax-payer will ultimately pay it, even if by a progressive income tax. Any tax credits offered to industries for cleaner effluents are really another form of subsidy for pollution control. The third alternative—lowering the corporate profits—seems unlikely, given the power, prestige of, and lack of public controls over large corporations. If profits were somehow substantially reduced, however, industrial expansion would slow down. Of the three alternatives, the first seems to be the most likely. Yet increasing the price of the products will affect the poor most severely, unless we make special allowances or adopt new pricing mechanisms.

In order to have economic justice and ecological sanity we might have to revamp radically our pricing structure. For instance, we now pay less for additional units of electric power consumption, which means that the tenth electrical appliance is actually cheaper (per kilowatt hour) to operate than the first. We are enticed into consuming increasing amounts of electric power that result in environmental contamination. In order to preserve a sound environment with economic justice, the basic units of power should be offered at the cheapest possible rates. Then a graduated price scale might be imposed on additional amounts so that the ninth appliance (a freezer?) will be more costly to operate than the first (a refrigerator?). The inversion of the rate structure would discourage profligate use of power.

Economic Growth and Environmental Destruction
An increasing Gross National Product (GNP) has functioned in American society as a God-concept does in a religious society. In short, Americans worship economic growth. Yet increased economic growth which comes about by increased material and power consumption is always accompanied by increased pollution. Hence, many ecologists and others believe that we must begin to deal with root causes and not symptoms. And perpetually increasing consumption levels of power and material goods (compounded by the population explosion) are the root causes.

But will not more technology solve the population problem? Our perennial faith in the "technical fix" to solve all of our pollution problems is being shattered. That notion naively assumes that no matter how badly the side effects of current technology destroy the environment, new technologies will appear that will fully ameliorate the damages. Just as the drug user becomes addicted to heroin, our society has become addicted to the technical fix. Technology, of course, can be useful in developing pollution control devices, but exclusive reliance on new technologies to extricate us from our follies has not and will not work repeatedly. We produce new problems faster than we solve old ones. In many instances *initial steps that produced the pollution will have to be stopped.* In fact, sometimes the technical fix creates problems that are more dangerous than the ones it tried to remedy. For example, the detergent used to free the ocean of the oil from the Torrey Canyon did more damage to marine life than the oil spilled!

There is a growing pool of data that shows that increased production will cause increased environmental contamination, even after the best pollution control devices are installed. Our current methods, for instance, extract raw materials from the earth and turn them into products that soon become obsolete. The disposal of these products often presents serious environmental problems. A classic case is that of bauxite ore which is extracted in Latin America and converted into billions of aluminum cans per year. Their disposal presents a fantastic problem since the cans do not decompose. Hence, many of our most secluded wildernesses are strewn with beer cans!

In order to conserve our natural resources a tax on extracting raw materials needs to be imposed as well as a tax on the disposal of the product. That is, the real cost of depleting natural resources and the cost of disposing of manufactured products should be included in the costs of production. Obviously, taxing the origin and the end of the production processes would make recycling of products a more competitive operation. This would allow us to move to what the economist Kenneth Boulding has called, the "spaceship earth" society. Boulding believes that the U.S. is now wedded to a "cowboy" economy which knows no limits on natural resources and has no ecological constraints.[10] A spaceship earth concept is one where the materials are recycled, just as occurs on space flights.

But a massive recycle industry cannot be developed without power consumption and environmental deterioration. Massive recycle industries would allow us to preserve natural resources and help solve the disposal problem, but the second law of thermodynamics cannot be reversed. Any power generating operation has some heat loss, and that is always a form of pollution! So increased recycling cannot be viewed as an unlimited process. Thus, some scientists are calling for a slowdown in economic growth.

Ecologists, who challenge the notion of endless material

economic growth, are being joined by a host of others. For instance, former Secretary of Interior Stewart Udall speaks freely of the madness involved in equating the GNP with national well-being. The geologist, Preston Cloud, speaking in Boston to the last meeting of the American Association for the Advancement of Science, remarked that "growth is a Trojan horse, with the diplomatic privileges of a sacred cow." Even the ecology features in *Time* (2 February, 1970 and 2 March, 1970) noted that the whirling dervish doctrine of perpetual growth should be challenged. The biologist René Dubos has commented on the insanity of such a notion as: "Produce more than you consume, so that you can consume more."[11] There is a serious question whether ecological constraints will allow growth to increase indefinitely. Although the idea strikes at the heart of Keynesian economics, it is being espoused by responsible physical, biological, and social scientists, who are not ordinarily viewed as "kooks" or "alarmists."

Before proceeding, it should be first specified that not all economic growth results in pollution. Increased sales of pollution control equipment and gains in the "service" sector also increase the GNP. But growth in sectors that cause vast pollution should be restrained. Thus the issue is not growth or no growth, but what kind of growth.

Economic Growth and High Employment Levels
A cutback in material production, however, would have profound repercussions on the poor and lower income groups. Those who have doubts about this should observe the rising unemployment which is a result of our current attempt to "cool off" an inflationary economy. (Unemployment rates have already risen from 3.3 percent to over 5 percent.)[12] Also, most industrialized nations finance their poverty programs via incremental economic growth or a growth dividend.[13] More growth means more jobs for all (especially the poor and lower middle income groups) and more public funds available to finance welfare programs (i.e., without further tax increases). We are addicted to the "trickle down theory," i.e., everyone must receive more if the poor are to receive more. That this theory has not been fully effective in ending poverty is irrelevant; it has worked in part. The poor may not have been helped appreciably by economic growth, but they certainly will suffer acutely if the growth rate

declines. This paradox, which can lead to a host of questions about the structural injustices in our economic system, cannot be pursued at this juncture.[14]

These effects on the poor and lower middle income families are most severe in an automated society. For years there has been a stalemate in the debate: "Does automation produce or reduce jobs?" The experts have argued on both sides of the issue. But from the maze of data some clear trends are discernible. During the Eisenhower years when economic growth was slow, unemployment rates soared (3 percent in 1953 to 5 percent in 1960). From 1962–68 (a period of economic growth) the unemployment rates dropped from 5.6 percent in 1962 to 3.5 percent in 1968. Such statistics led the "pro-automation" experts to say: "See! Automation produces more jobs, as long as economic growth is sustained." But if the ecological problems are as serious as many believe, then that provisional clause "as long as economic growth is sustained" radically alters the debate. For automation always increases productivity (i.e., units produced per man hour). If automation did not, it would be senseless to add new machinery. With a stagnant growth rate and increasing productivity, the logical result must be higher levels of unemployment as well as a shorter work week.

As our society becomes more industrialized, there is a shift from the "goods" to the "service" sector. As productivity increases (due to automation), more jobs will be available in the service sector. However, reliance on the service sector to take up all of the economic slack is another myth. With a slow industrial growth rate, the entire economy will slow down. Hence, the problems of unemployment that will result from the slowing down of economic growth, the necessity of an adequate guaranteed annual income for all, and the need for a redistribution of national income, must be included in all serious ecology debates.

The challenges should be clear to us. Although environmental problems are becoming critical, they must be interpreted in light of other problems and priorities. If the cost of pollution control is passed directly on to the consumer on all items, low-income families will be affected disproportionately. If new technologies cannot solve the environmental crisis and a slowdown in material production is demanded, the low income families will again bear the brunt of it, as more and more of them will join the ranks of the unemployed.

In the first instance, new pricing schemes are necessary in order to have ecological sanity and economic justice. In the latter case, we must either radically revamp our schemes for the distribution of national wealth and income *or* use ecology as a club over the heads of the poor and lower-middle income families. There are no other alternatives unless one decides that ecology is not a real problem. The mounting scientific evidence, however, stands as a staunch testimony against those who claim that ecology is a "faddish" and "overrated" issue.

Global Ecology and Economic Justice: The Challenge to Social Ethics

The ethical implications of the above discussion are obvious—man must be a steward of God's creation at the same time he works for social and economic justice for *all*. We can sacrifice neither the God of Genesis nor the God of the prophets. We should realize, therefore, that the problems from the outset are not just national but global. As a result ecology and distributive justice have to be considered in an international context. Unfortunately, the wider global aspects of economic development of poor nations, the gap between the rich and poor nations, the ecological problems associated with full world-wide industrialization, cannot be explored in detail here.

One point, however, should be touched upon, i.e., the disproportionate consumption of the earth's resources by Americans. The U.S., with 6 percent of the world's population, now uses roughly 40–60 percent of the non-renewable resources utilized each year.[15] In order to sustain our increasing "standard of living," by 1980, with around 5 percent of the world's population, the U.S. will need roughly 55–70 percent of the non-renewable resources used each year. Can economic justice be a global reality if this trend continues? Is development of the third world precluded by our need for their raw materials?[16] After all, non-renewable resources are finite, and took billions of years of evolution to reach their current state, and hence should be used sparingly and justly.

Therefore, the current American life styles should be challenged. Concern for economic justice should lead an affluent American to say: "We must consume less, enjoy it more, and share our abundance with others at home and abroad." To some, that might sound naïve, soft-headed, unrealistic, and unpragmatic. Despite name calling, it may point to a central and essential ecological fact which is consonant with our theological and ethical heritage. In order to attain economic justice the gap between the rich and the poor should be closed. With modern technology, managerial skills, and capital resources largely concentrated in the hands of industrialized nations, the rich-poor gap is widening. For example, from 1967 to 1969 the per capita income in the U.S. rose from $3,270 to $3,800, an increase of $530. Even discounting for inflation, that increase was about twice that of the entire annual per capita income in Guatemala which stagnated around $250. Some African and Asian nations are even poorer.

Many believe that it was the Judeo-Christian mandate that "man should have dominion" (*Gen.* 1:26) over nature which led to the ecological crisis.[17] Thus, a reformation of a theology and ethic of nature is necessary. But this should not be done divorced from the notions of distributive justice especially in the economic realm. And the above statistics clearly point out the need.

A responsible environmental ethic would recognize man's finitude and his place in the cosmos. He has been selected to be a custodian of God's creation and to transform the natural order for human welfare. But he must appreciate the limits of technical transformation. The side-effects of all of his actions must be carefully calculated, and appropriate plans made to offset their negative effects. He must further understand that even the positive aspects of his technical transformations affect various people differently. The costs and the benefits of each technical modification are not shared equally, so the question of *who pays the costs and who receives the benefits is essential.* A new environmental ethic would attempt to distribute the costs and benefits justly.

In order to manifest our ethical concerns, four things should be done simultaneously:

1. We should direct citizens to see the root causes of the ecological crisis. The nation must move beyond the anti-pollution fad and deal with causes not symptoms. The myth that equates increased material prosperity with the "good life" has to be challenged.

2. We should expose and oppose those who would use the current momentum of the ecology movement as the issue of the "silent majority," divorced from the needs of the poor. Rats, congested and dilapidated living spaces, and a repressive atmosphere are part of

urban ecology. The rat infested apartment should not receive less ecological emphasis than bird sanctuaries!

3. We should thoroughly investigate the allocation of the costs of pollution control. Often those who receive most of the benefits pay only a small portion of the costs, and vice versa. Passing the cost to the consumer might affect the poor unfairly.

4. We should insure that the consequences of altering the economic growth rate become an integral part of all ecology discussions. A new distribution of income and wealth must be reckoned with.

Yet we should move beyond the immediate American situation to visions of global ecology. America offers false hopes to many poor nations that they, too, can imitate the American model of development. That model may be extremely difficult to reproduce and suicidal if it is reproduced. For instance, if the current global population (3 billion) consumed at current American levels, the carbon dioxide and carbon monoxide levels would increase by a factor of 250 and sulfur dioxide by a factor of 200. The image of 7 billion people in 2000 consuming at even higher than American levels is horrendous even with extensive pollution control and recycling industries. There are limits to technology. Presently, America's over-consumption and over-pollution are made possible and sustained because of global injustice.

Can economic justice become a global reality as long as Americans are enamoured with an ever increasing "standard of living"? But if the entire world population were able to reach the consumption level of all Americans, would there be enough natural resources to sustain them? Would the resulting global pollution destroy the planetary life support systems? The answers to these questions depend on much scientific and technical data. But science and technology alone cannot provide the entire answer. Fundamentally, these are questions of human value and the human spirit. For example, the identity of increased "standard of living" with psychic well-being and the "good life," so firmly established in the U S. and industrialized nations, poses a spiritual as well as an economic problem. Theological and ethical reflection must link together ecology and distributive justice and move beyond national to global concerns.

In summary, we can say that the ecological crisis is grave, far more serious than the current publicity indicates. Much of the current debate still focuses on symptoms, not causes. There is still rampant the pious hope that new technologies will save us from the foibles and over-application of old technologies. New and more radical solutions are necessary. But the consequences of the solutions on all segments of society and the structural changes needed to offset the consequences must be dealt with. If economic justice for all is not an essential part of the debate, the ecology issue, despite its importance, will inadvertently be used as a club over the heads of the poor and lower-middle income groups, which includes most of black America.

NOTES

1. In January—April, 1970, for example, *Look, Time, Newsweek, Life, Fortune* and many other popular and professional journals either devoted issues to or did feature stories on ecology. Since then there has been a constant bombardment via the mass media.
2. The science of ecology emphasizes the "web of life," i.e., man is just one species in a complex and interrelated biosphere. Hence, most ecologists reject the anthropocentric focus of much of traditional theology. When the ecologically minded do theology, they construct a new kind of "nature mysticism." See Fred Elder, *Crisis in Eden* (Nashville: Abingdon Press, 1970) and the works of ecological scientists—Loren Eiseley and Ian McHarg. Man's peculiar responsibility to transform as well as to protect the natural order is, unfortunately, de-emphasized. In addition, most of the writings on an ethic of ecology devote almost no space to the special environmental problems of the poor. See F. F. Darling and J. P. Milton, *The Future Environments of North America* (New York: Natural History Press, 1966).
3. United Nations report on the environment released on 22 June, 1969.
4. From a report issued by *U.S. News and World Report*, July, 1969, which was reprinted in the *Philadelphia Inquirer*, "The Spectacular 70s," 17 August, 1969.
5. See T. Roszak, *The Making of a Counter Culture* (Garden City, New York: Doubleday & Company, Inc., 1969) for a brilliant explication of the youth movement. His work stands in sharp contrast to black theologians and other black writers who emphasize political and economic justice in a racist society.
6. This comment was made at a meeting held by the Boston Industrial Mission in April 1970 between Boston Area Ecology Action and the Massachusetts Welfare Rights Organization.

7. The words are an "almost exact" quote from an address made by Eugene Jones in Trinity Lutheran Church, Roxbury, Massachusetts, during a memorial service to the late Dr. Martin Luther King, Jr., on 4 April, 1970. They were enthusiastically received by the predominantly black audience.

8. Delivered to the U.S. Congress on 22 January, 1970, and reproduced in *Vital Speeches*, 1 February, 1970, pp. 226–229.

9. Quoted in *Earth Day—The Beginning* (New York: Bantam Books, Inc., 1970), p. 216. The Boston Industrial Mission has explored with Dr. Wiley and others from the National Welfare Rights Organization and ecology groups possible avenues of cooperation between the two movements.

10. See Kenneth Boulding's "Economics of the Coming Spaceship Earth" in G. de Bell's *The Environmental Handbook* (New York: Ballantine Books, Inc., 1970), pp. 96–101. See also the brochure *The Boston Industrial Mission at Mid-Decade*, Cambridge, BIM, May, 1970.

11. *So Human An Animal* (New York: Charles Scribner & Sons, 1968).

12. Figures are from the Bureau of Labor Statistics, Dept. of Labor, Washington, D.C.

13. Increased economic growth means a bigger pie and a bigger slice for all. Most economists argue that economic growth avoids class tensions, since everyone appears to be getting more even if the relative gaps remain unchanged. For the relationships between economic growth and employment, see "Technology and The American Economy," *Report of the National Commission on Technology, Automation and Economic Progress* (Washington, D.C.: U.S. Government Printing Office, February, 1966). See also economic textbooks, especially those by Keynesian economists. For the futility of endless economic growth, see E. Mishan, *Technology and Growth: The Price We Pay* (New York: Frederick A. Praeger, Inc., 1970).

14. For an insightful analysis and critique of income distribution, see G. Kolko, *Wealth and Power in America* (New York: Frederick A. Praeger, Inc., 1962).

15. See Lincoln Day and Alice Day, *Too Many Americans* (Boston: Houghton-Mifflin Company, 1964), p. 31.

16. See Charles Park, *Affluence in Jeopardy: Minerals and The Political Economy* (San Francisco: Freeman, Cooper & Co., 1968) and P. Jallé, *The Pillage of The Third World* (New York: Monthly Review Press, 1968).

17. See Lynn White, "The Historical Roots of the Ecologic Crisis," *Science* (10 March, 1967) and in this book for an indictment of the Christian tradition. Man is the egocentric manipulator who cuts himself off from nature. White calls for a new theological vision, one which sees St Francis of Assisi as the patron saint of ecology.

13

PARTICIPATORY TECHNOLOGY
JAMES D. CARROLL

In recent decades the idea of the alienation and estrangement of man from society has emerged as one of the dominant ideas of contemporary social thought. While interpretations of the concept of social alienation vary, Etzioni[1] has expressed the core of the idea as "the unresponsiveness of the world to the actor, which subjects him to forces he neither comprehends nor guides. . . .Alienation . . . is not only a feeling of resentment and disaffection but also an expression of the objective conditions which subject a person to forces beyond his understanding and control."

There is considerable speculative and observational testimony and some empirical evidence[2] that the scope and complexities of science and technology are contributing to the development of social alienation in contemporary society. Keniston,[3] for example, suggests that technology and its effects have been a factor in the alienation of many young people. At the same time he notes that the attitude of many young people toward technology is ambivalent because a revolt against the effects of technology must inevitably exploit the technology it opposes. In a different vein, De Jouvenel[4] has testified to the adverse psychological impact of scientific and technological complexities on sustaining general confidence in one's judgment. "Because science saps such individual confidence, we have a problem, which I feel we can meet but which it would be imprudent to deny." In a more general observation Mesthene[5] recently has referred to "the antitechnology spirit that is abroad in the land."

The author is an attorney and professor of Public Administration and Political Science at Ohio State University. This discussion of political processes for controlling technology appeared in *Science*, Vol. 171, p. 647–653 (19 February, 1971). Copyright 1971 by the American Association for the Advancement of Science.

PARTICIPATORY TECHNOLOGY

In this article I analyze the incipient emergence of participatory technology as a countervailing force to technological alienation in contemporary society. I interpret participatory technology as one limited aspect of a more general search for ways of making technology more responsive to the felt needs of the individual and of society. The term *participatory technology* refers to the inclusion of people in the social and technical processes of developing, implementing, and regulating a technology, directly and through agents under their control, when the people included assert that their interests will be substantially affected by the technology and when they advance a claim to a legitimate and substantial participatory role in its development or redevelopment and implementation.   The basic notion underlying the concept is that participation in the public development, use, and regulation of technology is one way in which individuals and groups can increase their understanding of technological processes and develop opportunities to influence such processes in appropriate cases.   Participatory technology is not an entirely new social phenomenon, but the evidence reviewed below suggests that its scope and impact may be increasing in contemporary society.

I first analyze several facts of which people are becoming increasingly aware that suggest why participatory technology is emerging as a trend, and I then analyze different forms of this trend. Finally, I evaluate some of its implications.

UNDERLYING REALIZATIONS

One primary reason for the emergence of participatory technology is the realization that technology often embodies and expresses political value choices that, in their operations and effects, are binding on individuals and groups, whether such choices have been made in political forums or elsewhere.   In the language of contemporary political science, by "political value choices" I mean choices that result in the authoritative allocation of values and benefits in society. In its most significant forms politics culminates in the determination and expression of social norms and values in the form of public law, public order, and governmental action.   To an indeterminate extent, technological processes in contemporary society have become the equivalent of a form of law—that is, an authoritative or binding expression of social norms and values from which the individual or a group may have no immediate recourse. What is at issue in the case of the computer and privacy, the supersonic transport and noise levels, highway development and the city, the antiballistic missile and national security, and the car and pollution is the authoritative allocation of social values and benefits in technological form.

The second realization is a correlative of the first. Technological processes frequently are the de facto locus of political choice. They are often political processes in which issues are posed and resolved in technical terms. In the absence of appropriately structured political processes for identifying and debating the value choices implicit in what appear to be technical alternatives, technical processes become, by default, the locus of political value decisions. In the context of a concern for the environment, technical questions of waste disposal systems involve value choices. In the context of a concern for urban development, technical questions of highway location and development involve value choices. In the context of a concern for privacy, technical questions of data collection. and retrieval involve value choices. Technological processes often embody significant value questions that are difficult to identify and resolve in public forums because the processes are technically complex and occur in administrative organizations to which citizens do not have easy access.

Third, there is the realization that the public order of industrial society is not particularly well structured for identifying, publicizing, and resolving in public forums political questions implicit in technological processes. The public order of industrial society is founded on, and perpetuates, values, compromises, and perceptions that are being rendered obsolete by transformation of the social and political conditions from which they were derived. The public order of industrial society preeminently expresses perceptions of material need and the values of economic growth—perceptions and values rooted in the experience of material want and economic insecurity of past generations. Because of the development of powerful technologies of production, and because of other factors, these perceptions and values, as embedded and expressed in public institutions and processes, do not encompass the total area of concern, which is expanding to include the quality of the environment, race, urban development, population growth, educational opportunity, the direction of technology, and other matters. Established means of structuring and expressing political concern themselves often border on obsolescence, because they are often based on geographical and functional jurisdictions that are unrelated to the issues on which the public must take action. If these jurisdictions were otherwise defined—for example, were defined to include an entire metropolitan area—they might provide the structure for more effective representation of diverse views and might facilitate public action through bargaining and trade-offs.

Today, in the face of population growth and technological complexity, legislative bodies, except in unusual cases such as that of the antiballistic missile, delegate to administrative agencies the responsibility for regulating, developing, and controlling technology. The general objectives of these administrative agencies involve mixed questions of value and technique, and the agencies resolve such questions in terms of their bearing on realization of the general objectives. Often the general objectives further the interests of individuals and groups allied with a particular agency. To the Department of Defense the question of the desirability of developing, maintaining, and transporting chemical and biological agents is primarily a matter of national defense policy. It is not primarily a question of the humaneness of such agents, or of their ultimate effects on the environment, or of their value or threat to man in contexts other than that of national defense.

By default, the responsibility for scrutinizing mixed questions of technology and value from the perspective of societal well-being often passes to special-interest groups and to individuals who may or may not be in a position, or be well equipped, to learn of and to influence such decisions. This is one aspect of the more general phenomenon of the devolution of authority from public representatives and administrators to "private" groups and individuals in contemporary society.

Fourth, there is the realization that, in contemporary society, political action directed toward the achievement of political value objectives, such as the production of 2.6 million housing units a year, often depends on the ability to translate the desired objective into technical tasks. Marcuse[6] observes that "the historical achievement of science and technology has rendered possible the *translation of values* into technical tasks—the materialization of values. Consequently, what is at stake is the redefinition of values in *technical terms*, as elements in the technological process. The new ends, as technical ends, would then operate in the project and in the construction of the machinery, and not only in its utilization [emphasis in the original]."

To a considerable extent, the achievement of more effective processes of education, housing, delivery of health care, postal service, public safety, and urban development depends on the political and technological capacity of contemporary society to agree on, and to translate, value objectives into technological acts. Traditional legislative declarations of intent are not sufficient. The establishment of a right to a decent home in a suitable environment requires more than a legislative act declaring that such a right exists. It also depends on the development of technical capability to translate the right into reality.

This does not mean that, in the formulation of political objectives, a technological, problem-oriented mode of thought must replace humanistic, intuitive, moral, and other modes of thought. It means that other modes of thought often depend for realization in public life and action on their expression in technical form, and that the development and control of that form is itself a political value-oriented act.

Fifth, there is the realization that the status enjoyed by technology as an agent for both bringing about and legitimatizing social change contributes to the growth of participatory technology. There is a tendency, stressed by Ellul,[7] Rickover,[8] and others, for contemporary man to accept change in technological form as inevitable and irresistible. In some cases, new technologies probably are accepted because of the specific results they produce for the individual, such as the mobility that, under some conditions, is made possible by the automobile. But there seems to be an additional social, psychological, and economic element at work—what Ellul calls "technological anaesthesia"—that generates acceptance of technological innovation irrespective of the particular effects that may result. Many people seem willing to use cars in urban areas even though such use may contribute little to mobility and may adversely affect the environment and health. It seems paradoxical but true that, while some changes in institutions and behavior are strongly resisted, other changes often are readily accepted when a technological element in the situation is the agent of change.

Participatory technology is one limited way of raising questions about the specific technological forms in terms of which social change is brought about. It is directed toward the development of processes and forums that are consistent with the expectations and values of the participatory individuals, who may resort to them in the absence of other means of making their views known. In participatory technology, however, as in other participatory processes, the opportunity to be heard is not synonymous with the right to be obeyed.

I here analyze three kinds of activities to illustrate some of the empirical referents of the concept of participatory technology.

LITIGATION

The first is the citizen lawsuit, directed toward the control and guidance of technology. As Sax[9] indicates, "The citizen-initiated lawsuit is . . . principally an effort to open the decision-making process to a wider constituency and to force decision-making into a more open and responsive forum. . . . [The] courts are sought out as an instrumentality whereby complaining citizens can obtain access to a more appropriate forum for decision-making."

The courts, of course, rely heavily on adversary proceedings, various forms of which have been suggested[10] as appropriate for handling scientific and technological issues involving the public interest. Not only can litigation restrict the use of technology, it can also lead to the modification and redevelopment of existing technology and stimulate the development of new technology to satisfy social values expressed in the form of legal norms, such as a right to privacy.

The legal response to cases involving technology has taken two forms. The first is an extension of those aspects of the legal doctrine of standing which determine who has a right to be heard in court on particular issues involving activities undertaken or regulated by public agencies. The second is a search by legal scholars, practicing lawyers, and judges for systems of conceptual correspondence in the terms of which scientific and technological developments and activities can be conceptualized and evaluated as changes in social values and norms that may warrant a legal response. The appropriate role of law in the regulation of genetic experimentation is an example.

An extension of the doctrine of standing has occurred in several recent cases involving technology, although the extension is not limited to such cases. In the words of the United States Supreme Court,[11] "The question of standing is related only to whether the dispute sought to be adjudicated will be presented in an adversary context and in a form historically viewed as capable of judicial resolution." The basic question is "whether the interest sought to be protected by the complainant is arguably within the zone of interests to be protected or regulated by the statute or constitutional guarantee in question.[12] The question of standing is a question not of whether a party should win or lose but of whether he should be heard.

The current extension of the doctrine is sometimes called the "private attorney general" concept. Under this concept a private citizen is allowed to present a case as an advocate of the public interest. A leading case is Scenic Hudson Preservation Conference v. Federal Power Commission,[13] decided by the Second Circuit of the United States Court of Appeals on 29 December 1965. On 9 March 1965 the Federal Power Commission granted a license to Consolidated Edison Company to construct a pumped storage hydroelectric project on the west side of the Hudson River at Storm King Mountain in Cornwall, New York. A pumped storage plant generates electric energy for use during peak load periods by means of hydroelectric units driven by water from a headwater pool or reservoir. The Storm King Project, as proposed by Consolidated Edison, would have required the placement of overhead transmission lines on towers 100 to 150 feet (30 to 45 meters) high. The towers would have required a path some 125 feet wide through Westchester and Putnam counties from Cornwall to the Consolidated Edison's facilities in New York City—a distance of 25 miles (40 kilometers). The petitioners were conservation and other groups and municipalities who claimed that the project, as designed by Consolidated Edison and as approved by the Federal Power Commission, would destroy the character of the land and the beauty of the area.

The Federal Power Commission argued, among other things, that the petitioners did not have standing to obtain judicial review of the legality of the license because they "make no claim of any personal economic injury resulting from the Commission's action."

The Court of Appeals held that the petitioners were entitled to raise the issue of the legality of the license and the licensing procedure even though they might not have a personal economic interest in the question. The court reasoned that a citizen has an interest in actions that affect the nature of the environment, and that this interest is arguably within the zone of interests that are or should be protected by law. On the merits of the case, the court held that the Federal Power Commission was required to give full consideration to alternative plans for the generation of peak-load electricity, including a plan proposed by one of the petitioners for the use of gas turbines.

The Scenic Hudson case is significant because it set a precedent for the enlargement of the opportunity of citizens, acting as citizens and not as private parties, to secure judicial review of the actions of public agencies, and of actions of the interests these agencies often regulate, in cases involving technology as well as other matters. The decision supports the proposition that, in certain cases, citizens will be recognized in court as advocates of a public interest, on the grounds that, as members of the public, they have been or may be injured by the actions complained of. They need not claim that they have been or will be injured economically or otherwise as private persons.[14]

The development of the "private attorney general" concept does not mean that substantive changes will automatically occur in the constitutional, statutory, and common law doctrines that regulate rights and duties pertaining to the development and use of science and technology. The work of analysts in the areas of law, science, and technology—analysts such as Patterson,[15] Frampton,[16] Cowan,[17] Miller,[18] Cavers,[19] Mayo and Jones,[20] Korn, [21] Green,[22] Ferry,[23] Wheeler,[24] and others[25]—indicates the difficulties of developing systems of conceptual correspondence between scientific and technological developments and legal concepts and doctrines. Scientific, technological, and legal systems often further different values and serve different purposes, and the reconciliation of conflicts in these values and purposes is only in part a juridical task. The "private attorney general" concept, however, does invite more active judicial scrutiny of such conflicts and may contribute to substantive changes in legal doctrine in the future[26] in areas such as the computer and privacy; air and water supply and pollution; noise control; medical, genetic, and psychological experimentation; drug testing and use; nuclear energy and radiation; food purity and pesticides; and the control and handling of chemical and biological weapons.

While the legal form of citizen participation in the control and development of technology has severe limitations because it tends to be (i) reactive rather than anticipatory, (ii) controlled by restrictive rules of evidence, and (iii) subject to dilatory tactics, litigation has proven, over time, to be a significant element in the efforts of individuals and groups to influence the processes and institutions that affect them.

TECHNOLOGY ASSESSMENT

A second form of participatory technology comes within the scope of existing and proposed processes of "technology assessment." While the concept of technology assessment can be interpreted to include the kinds of legal action I have discussed,[27] the term usually is used to refer to activities that are somewhat more anticipatory in nature and broader in scope.

To some extent "technology assessment" is a new label for an old activity—the attempt to comprehend, and to make informed decisions about, the implications of technological development. The movement to formalize and improve this activity in a public context was initiated in 1967 by Senator Edmund Muskie[28] in the Senate and by Representative Emilio Q. Daddario[29] in the House of Representatives. This movement has successfully directed attention to some limitations in the way technological questions are currently considered in the American system of politics and government.

"Technology assessment" was defined in the bill introduced by Daddario in the House of Representatives on 7 March, 1967 as a "method for identifying, assessing, publicizing, and dealing with the implications and effects of applied research and technology." The bill asserted that there is a need for improved methods of "identifying the potentials of applied research and technology and promoting ways and means to accomplish their transfer into practical use, and identifying the undesirable by-products and side effects of such applied research and technology in advance of their crystallization, and informing the public of their potential danger in order that appropriate steps may be taken to eliminate or minimize them."

The strengths and weaknesses of various forms of existing and proposed technology assessment are extensively analyzed in the hearings conducted by the Muskie[30] and Daddario[31] subcommittees; in the studies undertaken for the Daddario subcommittee by the National Academy of Sciences,[32] the National Academy of Engineering,[33] and the Science Policy Research Division of the Legislative Reference Service[34]; and in related analyses, such as those made by the Program of Policy Studies in Science and Technology of George Washington University.[35]

In these hearings and reports, citizen participation in technology assessment is both described and advocated. The analysis by Coates[36] of 15 case histories of technology assessments identifies one case that involved direct citizen participation—the examination of consumer products undertaken by the National Commission on Product Safety, which was established by Congress on 20 November, 1967. In 1968 and 1969, the commission investigated the safety of such products as toys and children's furniture, architectural glass, power mowers, power tools, glass bottles, and aerosol cans. Citizens testified before the commission and directed the commission's attention to various incidents and problems. Coates observes that citizens participated in this particular assessment because the experience of members of the public with various products was itself part of the subject matter of the inquiry. There was no direct citizen participation in the other assessments examined by Coates, but the subject matter of several of the assessment processes suggests that some form of citizen contribution, either direct or through representative intermediaries, would have been appropriate. This is true, for example, of the assessments of environmental noise, and of future public transportation systems of advanced type.

In his written testimony submitted to the Daddario subcommittee, Mayo[37] stresses the importance, in assessment processes, of direct participation or representation of persons affected by a technology. He emphasizes the fact that technology assessment has a dimension beyond the identification and analysis of the impacts of technology. This is the dimension of evaluation of the social desirability or undesirability of such impacts. Since different segments of the public may view the impacts in various ways, as beneficial or detrimental, comprehensive evaluation is difficult without direct inputs from such segments. While special-interest groups can be relied on to express their views, they cannot safely be regarded as representative of the views of all major segments of the public that may be concerned.

Of the various hearings and reports generated by the Daddario subcommittee, the report of the technology assessment panel of the National Academy of Sciences places the greatest emphasis on citizen participation and representation. This panel asserts that legislative authorization and appropriation processes are inadequate as technology assessment processes because legislative processes frequently consider only the contending views of well-organized interest groups and often do not direct attention to long-range consequences. The panel further argues that, while technology assessment occurs in industry and in government agencies, with few exceptions the basic questions considered concern the probable economic and institutional effects of a technology on those who are deciding whether to exploit it. Existing processes fail to give adequate weight to "the full spectrum of human needs" because not enough spokesmen for diverse needs have access to the appropriate decision-making processes.

In the judgment of the panel, extensive citizen participation and representation in the assessment process is necessary both for practical reasons and for reasons of democratic theory. There are two practical reasons. First, citizen participation in the early stages of the development of a technology may help to avoid belated citizen opposition to a technological development after heavy costs have been incurred. Second, "objective evaluation" is impossible unless the diverse views of interested parties have been considered. On the level of political theory, the panel suggests that, in a democratic framework, it is necessary to consider the views of those who will be affected by a particular course of action

The National Academy of Sciences panel explicitly acknowledges that technology assessment in some of its aspects is a political process because it involves questions of value: "We can hope to raise the level of political discourse; we must not seek to eliminate it." The panel concludes that there is a "need to accompany any new assessment mechanism with surrogate representatives or ombudsmen to speak on behalf of interests too weak or diffuse to generate effective spokesmen of their own. . . . Means must also be devised for alerting suitable representatives of interested groups to the fact that a decision potentially affecting them is about to be made. . . . *Whatever structure is chosen, it should provide well-defined channels through which citizens' groups, private associations, or surrogate representatives can make their views known. . . . It is particularly important to couple improved assessment with improved methods of representing weak and poorly organized interest groups* [emphasis in the original]."

As the National Academy of Sciences report states, and as Folk[38] stresses, to be effective technology assessment must function as part of the political process. What is at issue is the distribution and exercise of a form of decision-making power over technology. New technology assessment processes and structures probably would open decision-making processes to a wider constituency than now exists, and might change the distribution of power over some decisions involving technology. At the very least, new processes and structures might make it difficult for those accustomed to making technological decisions to do so without the knowledge of many other concerned people. It is doubtful that new assessment processes would be regarded as neutral either by those who now dominate technological decision-making processes or by those who might disagree with the results. Even though every effort were made to analyze questions of value as dispassionately as possible, or to exclude such questions entirely from assessment processes, dissatisfied parties almost certainly would attack the results and seek to offset them by other forms of political action.

Persuasion, bargains, and trade-offs in values are at the heart of political processes. Whether effective assessment can or should attempt to avoid these processes is questionable. Because technology assessment is to some extent a political process, the participation or representation of citizens may be not only desirable from the perspective of democratic theory but also necessary in political practice. Even such participation may not assure the effectiveness of the process in a larger political context.

AD HOC ACTIVITY

A third form of participatory technology encompasses a variety of ad hoc activities of individuals and groups beyond the scope of structured processes of litigation and assessment. This form includes activist intellectualism of the sort undertaken by Carson,[39] Nader,[40] and Commoner[41]; quasi-official action of the kind undertaken by Congressman R. D. McCarthy concerning chemical and biological warefare[42]; political and informational activities[43] of the sort undertaken by such groups as the Citizens' League Against the Sonic Boom, the Scientists' Institute for Public Information, the Sierra Club, Friends of the Earth, and Zero Population Growth; and sporadic activities of loose coalitions of individuals and groups energized by particular situations and issues.

Rather than attempt to survey such ad hoc activities, I here briefly describe and analyze an example of abortive participation that occurred in 1967 and 1968 in the initial efforts to develop a new town on the site of Fort Lincoln in Washington, D.C.[44] In some ways the Fort Lincoln example is typical of problems that often arise in processes of citizen participation in urban development. In other ways the case is distinctive because the primary purpose of the Fort Lincoln project was to demonstrate on a national basis the potentials of technological and administrative innovation for urban development.

On 30 August, 1967, President Johnson publicly requested several members of his administration and of the government of the District of Columbia to begin at once to develop a new community on the site of Fort Lincoln, which consists of 345 acres of nearly vacant land in the northeast section of Washington, D.C. The President explained the purpose of the project as the development of a community that would demonstrate the potentials of administrative and technological innovation in urban development. The Fort Lincoln project was conceptualized as the leading project in a national program to develop "new towns intown" on federally owned land in various cities throughout the country.

On 25 January, 1968, Edward J. Logue, who had achieved national recognition as an urban development administrator in New Haven and Boston, was retained as principal development consultant for Fort Lincoln. In the following 10 months, Logue and his associates developed an ambitious and innovative plan[45] that was based on, among other things, a thorough analysis[46] of the potentials for technological innovation in the development of Fort Lincoln and on a proposal[47] for an innovative educational system for the new community.

Fort Lincoln was a federal urban renewal project. Some form of citizen participation in urban renewal projects is required by law. Logue and the government officials involved in the Fort Lincoln project had had extensive experience with citizen participation in other urban development projects, including a model cities project in Washington, D.C. In developing the plans for Fort Lincoln, they made extensive efforts to fashion a participatory structure that would be acceptable to the citizens of the northeast section of Washington. For the most part they failed. Political activists in the area perceived the technical planning process as the locus of political opportunity and choice concerning such questions as the number of low-income families to be housed on the site. Although these activists disagreed over who could speak for the citizens, they agreed that the residents of the area should be granted funds to hire professionals to participate with and for them in the technical planning and development processes. At one point the Department of Housing and Urban Development offered to grant money for this purpose to the council that represented the citizens, but for various reasons the council rejected the offer

The Nixon Administration suspended development of Fort Lincoln in September 1969, pending further study. One analyst[48] has argued that the project was suspended because neither federal nor local officials believed that the development plan was either technologically or politically feasible. Other analysts[49] have suggested that the project was suspended because members of the Nixon Administration regarded it as a personal undertaking of President Johnson's and as an example of the overly ambitious social engineering activities of "the Great Society."

The struggle over citizen participation diminished support for the project in the neighborhood and among its potential supporters in other areas of the city. No strong political constituency favored the project. The Nixon Administration could and did suspend it without antagonizing any strong or vocal interest group.

Fort Lincoln is one example of the extent to which technical planning and development processes can become the locus of political conflict when these processes are perceived as the de facto locus of political choice. It is also an example of some of the difficulties that can arise in the course of efforts to reconcile the dictates of administrative and technological reasoning with the dictates of the political thinking of participating individuals in particular situations.

PROBLEMS
Like many other participatory processes, participatory technology

raises questions about the adequacy of the theory and practice of representative government.

According to traditional theories of American public life, citizens should express their demands for public action to their political and governmental representatives. Conflicting demands should be reconciled by persons elected or appointed to policy-making positions in which they are publicly accountable for their actions. Administrative and technical processes are not, in theory, the appropriate locus for the exercise of political influence and the reconciliation of political conflicts, because these processes are not usually structured as open political forums, and because most administrators and technical people are not directly accountable to electorates.

This theory of government is a prescriptive rather than a descriptive one. It does not correspond well with the realities of the exercise of political power in and through administrative and technical activities. Among other things, increases in population, the expansion of the public sector, and the increase in technological complexity have changed the number and, to some extent, the nature of demands and possibilities for governmental action in recent decades. While legislative bodies and individual elected officials continue to respond to some of these demands, many other demands are considered and resolved in administrative processes of limited visibility. The very act of translating most legislation into specific processes usually involves an exercise of political choice. Furthermore, agencies often invite demands upon themselves as a way of expanding the scope of their support and powers.

The politicalization of administration in this century, especially in response to the activities of interest groups, is a widely recognized phenomenon.[50]

Participatory technology is an attempt to influence public agencies directly, and, through them, the quasi-public and private interests they often influence and regulate. Like other participatory processes, participatory technology in some of its forms circumvents traditional processes of expressing demands through elected representatives and of relying on representatives to take appropriate action.

The hazards of participatory technology are many. On the one hand it can be used by administrative and technical people in a manipulative way to generate the illusion of citizen support of a particular course of action. On the other hand it can degenerate into forums for the exercise of obstructionist, veto-power techniques and paralyze public action. It can generate an overload of demands that agencies are not equipped to handle. It can be used as an instrument by an aggressive minority to capture decision-making processes and to impose minority views on a larger community. It can simply shift the locus for the exercise of "the tyranny of small decisions"[51] from one group to another or merely enlarge the core group that exercises control. Finally, it can lead to the dominance of technological know-nothing over the judgments of qualified individuals who are legally responsible for, are dedicated to, and understand processes of public action.

At the same time, as Spiegel and Mittenthal[52] observe, "Citizen participation can occur in partnerships with a governmental unit as well as against it. Its nature can be cooperative and integrative or conflicting and oppositional. . . ." Participatory technology, if appropriately structured, can contribute to decision-making processes that take into account alternative points of view, and can help an agency perform its functions in a more effective and open manner. It can provide a means by which the individual who feels powerless in the face of technological complexity can find a forum for the expression of his views.

The basic questions are these: In what cases is citizen participation in technological processes warranted, and according to what rationale? How should participation be structured and conducted? How much weight should participation be given in decision-making processes?

To provide a priori answers to these questions is impossible because of the variety of situations to which they apply. For this reason it is recommended that public agencies, scientific and technical associations, and individual members of the scientific, technological, and political communities undertake analyses of these questions in the various situations for which they have responsibility or to which they have access. No single activity by a particular organization such as the National Academy of Sciences can meet the need. The analysis must be as broad-based as the activities to which these questions apply.

At the same time, the men responsible for policy making in

foundations should consider the establishment of an experimental center for responsive technology. Such a center would analyze, on a continuing basis, the question of the ways in which public participation in technological decisions involving a public interest can be structured, and would support such participation in appropriate cases. The center might also support the education of proponents of technology, who would be qualified to recognize alternative conceptions of the public interest in technological matters and to present these conceptions to decision-making bodies.

SUMMARY

The hunger to participate that exists today in various segments of the American public is in part a response to what some people perceive as an unresponsiveness of institutions and processes to the felt needs of the individual and of society. It is also, in part, an expression of a desire for a redistribution of power in American public life.

Technology is one of the major determinants of the nature of public as well as private life in contemporary society. Participatory technology is an attempt on the part of diverse individuals and groups to influence technological processes through participation in existing or new public processes by which technology is or can be developed, controlled, and implemented. Like other processes of direct citizen participation in governmental decision making, it raises many questions about the adequacy of existing theories and practices of representative government. These questions cannot be answered on an a priori basis. Members of the educational, scientific, technical, and governmental communities should analyze these questions in an effort to develop answers that are appropriate to the particular situations for which they are responsible and with which they are concerned.

NOTES

1. A. Etzioni, *The Active Society* (Free Press, New York, 1968), pp. 617–622.
2. The best review is E. Chaszer, *Science and Technology in the Theories of Social and Political Alienation* (George Washington Univ., Washington, D.C., 1969). See also V. C. Ferkiss, *Technological Man: The Myth and the Reality* (Braziller, New York, 1969), and H. M. Sapolsky, *Science* **162,** 427 (1968).

3. K. Keniston, *The Uncommitted: Alienated Youth in American Society* (Harcourt, Brace & World, New York, 1968); *Young Radicals* (Harcourt, Brace & World, New York, 1968). See also T. Roszak, *The Making of a Counter Culture* (Doubleday, New York, 1969).

4. B. de Jouvenel, in *Science and Society*. E. Vavoulis and A. Colver, Eds. (Holden-Day, San Francisco, 1966), p. 85.

5. E. Mesthene, *Technology Assessment* (hearings before the Subcommittee on Science, Research, and Development of the House Committee on Science and Astronautics, 91st Congress, 1st Session) (Government Printing Office, Washington, D.C., 1969), p. 246.

6. H. Marcuse, *One Dimensional Man* (Beacon, Boston, 1964), p. 232.

7. J. Ellul, *The Technological Society* (Knopf, New York, 1964).

8. H. Rickover, *Amer. Behav. Scientist* **8,** 3 (1965).

9. J. Sax, *Ann. Amer. Acad. Polit. Soc. Sci.* **389,** 72 (1970).

10. J. Conant, *Science and Common Sense* (Yale Univ. Press, New Haven, 1961); J. Killian, in *Science as a Cultural Force*, H. Woolf, Ed. (Johns Hopkins Press, Baltimore, 1964); A. Kantrowitz, *Science* **156,** 763 (1967); H. Wheeler, *Center Mag.* **2,** 59 (1969); H. Green, in *Technology Assessment: The Proceedings of a Seminar Series*, R. C. Kasper, Ed. (George Washington Univ., Washington, D.C., 1969). See also H. W. Jones, Ed., *Law and the Social Role of Science* (Rockefeller Univ. Press, New York, 1966); L. Mayo, *Scientific Method, Adversarial System, and Technology Assessment* (George Washington Univ., Washington, D.C., 1970).

11. Flast *v.* Cohen, *United States Supreme Court Rep. No. 392* (1968), p. 83.

12. Association of Data Processing Service Organizations *v.* Camp, *United States Law Week* **38,** 4194 (1970).

13. *Federal Reporter No. 354*, U.S. Court of Appeals, Second Circuit (1965), p. 608; certiorari denied, *United States Supreme Court Rep. No. 384* (1966), p. 941.

14. In several recent cases the Scenic Hudson doctrine has been applied to matters such as highway location, the displacement of people by urban renewal projects, the protection of navigable waters, and the protection of lumber preserves. See *Cornell Law Rev.* **55,** 761 (1970). The proposed Environment Protection Act of 1970, introduced in the U.S. Senate in early 1970 by Senators Hart and McGovern, would clarify and extend the right of private citizens to bring antipollution suits against government agencies, industries, and private citizens.

15. E. Patterson, *Law in a Scientific Age* (Columbia Univ. Press, New York, 1963).

16. G. Frampton, *Mich. Law Rev.* **63,** 1423 (1963).

17. T. Cowan, *George Washington Law Rev.* **33,** 3 (1964).

18. A. Miller, *ibid.*, p. 17.

19. D. Cavers, *Mich. Law Rev.* **63,** 1325 (1965).

20. L. Mayo and E. Jones, *George Washington Law Rev.* **33,** 318 (1964).

21. H. Korn, *Law and the Determination of Facts Involving Science and Technology* (Columbia Univ. Law School, New York, 1965).

22. H. Green, *Bull. Atom. Scientists* **23,** 12 (1967).

23. W. Ferry, *Saturday Rev.* **51,** 50 (1968).

24. H. Wheeler, *Center Mag.* **2,** 59 (Mar. 1969).

25. See *Vanderbilt Law Rev.* **17,** 1 (1963); *Report of a Conference on Law and Science* (David Davies Memorial Institute, London, 1964); *George Washington Law Rev.* **33,** 1 (1964); *Mich. Law Rev.* **63,** 1325 (1965); *Case Western Reserve Law Rev.* **19,** 1 (1967); *George Washington Law Rev.* **36,** 1033 (1968), *Univ. of California Los Angeles Law Rev.* **15,** 267 (1968); *Cornell Law Rev.* **55,** 663 (1970).

26. Suits initiated in recent years to affect the control of technology through new applications of, or substantive changes in, legal doctrines include actions to ban the use of pesticides; to prevent airlines from using jets that pollute the air at the Newark, New Jersey, airport; to enjoin offshore drilling; to order a paper company to provide air pollution controls at a pulp mill; and to prevent a gas company from extending pipelines across a wooded tract. Several of these and similar suits are discussed in J. W. Moorman, "Outline for the Practicing Environmental Lawyer" (Center for the Study of Responsive Law, Washington, D.C., 1969); L. J. Carter, *Science* **166,** 1487 (1969); *ibid.,* p. 1601.

27. See, for example, B. M. Portnoy, *Cornell Law Rev.* **55,** 861 (1970).

28. "Creation of a Select Committee on Technology and the Human Environment," Senate Resolution 68, 90th Congress, 1st Session, 25 January, 1967.

29. "Technology Assessment Board," House of Representatives Bill 6698, 90th Congress, 1st Session, 7 March, 1967. See also "Technology Assessment" (statement of Emilio Q. Daddario, chairman, Subcommittee on Science, Research, and Development of the House Committee on Science and Astronautics, 90th Congress, 1st Session) (Government Printing Office, Washington, D.C., 1968).

30. *Establish a Select Committee on Technology and the Human Environment* (hearings before the Subcommittee on Intergovernmental Relations of the Senate Committee on Government Operations, 90th Congress, 1st Session) (Government Printing Office, Washington, D.C., 1967).

31 *Technology Assessment Seminar* (proceedings before the Subcommittee on Science, Research, and Development of the House Committee on Science and Astronautics, 90th Congress, 1st Session) (Government Printing Office, Washington, D.C., 1967); *Technology Assessment* (hearings before the Subcommittee on Science, Research, and Development of the House Committee on Science and Astronautics, 91st Congress, 1st Session) (Government Printing Office, Washington, D.C., 1969).

32. National Academy of Sciences, *Technology: Processes of Assessment and Choice* (Government Printing Office, Washington, D.C., 1969).

33. National Academy of Engineering, *A Study of Technology Assessment* (Government Printing Office, Washington, D.C., 1969).

34. Science Policy Research Division, Legislative Reference Service, *Technical Information for Congress* (Government Printing Office, Washington, D.C., 1969). See also National Academy of Public Administration, *A Technology Assessment System for the Executive Branch* (Government Printing Office, Washington, D.C., 1970).

35. These analyses are described in *Report: 1967–1968* and *Report: 1968–1969* (George Washington Univ., Washington, D.C., 1970).

36. V. Coates, "Examples of Technology Assessments for the Federal Government," (George Washington Univ., Washington, D.C., 1970).

37. L. Mayo, *Technology Assessment* (hearings before the Subcommittee on Science, Research, and Development of the House Committee on Science and Astronautics, 91st Congress, 1st Session) (Government Printing Office, Washington, D.C., 1969), pp. 83–102.

38. H. Folk, paper presented at the Boston meeting of the AAAS, December 1969.

39. R. Carson, *Silent Spring* (Houghton Mifflin, Boston, 1962).

40. R. Nader, *Unsafe at Any Speed* (Grossman, New York, 1965).

41. B. Commoner, *Science and Survival* (Viking, New York, 1966).

42. See R. D. McCarthy, *The Ultimate Folly* (Vintage, New York, 1969).

43. See G. DeBell, Ed., *The Environmental Handbook* (Ballantine, New York, 1970); J. G. Mitchell and C. L. Stallings, Eds., *Ecotactics* (Pocket Books, Simon & Schuster, New York, 1970); R. Rienow and L. T. Rienow, *Moment in the Sun* (Ballantine, New York, 1967); W. A. Shurcliff, *SST and Sonic Boom Handbook* (Ballantine, New York, 1970).

44. The account given here is derived from a longer study: J. D. Carroll and J. Zuccotti, "The Siege of Fort Lincoln, circa 1969: A Study in Non-participatory Technology," paper presented at the Eastern Regional Conference on Science, Technology, and Public Programs, Boston, 1970. See also M. Derthick, *New Towns In-Town* (Urban Institute, Washington, D.C., 1970), and "Fort Lincoln," *The Public Interest, No. 20* (1970), p. 3.

45. *Fort Lincoln New Town Final Planning Report* (District of Columbia Redevelopment Land Agency, National Capital Planning Commission, and Government of the District of Columbia, Washington, D.C., 1969).

46. D. A. Crane, A. H. Keyes, F. D. Lethbridge, D. H. Condon, *Technologies Study: The Application of Technical Innovation in the Development of A New Community* (District of Columbia Redevelopment Land Agency, National Capital Planning Commission, and Government of the District of Columbia, Washington, D.C., 1968).

47. M. Fantini and M. A. Young, "A Design for a New and Relevant System of Education for Fort Lincoln New Town" (New York, 1968).
48. M. Derthick, *New Towns In-Town* (Urban Institute, Washington, D.C., 1970).
49. J. D. Carroll and J. Zuccotti, "The Siege of Fort Lincoln, circa 1969: A Study in Nonparticipatory Technology," paper presented at the Eastern Regional Conference on Science, Technology, and Public Programs, Boston, 1970.
50. See T. Lowi, *The End of Liberalism* (Norton, New York, 1969); see also J. C. Charlesworth, Ed., *Theory and Practice of Public Administration* (American Academy of Political and Social Science, Philadelphia, 1968).
51. A. E. Kahn, *Kyklos—Int. Rev. Soc. Sci.* **19,** 23 (1966).
52. H. Spiegel and S. Mittenthal, in *Citizen Participation in Urban Development*, H. Spiegel, Ed. (National Training Laboratories Institute for Applied Behavioral Science, Washington, D.C., 1968), vol. 1, pp. 12, 13. See also P. Davidoff, *J. Amer. Inst. Planners* **31,** 331 (1965); E. M. Burke, *ibid.* **34,** 287 (1968); S. R. Arnstein, *ibid.* **35,** 216 (1969); A. Altshuler, *Community Control* (Pegasus, New York, 1970).

14

CAN TECHNOLOGY BE HUMANE?
PAUL GOODMAN

On 4 March, 1969, there was a work stoppage and teach-in initiated by dissenting professors at the Massachusetts Institute of Technology, and followed at thirty other major universities and technical schools across the country, against misdirected scientific research and the abuse of scientific technology. Here I want to consider this event in a broader context than the professors did, indeed as part of a religious crisis. For an attack on the American scientific establishment is an attack on the world-wide system of belief. I think we are on the eve of a new Protestant Reformation, and no institution or status will go unaffected.

March 4 was, of course, only the latest of a series of protests in the twenty-five years since the Manhattan Project to build the atom bomb, during which time the central funding of research and innovation has grown so enormously and its purposes have become so unpalatable. In 1940 the federal budget for research and development was less than 100 million dollars, in 1967 17 billion. Hitler's war was a watershed of modern times. We are accustomed, as H. R. Trevor-Roper has pointed out, to write Hitler off as an aberration, of little political significance. But, in fact, the military emergency that he and his Japanese allies created confirmed the worst tendencies of the giant states, till now they are probably irreversible by ordinary political means.

After Hiroshima, there was the conscience-stricken movement of the Atomic Scientists and the founding of their *Bulletin*. The

American Association for the Advancement of Science pledged itself to keep the public informed about the dangerous bearings of new developments. There was the Oppenheimer incident. Ads of the East Coast scientists successfully stopped the bomb shelters, warned about the fallout, and helped produce the test ban. There was a scandal about the bombardment of the Van Allen belt. Scientists and technologists formed a powerful (and misguided) ad hoc group for Johnson in the 1964 election. In some universities, sometimes with bitter struggle, classified contracts have been excluded. There is a Society for Social Responsibility in Science. Rachel Carson's book on the pesticides caused a stir, until the Department of Agriculture rescued the manufacturers and plantation-owners. Ralph Nader has been on his rampage. Thanks to spectacular abuses like smog, strip-mining, asphalting, pesticides, and oil pollution, even ecologists and conservationists have been getting a hearing. Protest against the boom has slowed up the development of the supersonic transport. Most recent has been the concerted outcry against the antiballistic missiles.

The target of protest has become broader and the grounds of complaint deeper. The target is now not merely the military, but the universities, commercial corporations, and government. It is said that money is being given by the wrong sponsors to the wrong people for the wrong purposes. In some of the great schools, such funding is the main support, e.g., at MIT, 90 percent of the research budget is from the government, and 65 percent of that is military. Inevitably, such funding channels the brainpower of most of the brightest science students, who go where the action is, and this predetermines the course of American science and technology for the foreseeable future. At present nearly 200,000 American engineers and scientists spend all their time making weapons, which is a comment on, and perhaps explanation for, the usual statement that more scientists are now alive than since Adam and Eve. And the style of such research and development is not good. It is dominated by producing hardware, figuring logistics, and devising salable novelties. Often there is secrecy, always nationalism. Since the grants go overwhelmingly through a very few corporations and universities, they favor a limited number of scientific attitudes and preconceptions, with incestuous staffing. There is a premium on "positive results"; surprising "failures" cannot be pursued, so that science ceases to be a wandering dialogue with the unknown.

The policy is economically wasteful. A vast amount of brains and money is spent on crash programs to solve often essentially petty problems, and the claim that there is a spin-off of useful discoveries is derisory, if we consider the sums involved. The claim that research is neutral, and it doesn't matter what one works on, is shabby, if we consider the heavy funding in certain directions. Social priorities are scandalous: money is spent on overkill, supersonic planes, brand-name identical drugs, annual model changes of cars, new detergents, and color television, whereas water, air, space, food, health, and foreign aid are neglected. And much research is morally so repugnant, e.g., chemical and biological weapons, that one dares not humanly continue it.

The state of the behavioral sciences is, if anything, worse. Their claim to moral and political neutrality becomes, in effect, a means of diverting attention from glaring social evils, and they are in fact used—or would be if they worked—for warfare and social engineering, manipulation of people for the political and economic purposes of the powers that be. This is an especially sad betrayal since, in the not-too-distant past, the objective social sciences were developed largely to dissolve orthodoxy, irrational authority, and taboo. They were heretical and intellectually revolutionary, as the physical sciences had been in their own Heroic Age, and they weren't getting governmental grants.

This is a grim indictment. Even so, I do not think the dissenting scientists understand how deep their trouble is. They still take themselves too much for granted. Indeed, a repeated theme of the 4 March complaints was that the science budget was being cut back, especially in basic research. The assumption was that though the sciences are abused, Science would rightly maintain and increase its expensive preeminence among social institutions. Only Science could find the answers.

But underlying the growing dissent there is an historical crisis. There has been a profound change in popular feeling, more than among the professors. Put it this way: Modern societies have been operating as if religion were a minor and moribund part of the scheme of things. But this is unlikely. Men do not do without a system of "meanings" that everybody believes and puts his hope in even if, or especially if, he doesn't know anything about it; what Freud called a "shared psychosis," meaningful because shared, and with the power that resides in dream and longing. In fact, in advanced countries it is science and technology themselves that have gradually and finally triumphantly become the system of mass faith, not disputed by various political ideologies and nationalisms that have also been mass religions. Marxism called itself "scientific socialism" as against moral and utopian socialisms; and movements of national liberation have especially promised to open the benefits of industrialization and technological progress when once they have gotten rid of the imperialists.

For three hundred years, science and scientific technology had an unblemished and justified reputation as a wonderful adventure, pouring out practical benefits, and liberating the spirit from the errors of superstition and traditional faith. During this century they have finally been the only generally credited system of explanation and problem-solving. Yet in our generation they have come to seem to many, and to very many of the best of the young, as essentially inhuman, abstract, regimenting, hand-in-glove with Power, and even diabolical. Young people say that science is antilife, it is a Calvinist obsession, it has been a weapon of white Europe to subjugate colored races, and manifestly—in view of recent scientific technology—people who think that way become insane. With science, the other professions are discredited; and the academic "disciplines" are discredited.

The immediate reasons for this shattering reversal of values are fairly obvious. Hitler's ovens and his other experiments in eugenics, the first atom bombs and their frenzied subsequent developments, the deterioration of the physical environment and the destruction of the biosphere, the catastrophes impending over the cities because of technological falures and psychological stress, the prospect of a brainwashed and drugged 1984. Innovations yield diminishing returns in enhancing life. And instead of rejoicing, there is now widespread conviction that beautiful advances in genetics, surgery, computers, rocketry, or atomic energy will surely only increase human woe.

In such a crisis, in my opinion, it will not be sufficient to ban the military from the universities; and it will not even be sufficient, as liberal statesmen and many of the big corporations envisage, to beat the swords into ploughshares and turn to solving problems of transportation, desalinization, urban renewal, garbage disposal, and cleaning up the air and water. If the present difficulty is religious and historical, it is necessary to alter the entire relationship of science, technology, and social needs both in men's minds and in fact. This involves changes in the organization of science, in scientific education, and in the kinds of men who make scientific decisions.

In spite of the fantasies of hippies, we are certainly going to continue to live in a technological world. The question is a different one: is that workable?

PRUDENCE

Whether or not it draws on new scientific research, technology is a branch of moral philosophy, not of science. It aims at prudent goods for the commonweal and to provide efficient means for these goods. At present, however, "scientific technology" occupies a bastard position in the universities, in funding, and in the public mind. It is half tied to the theoretical sciences and half treated as mere know-how for political and commercial purposes. It has no principles of its own. To remedy this—so Karl Jaspers in Europe and Robert Hutchins in America have urged—technology must have its proper place on the faculty as a learned profession important in modern society, along with medicine, law, the humanities, and natural philosophy, learning from them and having something to teach them. As a moral philosopher, a technician should be able to criticize the programs given him to implement. As a professional in a community of learned professionals, a technologist must have a different kind of training and develop a different character than we see at present among technicians and engineers. He should know something of the social sciences, law, the fine arts, and medicine, as well as relevant natural sciences.

Prudence is foresight, caution, utility. Thus it is up to the technologists, not to regulatory agencies of the government, to provide for safety and to think about remote effects. This is what Ralph Nader is saying and Rachel Carson used to ask. An important aspect of caution is flexibility, to avoid the pyramiding catastrophe that occurs when something goes wrong in interlocking technologies, as in urban power failures. Naturally, to take responsibility for such things often requires standing up to the front office and urban politicians, and technologists must organize themselves in order to have power to do it.

Often it is clear that a technology has been oversold, like the cars. Then even though the public, seduced by advertising, wants more, technolgists must balk, as any professional does when his client wants what isn't good for him. We are now repeating the same self-defeating congestion with the planes and airports: the more the technology is oversold, the less immediate utility it provides, the greater the costs, and the more damaging the remote effects. As this becomes evident, it is time for technologists to confer with sociologists and economists and ask deeper questions. Is so much travel necessary? Are there ways to diminish it? Instead, the recent history of technology has consisted largely of a desperate effort to remedy situations caused by previous overapplication of technology.

Technologists should certainly have a say about simple waste, for even in an affluent society there are priorities—consider the supersonic transport, which has little to recommend it. But the moon shot has presented the more usual dilemma of authentic conflicting claims. I myself believe that space exploration is a great human adventure, with immense aesthetic and moral benefits, whatever the scientific or utilitarian uses. Yet it is amazing to me that the scientists and technologists involved have not spoken more insistently for international cooperation instead of a puerile race. But I have heard some say that except for this chauvinist competition, Congress would not vote any money at all.

Currently, perhaps the chief moral criterion of a philosophic technology is modesty, having a sense of the whole and not obtruding more than a particular function warrants. Immodesty is always a danger of free enterprise, but when the same disposition is financed by big corporations, technologists rush into production with neat solutions that swamp the environment. This applies to packaging products and disposing of garbage, to freeways that bulldoze neighborhoods, highrises that destroy landscape, wiping out a species for a passing fashion, strip mining, scrapping an expensive machine rather than making a minor repair, draining a watershed for irrigation because (as in Southern California) the cultivable land has been covered by asphalt. Given this disposition, it is not surprising that we defoliate a forest in order to expose a guerrilla and spray teargas from a helicopter on a crowded campus.

Since we are technologically overcommitted, a good general maxim in advanced countries at present is to innovate in order to simplify the technical system, but otherwise to innovate as sparingly as possible. Every advanced country is overtechnologized; past a certain point, the quality of life diminishes with new "improvements." Yet no country is rightly technologized, making efficient use of available techniques. There are ingenious devices for unimportant functions, stressful mazes for essential functions, and drastic dislocation when anything goes wrong, which happens with increasing frequency. To add to the complexity, the mass of people tend to become incompetent and dependent on repairmen—indeed, unrepairability except by experts has become a desideratum of industrial design.

When I speak of slowing down or cutting back, the issue is not whether research and making working models should be encouraged or not. They should be, in every direction, and given a blank check. The point is to resist the temptation to apply every new device without a second thought. But the big corporate organization of research and development makes prudence and modesty very difficult; it is necessary to get big contracts and rush into production in order to pay the salaries of the big team. Like other bureaucracies, technological organizations are run to maintain themselves but they are more dangerous because, in capitalist countries, they are in a competitive arena.

I mean simplification quite strictly, to simplify the *technical* system. I am unimpressed by the argument that what is technically more complicated is really economically or politically simpler, e.g., by complicating the packaging we improve the supermarkets; by throwing away the machine rather than repairing it, we give cheaper and faster service all around; or even by expanding the economy with trivial innovations, we increase employment, allay discontent, save on welfare. Such ideas may be profitable for private companies or political parties, but for society they have proved to be an accelerating rat race. The technical structure of the environment is too important to be a political or economic pawn; the effect on the quality of life is too disastrous; and the hidden social costs are not calculated, the auto graveyards, the torn-up streets, the longer miles of commuting, the advertising, the inflation, etc. As I pointed out in *People or Personnel*, a country with a fourth of our per capita income, like Ireland, is not necessarily less well off; in some respects it is much richer, in some respects a little poorer. If possible, it is better to solve political problems by political means. For instance, if teaching machines and audio-visual aids are indeed educative, well and good; but if they are used just to save money on teachers, then not good at all—nor do they save money.

Of course, the goals of right technology must come to terms with other values of society. I am not a technocrat. But the advantage of raising technology to be a responsible learned profession with its own principles is that it can have a voice in the debate and argue for *its* proper contribution to the community. Consider the important case of modular sizes in building, or prefabrication of a unit bathroom: these conflict with the short-run interests of manufacturers and craft unions, yet to deny them is technically an abomination. The usual recourse is for a government agency to set standards; such agencies accommodate to interests that have a strong voice, and at present technologists have no voice.

The crucial need for technological simplification, however, is not in the advanced countries—which can afford their clutter and probably deserve it—but in underdeveloped countries which must rapidly innovate in order to diminish disease, drudgery, and deepening starvation. They cannot afford to make mistakes. It is now widely conceded that the technological aid we have given to such areas according to our own high style—a style usually demanded by the native ruling groups—has done more harm than good. Even when, as frequently if not usually, aid has been benevolent, without strings attached, not military, and not dumping, it has nevertheless disrupted ways of life, fomented tribal wars, accelerated urbanization, decreased the food supply, gone wasted for lack of skills to use it, developed a do-nothing élite.

By contrast, a group of international scientists called Intermediate Technology argue that what is needed is techniques that use only native labor, resources, traditional customs, and teachable know-how, with the simple aim of remedying drudgery, disease, and hunger, so that people can then develop further in their own style. This avoids cultural imperialism.   Such intermediate techniques may be quite primitive, on a level unknown among us for a couple of centuries, and yet they may pose extremely subtle problems, requiring exquisite scientific research and political and human understanding, to devise a very simple technology.   Here is a reported case (which I trust I remember accurately): In Botswana, a very poor country, pasture was overgrazed, but the economy could be salvaged if the land were fenced.   There was no local material for fencing, and imported fencing was prohibitively expensive. The solution was to find the formula and technique to make posts out of mud, and a pedagogic method to teach people how to do it.

In *The Two Cultures*, C. P. Snow berated the humanists for their irrelevance when two-thirds of mankind are starving and what is needed is science and technology.   They have perhaps been irrelevant; but unless technology is itself more humanistic and philosophical, it is of no use.   There is only one culture.

Finally, let me make a remark about amenity as a technical criterion. It is discouraging to see the concern about beautifying a highway and banning billboards, and about the cosmetic appearance of the cars, when there is no regard for the ugliness of bumper-to-bumper traffic and the suffering of the drivers.   Or the concern for preserving an historical landmark while the neighborhood is torn up and the city has no shape.   Without moral philosophy, people have nothing but sentiments.

ECOLOGY

The complement to prudent technology is the ecological approach to science.   To simplify the technical system and modestly pinpoint our artificial intervention in the environment makes it possible for the environment to survive in its complexity evolved for a billion years, whereas the overwhelming instant intervention of tightly interlocked and bulldozing technology has already disrupted many of the delicate sequences and balances. The calculable consequences are already frightening, but of course we don't know enough, and won't in the foreseeable future, to predict the remote effects of much of what we have done. The only possible conclusion is to be prudent; when there is serious doubt, to do nothing.

Cyberneticists—I am thinking of Gregory Bateson—come to ɪɴᴇ same cautious conclusion. The use of computers has enabled us to carry out crashingly inept programs on the bases of willful analyses. But we have also become increasingly alert to the fact that things respond, systematically, continually, cumulatively; they cannot simply be manipulated or pushed around. Whether bacteria or weeds or bugs or the technologically unemployed or unpleasant thoughts, they cannot be eliminated and forgotten; repressed, the nuisances return in new forms. A complicated system works most efficiently if its parts readjust themselves decentrally, with a minimum of central intervention or control, except in case of breakdown. Usually there is an advantage in a central clearinghouse of information about the gross total situation, but decision and execution require more minute local information. The fantastically simulated moon landing hung on a last split-second correction on the spot. In social organization, deciding in headquarters means relying on information that is cumulatively abstract and irrelevant, and chain-of-command execution applies standards that cumulatively do not fit the concrete situation. By and large it is better, given a sense of the whole picture, for those in the field to decide what to do and do it (cf. *People or Personnel*, Chapter III).

But with organisms too, this has long been the bias of psychosomatic medicine, the Wisdom of the Body, as Cannon called it. To cite a classical experiment of Ralph Hefferline of Columbia: a subject is wired to suffer an annoying regular buzz, which can be delayed and finally eliminated if he makes a precise but unlikely gesture, say by twisting his ankle in a certain way; then it is found that he adjusts quicker if he is *not* told the method and it is left to his spontaneous twitching than if he is told and tries deliberately to help himself. He adjusts better without conscious control, his own or the experimenter's.

Technological modesty, fittingness, is not negative. It is the ecological wisdom of cooperating with Nature rather than trying to master her. (The personification of "Nature" is linguistic wisdom.) A well-known example is the long-run superiority of partial pest-control in farming by using biological deterrents rather than chemical ones. The living defenders work harder, at the right moment, and with more pin-pointed targets. But leᴛ e giveᴇ another example because it is so lovely— though I have forgotten the name of my informant: A tribe in Yucatan educates its children to identify and pull up all weeds in the region; then what is left is a garden of useful plants that have chosen to be there and now thrive.

In the life sciences there is at present a suggestive bifurcation in methodology. The rule is still to increase experimental intervention, but there is also a considerable revival of old-fashioned naturalism, mainly watching and thinking, with very modest intervention. Thus, in medicine, there is new diagnostic machinery, new drugs, spectacular surgery; but there is also a new respect for family practice with a psychosomatic background, and a strong push, among young doctors and students, for a social-psychological and sociological approach, aimed at preventing disease and building up resistance. In psychology, the operant conditioners multiply and refine their machinery to give maximum control of the organism and the environment (I have not heard of any dramatic discoveries, but perhaps they have escaped me). On the other hand, the most interesting psychology in recent years has certainly come from animal naturalists, e.g., pecking order, territoriality, learning to control aggression, language of the bees, overcrowding among rats, trying to talk to dolphins

On a fair judgment, both contrasting approaches give positive results. The logical scientific problem that arises is, What is there in the nature of things that makes a certain method, or even moral attitude, work well or poorly in a given case? This question is not much studied. Every scientist seems to know what "the" scientific method is.

Another contrast of style, extremely relevant at present, is that between Big Science and old-fashioned shoestring science. There is plenty of research, with corresponding technology, that can be done only by Big Science; yet much, and perhaps most, of science will always be shoestring science, for which it is absurd to use the fancy and expensive equipment that has gotten to be the fashion.

Consider urban medicine. The problem, given a shortage of doctors and facilities, is how to improve the level of mass health, the vital statistics, and yet to practice medicine, which aims at the maximum possible health for each person. Perhaps the most efficient use of Big Science technology for the general health would be compulsory biennial checkups—as we inspect cars—for early diagnosis and to forestall chronic conditions with accumulating costs. Then an excellent machine would be a total diagnostic bus to visit the neighborhoods, as we do chest X-rays. On the other hand, for actual treatment and especially for convalescence, the evidence seems to be that small personalized hospitals are best. And to revive family practice, maybe the right idea is to offer a doctor a splendid suite in a public housing project.

Our contemporary practice makes little sense. We have expensive technology stored in specialists' offices and big hospitals, really unavailable for mass use in the neighborhoods; yet every individual, even if he is quite rich, finds it almost impossible to get attention to himself as an individual whole organism in his setting. He is sent from specialist to specialist and exists as a bag of symptoms and a file of test scores.

In automating there is an analogous dilemma of how to cope with masses of people and get economies of scale, without losing the individual at great consequent human and economic cost. A question of immense importance for the immediate future is, Which functions should be automated or organized to use business machines, and which should not? This question also is not getting asked, and the present disposition is that the sky is the limit for extraction, refining, manufacturing, processing, packaging, transportation, clerical work, ticketing, transactions, information retrieval, recruitment, middle management, evaluation, diagnosis, instruction, and even research and invention. Whether the machines can do all these kinds of jobs and more is partly an empirical question, but it also partly depends on what is meant by doing a job. Very often, e.g., in college admissions, machines are acquired for putative economics (which do not eventuate); but the true reason is that an overgrown and over-centralized organization cannot be administered without them. The technology conceals the essential trouble, e.g., that there is no community of scholars and students are treated like things. The function is badly performed, and finally the system breaks down anyway. I doubt that enterprises in which interpersonal relations are important are suited to much programming.

But worse, what can happen is that the real function of the enterprise is subtly altered so that it is suitable for the mechanical system. (E.g., "information retrieval" is taken as an adequate re-placement for critical scholarship.) Incommensurable factors, individual differences, the local context, the weighting of evidence are quietly overlooked though they may be of the essence. The system, with its subtly transformed purposes, seems to run very smoothly; it is productive, and it is more and more out of line with the nature of things and the real problems. Meantime it is geared in with other enterprises of society, e.g., major public policy may depend on welfare or unemployment statistics which, as they are tabulated, are blind to the actual lives of poor families. In such a case, the particular system may not break down; the whole society may explode.

I need hardly point out that American society is peculiarly liable to the corruption of inauthenticity, busily producing phony prod-ucts. It lives by public relations, abstract ideals, front politics, show-business communications, mandarin credentials. It is pre-eminently overtechnologized. And computer technologists espe-cially suffer the euphoria of being in a new and rapidly expanding field. It is so astonishing that the robot can do the job at all or seem to do it, that it is easy to blink at the fact that he is doing it badly or isn't really doing quite that job.

DECENTRALIZATION
The current political assumption is that scientists and inventors, and even social scientists, are "value-neutral," but their discoveries are "applied" by those who make decisions for the nation. Counter to this, I have been insinuating a kind of Jeffersonian democracy or guild socialism, that scientists and inventors and other workmen are responsible for the uses of the work they do, and ought to be com-petent to judge these uses and have a say in deciding them. They usually are competent. To give a striking example, Ford assembly line workers, according to Harvey Swados, who worked with them, are accurately critical of the glut of cars, but they have no way to vent their dissatisfactions with their useless occupation except to leave nuts and bolts to rattle in the body.

My bias is also pluralistic. Instead of the few national goals of a few decision-makers, I propose that there are many goods of many activities of life, and many professions and other interest groups each with its own criteria and goals that must be taken into account.

A society that distributes power widely is superficially conflictful but fundamentally stable.

Research and development ought to be widely decentralized, the national fund for them being distributed through thousands of centers of initiative and decision. This would not be chaotic. We seem to have forgotten that for four hundred years Western science majestically progressed with no central direction whatever, yet with exquisite international coordination, little duplication, almost nothing getting lost, in constant communication despite slow facilities. The reason was simply that all scientists wanted to get on with the same enterprise of testing the boundaries of knowledge, and they relied on one another.

What is as noteworthy is that something similar holds also in invention and innovation, even in recent decades when there has been such a concentration of funding and apparent concentration of opportunity. The majority of big advances have still come from independents, partnerships, and tiny companies. (Evidence published by the Senate Subcommittee on Antitrust and Monopoly, May 1965.) To name a few, jet engines, xerography, automatic transmission, cellophane, air-conditioning, quick freeze, antibiotics, and tranquilizers. The big technological teams must have disadvantages that outweigh their advantages, like lack of single-mindedness, poor communications, awkward scheduling. Naturally, big corporations have taken over the innovations, but the Senate evidence is that 90 percent of the government subsidy has gone for last-stage development for production, which they ought to have paid out of their own pockets.

We now have a theory that we have learned to learn, and that we can program technical progress, directed by a central planning board. But this doesn't make it so. The essence of the new still seems to be that nobody has thought of it, and the ones who get ideas are those in direct contact with the work. *Too precise* a preconception of what is wanted discourages creativity more than it channels it; and bureaucratic memoranda from distant directors don't help. This is especially true when, as at present, so much of the preconception of what is wanted comes from desperate political anxiety in emergencies. Solutions that emerge from such an attitude rarely strike out on new paths, but rather repeat traditional thinking with new gimmicks; they tend to compound the problem. A price-less advantage of widespread decentralization is that it engages more minds, and more mind, instead of a few panicky (or greedy) corporate minds.

A homespun advantage of small groups, according to the Senate testimony, is that co-workers can talk to one another, without schedules, reports, clock-watching, and face-saving.

An important hope from decentralizing science is to develop knowledgeable citizens, and provide not only a bigger pool of scientists and inventors but also a public better able to protect itself and know how to judge the enormous budgets asked for.   The safety of the environment is too important to be left to scientists, even ecologists.   During the last decades of the nineteenth century and the first decade of the twentieth, the heyday of public faith in the beneficent religion of science and invention, say from Pasteur and Huxley to Edison and the Wright Brothers, philosophers of science had a vision of a "scientific way of life," one in which people would be objective, respectful of evidence, accurate, free of super-stition and taboo, immune to irrational authority, experimental. All would be well, is the impression one gets from Thomas Huxley, if everybody knew the splendid Ninth Edition of the *Encyclopaedia Britannica* with its articles by Darwin and Clerk Maxwell. Veblen put his faith in the modesty and matter-of-factness of engineers to govern.   Sullivan and Frank Lloyd Wright spoke for an austere functionalism and respect for the nature of materials and industrial processes.   Patrick Geddes thought that new technology would finally get us out of the horrors of the Industrial Revolution and produce good communities.   John Dewey devised a system of education to rear pragmatic and experimental citizens to be at home in the new technological world rather than estranged from it. Now fifty years later, we are in the swamp of a scientific and technological environment and there are more scientists alive, etc., etc. But the mention of the "scientific way of life" seems like black humor.

Many of those who have grown up since 1945 and have never seen any other state of science and technology assume that rationalism itself is totally evil and dehumanizing. It is probably more signi-ficant than we like to think that they go in for astrology and the Book of Changes, as well as inducing psychedelic dreams by technological means. Jacques Ellul, a more philosophic critic, tries to show that technology is necessarily over-controlling, standardizing, and voraciously inclusive, so that there is no place for freedom. But I doubt that any of this is intrinsic to science and technology. The crude history has been, rather, that they have fallen willingly under the dominion of money and power. Like Christianity or communism, the scientific way of life has never been tried.

To satisfy the 4 March dissenters, to break the military-industrial corporations and alter the priorities of the budget, would be to restructure the American economy almost to a revolutionary extent. But to meet the historical crisis of science at present, for science and technology to become prudent, ecological, and decentralized, requires a change that is even more profound, a kind of religious transformation. Yet there is nothing untraditional in what I have proposed; prudence, ecology, and decentralization are indeed the high tradition of science and technology. Thus the closest analogy I can think of is the Protestant Reformation, a change of moral allegiance, liberation from the Whore of Babylon, return to the pure faith.

Science has long been the chief orthodoxy of modern times and has certainly been badly corrupted, but the deepest flaw of the affluent societies that has alienated the young is not, finally, their imperialism, economic injustice, or racism, bad as these are, but their nauseating phoniness, triviality, and wastefulness, the cultural and moral scandal that Luther found when he went to Rome in 1510. And precisely science, which should have been the wind of truth to clear the air, has polluted the air, helped to brainwash, and provided weapons for war. I doubt that most young people today have even heard of the ideal of the dedicated researcher, truculent and incorruptible, and unrewarded, for instance the "German scientist" that Sinclair Lewis described in *Arrowsmith*. Such a figure is no longer believable. I don't mean, of course, that he doesn't exist; there must be thousands of him, just as there were good priests in 1510.

The analogy to the Reformation is even more exact if we consider the school system, from educational toys and Head Start up through the universities. This system is manned by the biggest horde of monks since the time of Henry VIII. It is the biggest industry in the country. I have heard the estimate that 40 percent of the national product is in the Knowledge Business. It is mostly hocus-pocus. Yet the belief of parents in this institution is quite delusional and school diplomas are in fact the only entry to licensing and hiring in every kind of job. The abbots of this system are the chiefs of science, e.g., the National Science Foundation, who talk about reform but work to expand the school budgets, step up the curriculum, and inspire the endless catechism of tests.

These abuses are international, as the faith is. For instance, there is no essential difference between the military-industrial or the school system of the Soviet Union and the United States. There are important differences in way of life and standard of living, but the abuses of technology are very similar: pollution, excessive urbanization, destruction of the biosphere, weaponry, and disastrous foreign aid. Our protesters naturally single out our own country, and the United States is the most powerful country, but the corruption we are speaking of is not specifically American nor even capitalist; it is a disease of modern times.

But the analogy is to the Reformation, it is not to primitive Christianity or some other primitivism, the abandonment of technological civilization. There is indeed much talk about the doom of Western civilization, and a few Adamites actually do retire into the hills; but for the great mass of mankind, and myself, that's not where it's at. There is not the slightest interruption to the universalizing of Western civilization, including most of its delusions, into the so-called Third World. (If the atom bombs go off, however?)

Naturally the exquisitely interesting question is whether or not this Reformation will occur, how to make it occur, against the entrenched world-wide system of corrupt power that is continually aggrandizing itself. I don't know. In my analogy I have deliberately been choosing the date 1510, Luther in Rome, rather than 1517 when, in the popular story, he nailed his Theses on the cathedral door. There are everywhere contradictory signs and dilemmas. The new professional and technological class is more and more entangled in the work, statuses, and rewards of the system, and yet this same class, often the very same people, are more and more protestant. On the other hand, the dissident young, who are unequivocally for radical change, are so alienated from occupation, function, knowledge, or even concern, that they often seem to be simply irrelevant to the underlying issues of modern times. The monks keep "improving" the schools and getting bigger budgets to do so, yet it is clear that high schools will be burned down, twelve-year-olds will play truant in droves, and the taxpayers are already asking what goes on and voting down the bonds.

The interlocking of technologies and all other institutions makes it almost impossible to reform policy in any part; yet this very interlocking that renders people powerless, including the decision-makers, creates a remarkable resonance and chain reaction if any determined group, or even determined individual, exerts force. In the face of overwhelmingly collective operations like the space exploration, the average man must feel that local or grassroots efforts are worthless, there is no science but Big Science, and no administration but the State. And yet there is a powerful surge of localism, populism, and community action, as if people were determined to be free even if it makes no sense. A mighty empire is stood off by a band of peasants, and *neither* can win—this is even more remarkable than if David beats Goliath; it means that neither principle is historically adequate. In my opinion, these dilemmas and impasses show that we are on the eve of a transformation of conscience.

15

THE POWER TO DESTROY,
THE POWER TO CREATE

ECOLOGY ACTION EAST

The Power to Destroy

The power of this society to destroy has reached a scale unprecedented in the history of humanity—and this power is being used, almost systematically, to work an insensate havoc upon the entire world of life and its material bases.

In nearly every region, air is being befouled, waterways polluted, soil washed away, the land desiccated, and wildlife destroyed. Coastal areas and even the depths of the sea are not immune to widespread pollution. More significantly in the long run, basic biological cycles such as the carbon cycle and nitrogen cycle, upon which all living things (including humans) depend for the maintenance and renewal of life, are being distorted to the point of irreversible damage. The wanton introduction of radioactive wastes, long-lived pesticides, lead residues, and thousands of toxic or potentially toxic chemicals in food, water, and air; the expansion of cities into vast urban belts, with dense concentrations of populations comparable in size to entire nations; the rising din of background noise; the stresses created by congestion, mass living, and mass manipulation; the immense accumulations of garbage, refuse, sewage, and industrial wastes; the congestion of highways and city streets with vehicular traffic; the profligate destruction of precious raw materials; the scarring of the earth by real estate speculators, mining and lumbering barons, and highway construction bureaucrats—all, have wreaked a damage in a single generation that exceeds the damage inflicted by thousands

Reprinted by permission of Ecology Action East, a writing collective, from the January 1970 issue of *Rat*.

of years of human habitation on this planet. If this tempo of destruction is borne in mind, it is terrifying to speculate about what lies ahead in the generation to come.

The essence of the ecological crisis in our time is that this society —more than any other in the past—is literally undoing the work of organic evolution. It is a truism to say that humanity is part of the fabric of life. It is perhaps more important at this late stage to emphasize that humanity depends critically upon the complexity and variety of life, that human well-being and survival rest upon a long evolution of organisms into increasingly complex and interdependent forms. The development of life into a complex web, the elaboration of primal animals and plants into highly varied forms, has been the precondition for the evolution and survival of humanity itself and for a harmonized relationship between humanity and nature.

Technology and Population

If the past generation has witnessed a despoliation of the planet that exceeds all the damage inflicted by earlier generations, little more than a generation may remain before the destruction of the environment becomes irreversible. For this reason, we must look at the roots of the ecological crisis with ruthless honesty. Time is running out and the remaining decades of the twentieth century may well be the last opportunity we will have to restore the balance between humanity and nature.

Do the roots of the ecological crisis lie in the development of technology? Technology has become a convenient target for bypassing the deep-seated social conditions that make machines and technical processes harmful.

How convenient it is to forget that technology has served not only to subvert the environment but also to improve it. The Neolithic Revolution which produced the most harmonious period between nature and postpaleolithic humanity was above all a technological revolution. It was this period that brought to humanity the arts of agriculture, weaving, pottery, the domestication of animals, the discovery of the wheel, and many other key advances. True, there are techniques and technological attitudes that are entirely destructive of the balance between humanity and nature. Our responsibilities are to separate the promise of technology—its creative potential—

from the capacity of technology to destroy. Indeed, there is no such word as "technology" that presides over all social conditions and relations; there are different technologies and attitudes toward technology, some of which are indispensable to restoring the balance, others of which have contributed profoundly to its destruction. What humanity needs is not a wholesale discarding of advanced technologies, but a sifting, indeed a further development of technology along ecological principles that will contribute to a new harmonization of society and the natural world.

Do the roots of the ecological crisis lie in population growth? This thesis is the most disquieting, and in many ways the most sinister, to be advanced by ecology action movements in the United States. Here, an *effect* called "population growth," juggled around on the basis of superficial statistics and projections, is turned into a *cause*. A problem of secondary proportions at the present time is given primacy, thus obscuring the fundamental reasons for the ecological crisis.   True, if present economic, political and social conditions prevail, humanity will in time overpopulate the planet and by sheer weight of numbers turn into a pest in its own global habitat.   There is something obscene, however, about the fact that an effect, "population growth," is being given primacy in the ecological crisis by a nation which has little more than 7 percent of the world's population, wastefully devours more than 50 percent of the world's resources, and is currently engaged in the depopulation of an Oriental people that has lived for centuries in sensitive balance with its environment.

We must pause to look more carefully into the population problem, touted so widely by the white races of North America and Europe—races that have wantonly exploited the peoples of Asia, Africa, Latin America, and the South Pacific. The exploited have delicately advised their exploiters that what they need are not contraceptive devices, armed "liberators," and Prof. Paul R. Ehrlich to resolve their population problems; rather, what they need is a fair return on the immense resources that were plundered from their lands by North America and Europe. To balance these accounts is more of a pressing need at the present time than to balance birth rates and death rates. The peoples of Asia, Africa, Latin America, and the South Pacific can justly point out that their American "advisors" have shown the world how to despoil a virgin continent in less than a century and have added the words "built-in obsolescence" to the vocabulary of humanity.

This much is clear: when large labor reserves were needed during the Industrial Revolution of the early nineteenth century to man factories and depress wages, population growth was greeted enthusiastically by the new industrial bourgeoisie. And the growth of population occurred despite the fact that, owing to long working hours and grossly overcrowded cities, tuberculosis, cholera, and other diseases were pandemic in Europe and the United States. If birth rates exceeded death rates at this time, it was not because advances in medical care and sanitation had produced any dramatic decline in human mortality; rather, the excess of birth rates over death rates can be explained by the destruction of preindustrial family forms, village institutions, mutual aid, and stable, traditional patterns of life at the hands of capitalist "enterprise." The decline in social morale ushered in by the horrors of the factory system, the degradation of traditional agrarian peoples into grossly exploited proletarians and urban dwellers, produced a concomitantly irresponsible attitude toward the family and the begetting of children. Sexuality became a refuge from a life of toil on the same order as the consumption of cheap gin; the new proletariat reproduced children, many of whom were never destined to survive into adulthood, as mindlessly as it drifted into alcoholism. Much the same process occurred when the villages of Asia, Africa, and Latin America were sacrificed on the holy altar of imperialism.

Today, the bourgeoisie "sees" things differently. The roseate years of "free enterprise" and "free labor" are waning before an era of monopoly, cartels, state-controlled economies, institutionalized forms of labor mobilization (trade unions), and automatic or cybernetic machinery. Large reserves of unemployed labor are no longer needed to meet the needs of capital expansion, and wages are largely negotiated rather than left to the free play of the labor market. From a need, idle labor reserves have now turned into a threat to the stability of a managed bourgeois economy. The logic of this new "perspective" found its most terrifying expression in German fascism. To the Nazis, Europe was already "overpopulated" in the thirties and the "population problem" was "solved" in the gas chambers of Auschwitz. The same logic is implicit in many of the new-Malthusian arguments that masquerade as ecology today. Let there be no mistake about this conclusion.

Sooner or later the mindless proliferation of human beings will have to be arrested, but population control will either be initiated by "social controls" (authoritarian or racist methods and eventually by systematic genocide) or by a libertarian, ecologically oriented society (a society that develops a new balance with nature out of a reverence for life). Modern society stands before these mutually exclusive alternatives and a choice must be made without dissimulation. Ecology action is fundamentally social action. Either we will go directly to the social roots of the ecological crisis today or we will be deceived into an era of totalitarianism.

Ecology and Society

The basic conception that humanity must dominate and exploit nature stems from the domination and exploitation of man by man. Indeed, this conception goes back earlier to a time when men began to dominate and exploit women in the patriarchal family. From that point onward, human beings were increasingly regarded as mere resources, as objects instead of subjects. The hierarchies, classes, propertied forms, and statist institutions that emerged with social domination were carried over conceptually into humanity's relationship with nature. Nature too became increasingly regarded as a mere resource, an object, a raw material to be exploited as ruthlessly as slaves on a latifundium. This "world-view" permeated not only the official culture of hierarchical society; it became the way in which slaves, serfs, industrial workers and women of all social classes began to view themselves. As embodied in the "work ethic," in a morality based on denial and renunciation, in a mode of behavior based on the sublimation of erotic desires, and in other worldly outlooks (be they European or Asian), the slaves, serfs, workers, and female half of humanity were taught to police themselves, to fashion their own chains, to close the doors on their own prison cells.

If the world view of hierarchical society is beginning to wane today, this is mainly because the enormous productivity of modern technology has opened a new vision: the possibility of material abundance, an end to scarcity, and an era of free time (so-called "leisure time") with minimal toil. Our society is becoming permeated by a tension between "what-is" and "what-could-be," a tension exacerbated by the irrational, inhuman exploitation and destruction of the earth and its inhabitants. The greatest impediment that obstructs a solution of this tension is the extent to which hierarchical society still fashions our outlook and actions. It is easier to take refuge in critiques of technology and population growth; to deal with an archaic, destructive social system as the premises on which all thinking must rest. Without shedding these premises, all discussions of ecological balance must remain palliative and self-defeating.

The Power to Create

By virtue of its unique cultural baggage, modern society—our profit-oriented bourgeois society—tends to exacerbate humanity's conflict with nature in a more critical fashion than preindustrial societies of the past. In bourgeois society, humans are not only turned into objects; they are turned into commodities; into objects explicitly designed for sale on the market place. Competition between human beings, qua commodities, becomes an end in itself, together with the production of utterly useless goods. Quality is turned into quantity, individual culture into mass culture, personal communication into mass communication. The natural environment is turned into a gigantic factory, the city into an immense market place; everything from a redwood forest to a woman's body has "a price." Everything is equatable in dollars-and-cents, be it a hallowed cathedral or individual honor. Technology ceases to be an extension of humanity; humanity becomes an extension of technology. The machine does not expand the power of the worker; the worker expands the power of the machine, indeed, he becomes a mere part of the machine.

Is it surprising, then, that this exploitative, degrading, quantified society pits humanity against itself and against nature on a more awesome scale than any other in the past?

Yes, we need change, but change so fundamental and far-reaching that even the concept of revolution and freedom must be expanded beyond all earlier horizons. No longer is it enough to speak of new techniques for conserving and fostering the natural environment; we must deal with the earth communally, as a human collectivity, without those trammels of private property that have distorted humanity's vision of life and nature since the breakup of tribal society. We must eliminate not only bourgeois hierachy, but hierarchy as such; not only the patriarchal family, but *all* modes of sexual and parental domination; not only the bourgeois class and propertied system, but *all* social classes and property; humanity must come into possession of itself, individually and collectively, so that all human beings attain control of their everyday lives. Our cities must be decentralized into communities, or ecocommunities, exquisitely and artfully tailored to the carrying capacity of the eco-systems in which they are located. Our technologies must be re-adapted and advanced into ecotechnologies, exquisitely and artfully adapted to make use of local energy sources and materials, with minimal or no pollution of the environment. We must recover a new sense of our needs—needs that foster a healthful life and express our individual proclivities, not "needs" dictated by the mass media. We must restore the human scale in our environment and in our social relations, replacing mediated by direct personal relations in the management of society. Finally, all modes of domination—social or personal—must be banished from our conceptions of ourselves, our fellow humans, and nature. The administration of humans must be replaced by the administration of things. The revolution we seek must encompass not only political institutions and economic relations, but consciousness, life style, erotic desires, and our inter-pretation of the meaning of life.

What is in the balance, here, is the age-long spirit and systems of domination and repression that have not only pitted human against human, but humanity against nature. The conflict between humanity and nature is an extension of the conflict between human and human. Unless the ecology movement encompasses the problem of domina-tion in all its aspects, it will contribute nothing toward eliminating the root causes of the ecological crisis of our time. If the ecology movement stops at mere reforms in pollution and conservation con-trol without dealing radically with the need for an expanded concept of revolution it will merely serve as a safety valve for the existing system of natural and human exploitation.

Goals

In some respects the ecology movement today is waging a delaying action against the rampant destruction of the environment. In other respects its most conscious elements are involved in a creative move-ment to totally revolutionize the social relations of humans to each other and of humanity to nature.

Although they closely interpenetrate, the two efforts should be distinguished from each other. Ecology Action East supports every effort to conserve the environment: to preserve clean air and water, to limit the use of pesticides and food additives, to reduce vehicular traffic in streets and on highways, to make cities more wholesome physically, to prevent radioactive wastes from seeping into the environment, to guard and expand wilderness areas and domains for wildlife, to defend animal species from human depredation.

But Ecology Action East does not deceive itself that such delaying actions constitute a solution to the fundamental conflict that exists between the present social order and the natural world. Nor can such delaying actions arrest the overwhelming momentum of the existing society for destruction.

This social order plays games with us. It grants long-delayed, piecemeal, and woefully inadequate reforms to deflect our energies and attention from larger acts of destruction. In a sense, we are "offered" a patch of redwood forest in exchange for the Cascades. Viewed in a larger perspective, this attempt to reduce ecology to a barter relationship does not rescue anything; it is a cheap *modus operandi* for trading away the greater part of the planet for a few islands of wilderness, for pocket parks in a devastated world of concrete.

Ecology Action East has two primary aims: one is to increase in the revolutionary movement the awareness that the most destructive and pressing consequences of our alienating, exploitative society is the environmental crisis, and that any truly revolutionary society must be built upon ecological precepts; the other is to create, in the minds of the millions of Americans who are concerned with the destruction of our environment, the consciousness that the principles of ecology, carried to their logical end, demand radical changes in our society and our way of looking at the world.

Ecology Action East takes its stand with the life-style revolution that, at its best, seeks an expanded consciousness of experience and human freedom. We seek the liberation of women, of children, of the gay people, of black people and colonial peoples, and of working people in all occupations as part of a growing social struggle against the age-old traditions and institutions of domination—traditions and institutions that have so destructively shaped humanity's attitude toward the natural world. We support libertarian communities and struggles for freedom wherever they arise; we take our stand with every effort to promote the spontaneous self-development of the young; we oppose every attempt to repress human sexuality, to deny humanity the eroticization of experience in all its forms. We join in all endeavors to foster a joyous artfulness in life and work: the promotion of crafts and quality production, the design of new ecocommunities and ecotechnologies, the right to experience on a daily basis the beauty of the natural world, the open, unmediated, sensuous pleasure that humans can give to each other, the growing reverence for the world of life.

In short, we hope for a revolution which will produce politically independent communities whose boundaries and populations will be defined by a new ecological consciousness; communities whose inhabitants will determine for themselves, within the framework of this new consciousness, the nature and level of their technologies, the forms taken by their social structures, world-views, life styles, expressive arts, and all the other aspects of their daily lives.

But we do not delude ourselves that this life-oriented world can be fully developed or even partially achieved in a death-oriented society. American society, as it is constituted today, is riddled with racism and sits astride the entire world, not only as a consumer of its wealth and resources, but as an obstacle to all attempts at self-determination at home and abroad. Its inherent aims are production for the sake of production, the preservation of hierarchy and toil on a world scale, mass manipulation and control by centralized, statist institutions. This kind of society is unalterably counterposed to a life-oriented world. If the ecology movement does not draw these conclusions from its efforts to conserve the natural environment, then conservation becomes mere obscurantism. If the ecology movement does not direct its main efforts toward a revolution in all areas of life—social as well as natural, political as well as personal, economic as well as cultural—then the movement will gradually become a safety valve of the established order.

It is our hope that groups like our own will spring up throughout the country, organized like ourselves on a humanistic, libertarian basis, engaged in mutual action and a spirit of cooperation based on mutual aid. It is our hope that they will try to foster a new ecological attitude not only toward nature but also toward humans: a conception of spontaneous, variegated relations within groups and between groups, within society and between individuals.

We hope that ecology groups will eschew all appeals to the "heads of government" and to international or national state institutions, the very criminals and political bodies that have materially contributed to the ecological crisis of our time. We believe the appeals must be made to the people and to their capacity for direct action that can get them to take control of their own lives and destinies. For only in this way can a society emerge without hierarchy and domination, a society in which each individual is the master of his or her own fate.

The great splits which divided human from human, humanity from nature, individual from society, town from country, mental from physical activity, reason from emotion, and generation from generation must now be transcended. The fulfillment of the age-old quest for survival and material security in a world of scarcity was once regarded as the precondition for freedom and a fully human life. To live we had to survive. As Brecht put it: "First feed the face, then give the moral."

The situation has now begun to change. The ecological crisis of our time has increasingly reversed this traditional maxim. Today, if we are to survive, we must begin to live. Our solutions must be commensurable with the scope of the problem, or else nature will take a terrifying revenge on humanity.

16

THE CARRYING CAPACITY OF OUR GLOBAL ENVIRONMENT: A LOOK AT THE ETHICAL ALTERNATIVES
JORGEN RANDERS AND DONELLA MEADOWS

> For which of you, intending to build a tower,
> sitteth not down first, and counteth the cost,
> whether he have sufficient to finish it?
>
> *Luke* 14:28

The main thesis of this paper is very simple: because our environment—the earth—is finite, growth of human population and industrialization cannot continue indefinitely. This is a simple and obvious fact, but its consequences pose an unprecedented challenge to mankind. The challenge lies in deciding on the ethical basis for making the trade-offs which will confront us in the near future—trade-offs which arise because in a limited world we cannot maximize everything for everyone.

1. THE ENVIRONMENT IS FINITE

It should be quite unnecessary to point out that our environment is finite. However, most considerations of the world's future tend to lose sight of this fact. Thus, it will be worthwhile to spend some time discussing the physical limitations of the earth—especially because it is not generally recognized that we are already quite close to several physical limitations which define the carrying capacity of our globe.

The authors are members of the System Dynamics Group of the A. P. Sloan School of Management at the Massachusetts Institute of Technology. Their computer models of global systems are part of the Club of Rome's "Project on the Predicament of Mankind." An earlier version of this article appeared in *Sloan Management Review* (Winter 1972). Copyright © 1972 by Jørgen Randers.

Agricultural Land

The quantity which is most obviously in limited supply on our earth is arable land. There are about 3.2 billion hectares of land suitable for agriculture on the earth. Approximately half of that land is under cultivation today. The remaining half will require immense capital costs to settle, clear, irrigate, or fertilize before it can produce food. The costs will be so high that the United Nations Food and Agriculture Organization, which is seeking desperately to stimulate greater food production, has decided that in order to expand food output it must rely on more intensive use of currently cultivated land, not on new land development.

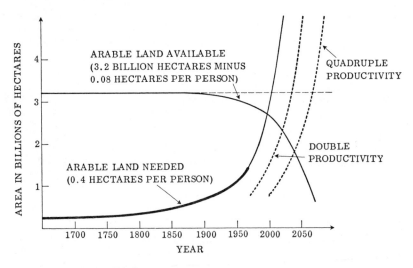

Fig. 1: Available and needed land area.

If we do decide to incur the costs to cultivate all possible arable land and to produce as much food as possible, how many people could we expect to feed? The lower curve in Figure 1 shows the amount of land *needed* to feed the growing world population, assuming that the present world average of 0.4 hectares per person is sufficient. (If we wanted to feed everyone at U.S. standards, we would require 0.9 hectares per person) The actual growth in population, and thus in land needed, from 1650 to 1970 is depicted with a heavy line; the projected growth at 2.1% per year after 1970 by a lighter line. The upper curve indicates the actual amount of arable land *available*. This line slopes downward because each additional person requires a certain amount of land (0.08 hectares assumed here) for housing, roads, waste disposal, power lines, and other uses which essentially "pave" land and make it unusable for farming.

The graph in Figure 1 tells us that, even with the optimistic assumption that we will utilize all possible land, we will still face a serious land shortage before the year 2000.

The graph also illustrates some very important facts about exponential growth within a limited space. First, it shows how we can move within a few years from a situation of great abundance to one of great scarcity. The human race has had an overwhelming excess of arable land for all of our history, and now within 30 years, or one population doubling time, we will be forced to deal with a sudden and serious shortage.

A second lesson to be learned from Figure 1 is that the exact numerical assumptions we make about the limits of the earth are essentially unimportant when we are faced with the inexorable progress of exponential growth. For example, we might assume that *no* arable land is taken for cities, roads, or other non-agricultural uses. In that case, the land available is constant, as shown by the horizontal dashed line, and the point at which the two curves cross is delayed by only about 10 years. Or we can suppose that we will double, or even quadruple the productivity of the land, through advances in agricultural technology. The effect of increasing productivity is shown by the dotted lines in Figure 1. Each doubling of productivity gains us just one population doubling time, or about 30 years.

Some people look to the sea to provide the extra food we will need as our population grows. But the total world fish catch in 1969 represented only a few percent of the world's caloric requirements, and the total catch in 1970 decreased from 1969. That was the first decrease since World War II, and it occurred in spite of increasing investment and technological developments in the fishing industry. Most experts agree that the world's fish banks have been over-exploited and that prospects are for further decline, not advances, in output from the sea. The seas thus cannot eliminate the constraints imposed on growth by limited land

Heat Release

We are faced with further obvious constraints in connection with natural resources like fresh water, metals, and fuels. Indications are that several of these will be in short supply even at higher prices within the next forty years, if present growth continues. However, it is argued that mining low grade ores and desalting the sea's water can alleviate these problems, and it may indeed be so, assuming that we can satisfy the enormous demands for energy that would result from such operations.

A consideration of the energy that will be necessary to meet man's growing needs leads us to a more subtle and much more fundamental physical limitation imposed by our environment. Even if we assume that we find the means to *generate* the energy needed—for instance, through controlled fusion—we are still faced with the fundamental thermodynamic fact that virtually all energy generated finally ends up as heat. An everyday example is the energy originally stored in the gas of your car. A significant part of this energy is immediately released as heat as it warms the engine and the radiator, because the engine is necessarily inefficient in converting the energy in the gas to useful motion of the wheels. But the point is that even the *useful* part of the energy finally is transferred to heat in the tires, the road, the brakes and ultimately in the surrounding air. On a larger scale we have the heat release from the condensation of distilled water in a desalination plant.

The final fate of the energy expended should not be confused with what is commonly called "thermal pollution," namely the waste heat produced locally at power plants in the generation of electric energy. The waste heat is due to inevitable inefficiencies in the generating process, and the consequent "thermal pollution" heats the environment, of course, but the point is that even the *useful* energy output from the power plant finally ends up as heat. This is so, regardless of whether the energy was generated by burning of coal or oil, or by nuclear reactions—and regardless of what the energy is being used for. It is theoretically impossible to avoid heat release if we want to consume energy. No technical gadgetry or scientific breakthrough will circumvent it.

The heat released from all of mankind's energy-using activities will begin to have worldwide climatic effects when the released amount reaches some appreciable fraction of the energy normally absorbed from the sun. Experts disagree on exactly what the fraction is. They do agree, however, that if we want to avoid major unpredictable changes in the climate there is a fundamental limit to the amount of energy we can consume on earth.

If worldwide energy consumption increases at 4% per year for another 130 years, we will at that point in time be releasing heat amounting to 1% of the incoming solar radiation—enough to increase the temperature of the atmosphere by an estimated 3/4°C. That may sound like an unimpressive figure, but on a worldwide basis it may amount to climatic upheavals like increased melting of the polar ice caps. Local weather perturbations may come much sooner. In just 30 years it is estimated that in the Los Angeles Basin heat released through energy consumption will be 18% of the normal incident solar energy of that area.

Pollution Absorption

A third limitation to population and industrial growth is our globe's finite absorptive capacity for pollution. Until quite recently our environment was considered essentially infinite. It seemed impossible that the use of soap for one's laundry or pesticides for one's roses could affect the workings of the world ecosystem. But after the death of Lake Erie, the global increase in atmospheric CO_2, and the prohibition in the U.S. of swordfish due to its content of mercury, it is becoming abundantly clear that our environment is only able to absorb and degrade a limited amount of emissions and waste every year. When we exceed this absorptive capacity, we not only cause pollutants to accumulate in nature, but we also run the risk of destroying the natural degradation processes themselves, and thus decreasing the future absorptive capacity. This general principle can be described in more practical terms. Discharging a small amount of waste into a pond will only slightly lower the water quality because the pond's microorganisms manage to degrade the pollution as it occurs. A higher, constant discharge rate will result in a lower but constant water quality. The absorptive capacity of the pond is exceeded, however, if we increase the discharge rate to the point where the absorbing microorganisms die because of oxygen depletion or accumulation of toxic wastes. When that happens, continued constant discharge to the pond will simply build up, making the water quality continually less.

Thus we realize that absorptive capacity—far from being a good in unlimited supply—is an extremely valuable, scarce resource, which in fact limits the total possible emissions from human activity.

2. THE PRESENT GLOBAL TREND: GROWTH

Growth in a Finite World

Having established the existence of purely physical limitations of our earth (and we have described here only a few of the many biological, physical, and social limits which exist), we may now ask whether mankind's present behavior takes into account their existence.

On a global scale we are presently experiencing an exponential growth in population and in what we will call capital—buildings, roads, cars, power plants, machinery, ships, etc. Some inevitable consequences of this growth are exponentially increasing demands for food and energy and also exponentially increasing emissions of pollution to the environment.

Since we know that there are upper limits to the supply of food and energy and also to the amount of pollution which can be absorbed by the environment, it seems obvious that the growth we are presently experiencing cannot continue indefinitely. More important, as we have already indicated, we will surpass several of these constraints within the next few generations.

Hence, we are led to ask: are there mechanisms in the world system as it is currently organized which will bring about a smooth shift from present growth trends to some other kind of acceptable behavior consistent with the world's finite capabilities? Or will the transition be relatively sudden and stressful?

These are the questions our group at M.I.T. set out to answer when we embarked on an effort to make a mathematical simulation model of population and capital growth in the world system.

The WORLD Model

Our model is a set of assumptions which relate world population, industry, pollution, agriculture and natural resources. The model explicitly represents the growth of population and industry as a function of the biological, political, economic, physical, and social factors which influence them. It also recognizes that population and industrial growth in turn feed back to alter each of those biological, political, economic, physical, or social factors.

The exponential growth of population and capital is inextricably linked with all our global problems—unemployment, starvation, disease, pollution, the threat of warfare, and resource shortages. All are influenced importantly by the dynamic interaction of population and capital. No attempt to understand our long-term options can succeed unless it is firmly based on an understanding of the relationships between these two forces and the ultimate limits to their growth.

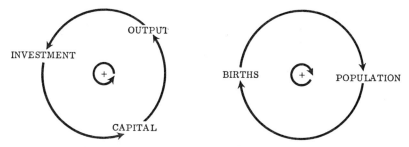

Fig. 2: The positive feedback loops governing the growth in population and capital.

Population and births constitute a positive feedback loop. If there are more people, there will be more births each year, and more births result in more people (Fig. 2). Wherever there is a dominant positive feedback loop of this form, exponential growth will be observed. Capital and investment constitute another positive feedback loop. Capital produces output of goods and services. Greater output, all else equal, results in a larger investment and thus in more capital. The interactions among population and capital determine the rate at which each of them grows. The interaction takes many forms (Fig. 3).

As a greater fraction of output is diverted from investment, the growth rate of capital decreases. Output may be diverted to consumption, to services, or to agricultural capital such as fertilizer, tractors, or irrigation ditches. As services increase, health and education improve, average lifetime becomes greater, deaths decrease, and population grows. Similarly, output diverted into agricultural capital results ultimately in more food and a higher average lifetime. The primary determinant of the fraction of output reinvested is the output per capita. Where production per capita is low, most of the

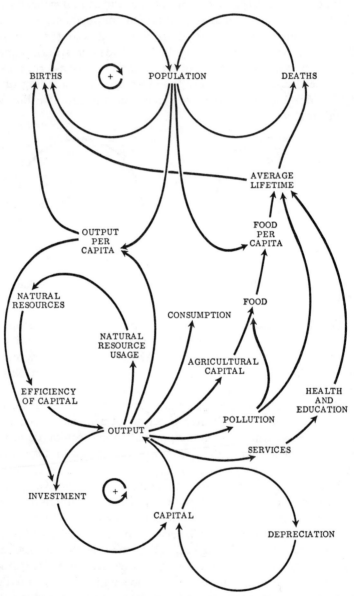

Fig. 3: Basic interactions between population growth and capital accumulation.

output must be diverted to consumption, services, and food. Those allocations reduce the rate of accumulation of the capital base and, at the same time, stimulate the growth of population. Population can increase much more easily than capital in traditional societies. Hence, output per capita remains low in these countries and they find it very difficult to achieve economic growth.

Output diverted into consumption subtracts capital from the system and does not generate future growth directly. Industrial output also leads to the depletion of natural resources. As natural resources decline, lower grade ores must be mined, and raw materials must be transported longer distances. Since more capital must be allocated to obtaining resources, the overall production efficiency of capital decreases, and the capital-output ratio goes down.

Output per capita is the single force acting here to slow the population explosion. As output per capita increases, the desired family size declines and birth control efficiency increases. The birth rate goes down (see Fig. 4) and the population growth rate typically decreases. The influence of this is accelerated somewhat by the fact that as death rates decline there is a further decrease in desired family size. A large portion of the world's parents bear children primarily as a source of support in their old age. If there is a high mortality rate, parents must bear three or four sons to ensure that one will live. Thus, as the perceived death rate decreases, birth rates also decline. Economic output has one additional impact. Output leads to the generation of pollution. Pollution may decrease food production and also decrease the average lifetime.

Most global problems have important roots in this simple set of interactions.[1] There are four advantages to collecting our assumptions about the world into a formal model of this sort (see Fig. 5). First, by listing the assumed interrelations explicitly, they are readily available for criticism and improvement by those with knowledge in each specific problem area. Second, it is possible, with the aid of a computer, to follow how this set of assumptions about the world system will behave as a function of time. Third, it is also possible through such simulation to test the effect of some change in the basic assumptions, and hence one may investigate which interrelations are critical to the system's behavior (and thus deserve close study) and which are not. And fourth, the model permits one to study the effects of policies believed to improve the behavior of the system.

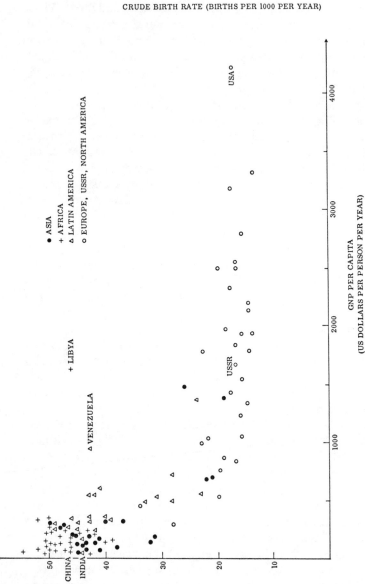

Fig. 4: The relationship oetween birth rate and GNP per capita. *Source of data: USAID, Population Program Assistance, AID Bureau for Technical Assistance, Office of Population, 1970.*

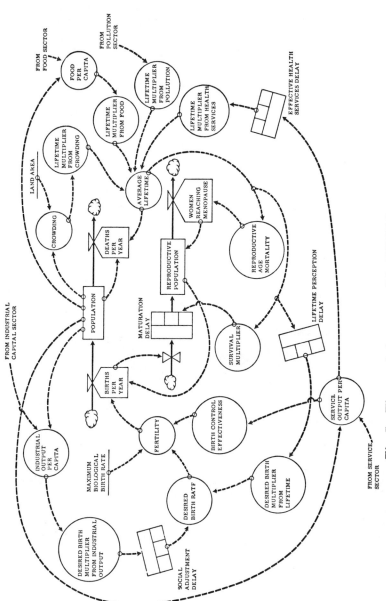

Fig. 5: The population sector of the WORLD model.

The computer is necessary only because the calculations necessary to consider all the inter-connections between variables are very tedious and time-consuming.

Figures 6, 7, 8, 9 and 10 show the differing behavior resulting from different policies with respect to natural resource usage, pollution control and allocation of capital investment.

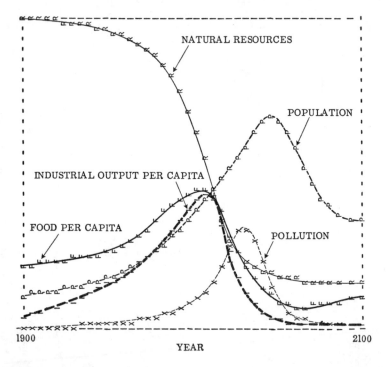

Fig. 6: The basic world model behavior, showing the tendency of population and industrialization to rise above the ultimate carrying capacity of the earth and then to collapse. This behavior mode is caused by the many time-delays in the natural feedback processes which oppose population and industrial growth. In this figure, growth is suppressed by the depletion of natural resources.

Please note: These computer simulations are not exact numerical predictions of the future. Rather they provide *qualitative* projections of possible future trends. The precise timing of events is thus less significant than the *changes* in behavior among simulations. The years are given only as approximate reference points.

Continued Growth leads to Collapse

Simulation runs like these have led us to conclude that there are no mechanisms currently existent that will bring the present growth to a smooth stop when we reach the maximum level consistent with our finite environment.

Of course this does not mean that growth will not stop. It only means that, instead of an orderly transition to some feasible final state, the human population is most likely to over-shoot the physical limitations of the earth and then be forced into a traumatic decline

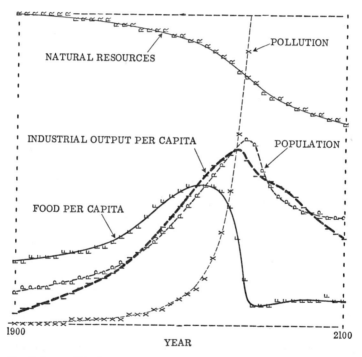

Fig. 7: It is possible that technological advances, such as recycling and new seabed discoveries, would avert the resource crisis shown in the previous figure. Here we simulate that possibility by doubling the amount of available resource reserves and reducing the natural consumption rate by 75% in 1971. The result is another collapse of population and industry, caused this time by a breakdown in pollution absorption.

See cautionary note under Fig. 6 concerning the interpretation of these computer simulations.

back down to some level of population and industrialization which can be supported by our physical environment—which by then will be sorely depleted. For once we exceed any natural constraint, tremendous pressures will develop to halt growth. If it so happens that we begin by exceeding the absorptive capacity for pollution, the pressures will take the form of increases in death rates due to impurities in food, water and air, decreases in crops and fish catches due to similar reductions in plant and animal life, and significant

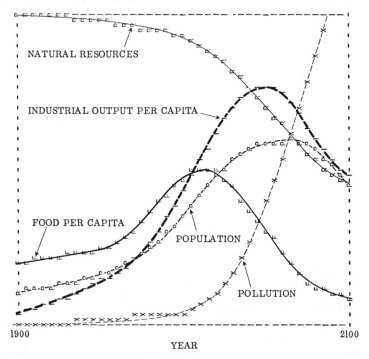

Fig. 8: In an attempt to avoid a pollution crisis, the normal rate of pollution generation is reduced by 50 percent in 1971. The 5 percent increase in capital investment needed for the pollution control is financed by a reduction in private and public consumption, and resource usage is as in Fig. 7. As a result of the pollution control, the population growth rate is reduced somewhat by lack of food before the pollution crisis occurs again, somewhat later than in Fig. 7.

See cautionary note under Fig. 6 concerning the interpretation of these computer simulations.

reduction in the effectiveness of investment, due to high costs of controlling the high pollution in all *input*-factors. These pressures will mount until population and industrialization finally involuntarily start to decline, and the pressures will only cease when levels are reached which are consistent with the supporting capacity of the physical environment.

If we attempt to continue growth by removing one set of pressures—for instance, by increasing food output with fertilizers and

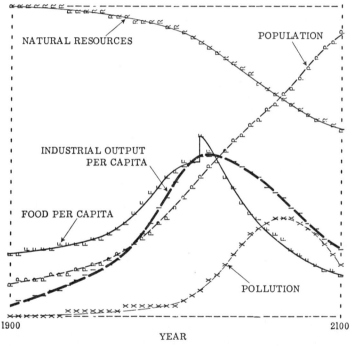

Fig. 9: Maintaining resource and pollution policies as in Fig. 8, an attempt is made at the point where food per capita starts to fall to avoid this decline by doubling the resources allocated to food production (at the expense of industrial production). The short-term effect is to increase per capita food availability significantly for a 20 year period. The long-term result of this policy is a population which is much larger (due to more food and less industrial pollution) and materially much poorer than in Fig. 8, but at the same subsistence food level.

See cautionary note under Fig. 6 concerning the interpretation of these computer simulations.

high-yield grains—we alleviate the situation only until we encounter the next constraint. If we manage to remove that constraint, we will soon reach another one. The situation is somewhat like growing taller in a room with infinitely many ceilings: one does not *solve* the problem by removing the first ceiling upon contact, nor by removing the second, third etc. The only solution to growth in a finite space is an end to growth. The end to growth can be deliberate and controlled, or it can be involuntary and uncontrollable.

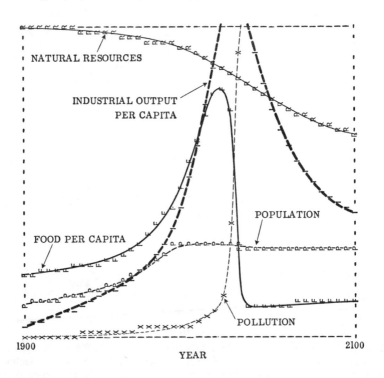

Fig. 10: Maintaining the resource and pollution policies as in Figure 8, the population is assumed to be stabilized in 1990. The short-term result is a significant increase in per capita material wealth and food. The rate of industrialization is high because of the low need for additional food, however, and results in a pollution crisis after a short period of time.

See cautionary note under Fig. 6 concerning the interpretation of these computer simulations.

3. THE ETHICAL BASIS FOR ACTION

The Short-Term Objective Function

Thus we are faced with the fact that continuation of current growth practices will inevitably lead us to some sort of collapse, with a subsequent decrease in the cultural and economic options of the human race. If this seems undesirable, one is naturally led to ask: What shall we do?

It is important to realize that our answer to this question is completely dependent on our choice of criteria for what is "good." If we do not know what we want to obtain, if we don't know our "objective function," it is meaningless to try to decide what to do in a given situation. If our objective is to maximize the benefits of the people alive today, our course of action will be quite different from our actions if the goal is to maximize the benefits of all people who are going to live on our planet over the next 200 years.

At least in principle (and it is clear that this is far from being a realized principle) present human behavior is guided by the general idea that all people alive *today* are equally important and that the objective function is to maximize the total current benefits for all these people. We have decided in the Western democracies that this objective is best served by letting each individual be free to pursue his own interest. It is assumed, very simply, that if every citizen and institution in our society acts to maximize his own position in the short term, the society as a whole will benefit.

This acceptance of "the Invisible Hand" has, however, introduced a strong emphasis on short-term benefits in our societies. When an action will bring both benefits and costs over time, individuals use the concept of net present value and discount the future implications so that they can determine whether an action is profitable—and hence should be taken. The result of this procedure is that we assign essentially zero value to anything happening more than twenty years from now. In other words, actions will be taken although their cost to society twenty years hence is going to be enormous—just because the benefits are larger than the costs in the short run (e.g., over the next decade).

If we choose to adhere strictly to the objective of maximizing the short-term rewards of the present generation, there are in fact no long-term environmental trade-offs to be made. In this case we would simply continue as before, maximizing the current benefits and neglecting any future costs which will result.

The question about use or non-use of DDT, for example, would be easily resolved. The fact that 1.3 billion people today can live in safety from malaria due to DDT would strongly outweigh the costs—for instance, in the form of inedible fish—inflicted upon future generations though our continued use of the chemical.

It is only this short-term objective function which can lead to the currently accepted conclusion that the value of an additional human being is infinite. The severe restrictions his existence will impose on the choices and perhaps even the lives of future generations—because of his consumption of non-renewable natural resources and his contribution to the destruction of the life support system of the globe—is completely neglected.

Thus we see that adherence to the short-term objective function resolves very simply all trade-offs between current benefits and future cost. Of course we will be left with the more usual trade-offs among people alive today—for instance, the choice between denying the firm upstream freedom to dump waste in the river and denying those who live downstream pure drinking water. But these short-term conflicts are not our concern here, because we *do* have mechanisms in our society to resolve conflicts between two people alive today.

We do *not* have, however, mechanisms or even moral guidelines for resolving conflicts between the current population and the people of the future. And at the same time our simulation model demonstrates that the present preoccupation with what seems pleasant or profitable in the short run will fuel the growth which is finally going to make the world overshoot some physical constraint, forcing us—and especially our descendants—into a period of abrupt and significant changes.

The Long-Term Objective Function

It is, however, possible to change the objective function—in the same way that Christianity changed the objective of man from selfish gratification to consideration for the welfare of all people living at the same point in time.

We could, for example, adopt as our cardinal philosophy the rule that no man or institution in our society may take any action which decreases the economic and social options of those who will live on the planet over the next 100 years. Perhaps only organized religion has the moral force to bring such a change, or perhaps it could come from an enlightened and widespread change in public education.

We are basically facing only one ethical question in the impending global crisis. Should we continue to let our actions be guided by the short-term objective function, or should we adopt a longer-term perspective? In other words, what time horizon should we use, when comparing the costs and benefits of current actions?

We feel that the moral and ethical leaders of our societies should adopt the goal of increasing the time-horizon implicit in mankind's activities—that is, introducing the longer-term objective function which maximizes the benefit of those living today, subject to the constraint that it does not decrease the economic and social options of those who will inherit this globe, our children and grandchildren.

This goal is of course not completely foreign to contemporary society. People in general feel some responsibility for the lives of their children, and the long-term objective function seems to be the value implicit in the actions of conservationists. However, ultimately it must be present in *all* our activities—as it is said to have been in the native tribes of Sierra Leone, where nothing could be done to the jungle which would leave it unfit for the use of *all* future generations.

4. GLOBAL EQUILIBRIUM—A DESIRABLE POSSIBILITY

A Lasting Solution

Assuming that we accept the long-term objective function as the guideline for our actions, what can we do about the approaching collision between our growing societies and the physical limits of the earth?

As soon as we are committed to the creation of a long-term, viable world system, our most important task becomes to avoid the trauma connected with actually exceeding any of the globe's limitations— food production capability, pollution absorption capacity, or resource supply. This can only be done through a deliberate decision to stop physical growth. We must engineer a smooth transition to a non-growth situation—a "global equilibrium," a steady state— which is in accordance with our globe's physical limits. We must ourselves halt the growth by developing and employing legal, economic or religious pressures as substitutes for those pressures which would otherwise have been exerted by nature to halt the uncontrolled growth.

By starting now we may still be able to *choose* the set of pressures we prefer to employ in stopping population and capital growth. We cannot avoid pressures. As we continue growing, nature will supply counter forces—forces which *will* rise until growth stops. However, a deliberate choice of the least objectionable counter-forces is likely to leave intact many more of our fundamental, long-term objectives than is the blind and random action of natural forces such as starvation or social breakdown.

The first requirement for a viable steady state is a constant level of population and capital—that is, the number of people and physical objects must remain constant. A second requirement is equally important. Since we want to create a system capable of existing for a long time, the state of global equilibrium must be characterized by minimal consumption of non-renewable materials and by minimal emissions of non-degradable waste. In this way we can maximize the time before resources are depleted and avoid a critical load on the environment.

One possible way of achieving such an equilibrium society is depicted in Fig. 11. Many different possible paths to global equilibrium exist, however, and the one to choose depends on our objectives. For instance: Do we want many people at a low material standard of living or few at a higher? Do we want fancy food or just the minimum daily ration of calories, protein and vitamins?

In this equilibrium mode of human civilization, science and technology will be busily developing ways of constructing products which last very long, do not emit pollution, and can be easily recycled. Competition among individual firms may very well continue, the only difference being that the total market for material goods will no longer expand. Emphasis will be on repair and maintenance rather than on new production.

Although global equilibrium implies non-growth of all *physical* activities, this need not be the case for cultural activities. Freed from preoccupation with material goods, people may throw their energy into development of the arts and sciences, into the enjoyment of unspoiled nature, and into meaningful interactions with their fellow man.

The Distribution of Wealth and Responsibility

Stopping the population explosion is becoming increasingly more accepted as an important task to be accomplished as fast as possible, but what about stopping physical growth? Can we really suggest a deliberate restriction of our production, leaving the world's poor in their present miserable situation?

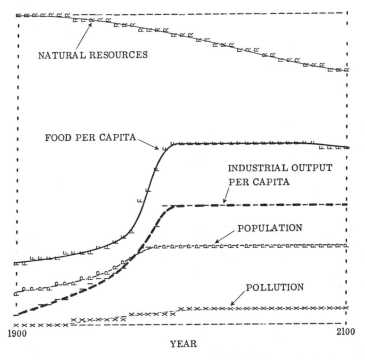

NATURAL RESOURCES

FOOD PER CAPITA

INDUSTRIAL OUTPUT PER CAPITA

POPULATION

POLLUTION

1900   2100

YEAR

Fig. 11: Global equilibrium is established by stabilizing population in 1980 and industrial capital in 1990. In addition, a societal value change allocates more of industrial output to services and food and slightly less to material goods. Material goods reach a relatively high level, however, by better product design, which allows a longer useful lifetime for each product. Resource and pollution policies are as in Fig. 8. Equilibrium population is 4 billion and GNP per capita is about twice the present world average. This is only one of several possible global equilibria, in which the relative levels of population, food, pollution, and industrialization can be set to reflect different social objectives.

See cautionary note under Fig. 6 concerning the interpretation of these computer simulations.

Striving towards global equilibrium does *not* imply "freezing" the world in its present configuration of rich and poor nations and peoples. It is *overall* growth which must finally stop, but that does not preclude redistribution of the world's existing wealth. One possibility is that the developed world deliberately stops its growth and possibly even lets itself "shrink" somewhat, while the developing world is allowed (and maybe helped) to grow economically to an acceptable, but not infinitely high level. Thus initially it will be the developed world which has to take the lead in the path towards *economic* equilibrium; however, the developing world will have serious responsibilities in attempting to stop its rapidly growing populations.

Many people believe that we must cling to the goal of maximizing physical growth, simply because we are still so *very* far from having attained the Utopia where everything is plentiful for everyone. However, we must remember our conclusion above that a continued reliance on short-term objectives and continued growth only makes it certain that there will be no acceptable future—for *any* country. In other words: such a Utopia does not exist, and striving towards it is futile.

Also it should be made quite clear that economic growth as we have experienced it over the last century in *no* way has resulted in increased equality among the world's people. To the contrary, growth in its present form simply widens the gap between the rich and poor, as can be seen from Fig. 12.

An end to overall economic growth, however, might very well ultimately lead to a more equitable distribution of wealth throughout the world—because no one would accept economic inequalities in the present under the (false) pretence that they would be removed through future growth. Of course the state of global equilibrium will also have its problems—mainly political and ethical. In the words of H. E. Daly,[2] the American economist:

For several reasons the important issue of the stationary state will be distribution, not production. The problem of relative shares can no longer be avoided by appeals to growth. The argument that everyone should be happy as long as his absolute share of the wealth increases, regardless of his relative share, will no longer be available. . . The stationary state would make fewer demands on our environmental resources, but much greater demands on our moral resources.

But these political problems have solutions, and we are certainly more likely to find those solutions in an equilibrium state than in a collapsing one.

Stopping the overall physical growth on our planet is not an attempt by the rich countries to divert attention from economic development to the protection of "their" environment. Rather global equilibrium is a necessity if mankind wants to have an equitable future on his small, fragile planet.

The Golden Age
The presence of global equilibrium could permit the development of an unprecedented golden age for humanity.   Freedom from the

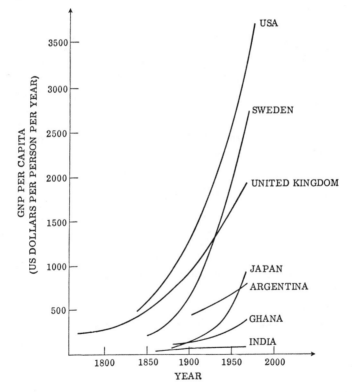

Fig. 12:   The economic growth of several countries.
Source of data: Simon Kuznets, *Economic Growth of Nations*, Harvard University Press, Cambridge, Mass., 1971.

pressures of providing for ever-increasing numbers of people would make it possible to put substantial effort into the self-realization and development of the individual. Instead of struggling merely to keep people alive, we could employ our energy in developing human culture—that is, in increasing the quality of life for the individual to a level high above the present subsistence. The few periods of equilibrium in the past—for example, the 300 years of Japan's classical period—often witnessed a profound flowering of the arts.

The freedom from ever-increasing capital—i.e., from more concrete, cars, dams and skyscrapers—would make it possible even for our great-grandchildren to enjoy solitude and silence. The desirable aspects of the steady state were realized long ago. John Stuart Mill[3] wrote in 1857:

It is scarcely necessary to remark that a stationary condition of capital and population implies no stationary state of human improvement. There would be as much scope as ever for all kinds of mental culture, and moral and social progress; as much room for improving the Art of Living and much more likelihood of its being improved, when minds cease to be engrossed by the art of getting on. Even the industrial arts might be as earnestly and as successfully cultivated, with this sole difference, that instead of serving no purpose but the increase of wealth, industrial improvements would produce their legitimate effect, that of abridging labor.

This, then, is the state of global equilibrium, which seems to be the logical consequence of the adoption of the long-term objective function.

The changes needed during the transition from growth to global equilibrium are tremendous, and the time is very short. But the results seem worth striving for, and the first step must be to increase our time horizon—to accept the long-term objective function.

NOTES

1. Further information about our modeling effort can be obtained from System Dynamics Program Office, A. P. Sloan School of Management, E40–214, Massachusetts Institute of Technology, Cambridge, Massachusetts 02139.
2. Herman E. Daly in *The Patient Earth*, John Harte and Robert Socolow, eds., Holt, Rinehart and Winston, 1971.
3. J. S. Mill, *Principles of Political Economy*, Vol. II, London: John W. Parker and Son, 1857.